366/2244

23. OCT 1976

26. FEB 1977

19. MAR 1977
16. APR 1977
30. JAN. 1979

-9. MAR. 1979

13. AUG. 1979

(S) 18.8.83

-4. OCT. 1983

-5. MAR. 1984

**LONDON BOROUGH OF ENFIELD
LIBRARY SERVICES**

This book to be RETURNED on or before the latest date stamped unless a renewal has been obtained by personal call, post or telephone, quoting the above number and the date due for return.

30126 01051552 3

PERGAMON INTERNATIONAL LIBRARY
of Science, Technology, Engineering and Social Studies
The 1000-volume original paperback library in aid of education,
industrial training and the enjoyment of leisure
Publisher: Robert Maxwell, M.C.

Strategic Planning
in London
The Rise and Fall of the
Primary Road Network

THE PERGAMON TEXTBOOK
INSPECTION COPY SERVICE

An inspection copy of any book published in the Pergamon International Library will gladly be sent to academic staff without obligation for their consideration for course adoption or recommendation. Copies may be retained for a period of 60 days from receipt and returned if not suitable. When a particular title is adopted or recommended for adoption for class use and the recommendation results in a sale of 12 or more copies, the inspection copy may be retained with our compliments. If after examination the lecturer decides that the book is not suitable for adoption but would like to retain it for his personal library, then a discount of 10% is allowed on the invoiced price. The Publishers will be pleased to receive suggestions for revised editions and new titles to be published in this important International Library.

Pergamon Urban and Regional Planning Advisory Committee

G. F. CHADWICK, PhD, MA, BScTech, FRTPI, FILA (Chairman),
   Planning Consultant,
   Sometime Professor of Town and Country Planning,
   University of Newcastle upon Tyne

D. R. DIAMOND, MA, MSc,
   Reader in Regional Planning, London School of Economics

A. K. F. FALUDI, Dipl-Ing, Dr techn,
   Professor of Planning Theory,
   Delft University of Technology

J. K. FRIEND, MA,
   Institute for Operational Research

D. C. GILL, BA, MRTPI,
   Director of Planning,
   Humberside County Council

B. GOODEY, BA, MA,
   Lecturer in Urban Studies,
   Centre for Urban and Regional Studies,
   University of Birmingham

D. N. M. STARKIE, BSc(Econ), MSc(Econ),
   Department of Geography,
   University of Reading

B. STYLES, BA, MCD, MRTPI,
   Divisional Planning Officer,
   City of Birmingham Planning Department

Strategic Planning in London
The Rise and Fall of the Primary Road Network

DOUGLAS A. HART, M.A., Ph.D.
Lecturer in Inter-Authority Relations
Institute of Local Government Studies
University of Birmingham

PERGAMON PRESS
Oxford · New York · Toronto
Sydney · Paris · Frankfurt

U. K.	Pergamon Press Ltd., Headington Hill Hall, Oxford OX3 0BW, England
U. S. A.	Pergamon Press Inc., Maxwell House, Fairview Park, Elmsford, New York 10523, U.S.A.
CANADA	Pergamon of Canada Ltd., P.O. Box 9600, Don Mills M3C 2T9, Ontario, Canada
AUSTRALIA	Pergamon Press (Aust.) Pty. Ltd., 19a Boundary Street, Rushcutters Bay, N.S.W. 2011, Australia
FRANCE	Pergamon Press SARL, 24 rue des Ecoles, 75240 Paris, Cedex 05, France
WEST GERMANY	Pergamon Press GmbH, 6242 Kronberg-Taunus, Pferdstrasse 1, Frankfurt-am-Main, West Germany

Copyright © Douglas Hart 1976

All Rights Reserved. No part of this publication may be reproduced, stored in a retrieval system or transmitted in any form or by any means: electronic, electrostatic, magnetic tape, mechanical, photocopying, recording or otherwise, without permission in writing from the publishers

First edition 1976

Library of Congress Cataloging in Publication Data

Hart, Douglas A
   Strategic planning in London.

(Urban and regional planning series; v. 12) (Pergamon international library of science, technology, engineering, and social studies)
Bibliography: p.
1. Roads—London metropolitan area. 2. Highway planning—London metropolitan area. I. Title.
II. Series.
HE363.G75L66   1975   388.4′11′09421   75-30723
ISBN 0-08-019780-9

Printed in Great Britain by A. Wheaton & Co. Exeter

To Bub and Beck

Contents

ABSTRACT	x
ACKNOWLEDGEMENTS	xi
ABBREVIATIONS USED IN THE TEXT	xiii
INTRODUCTION	1

CHAPTER 1. ORDERING CHANGE: PLANNING AS AN
    ITERATIVE PROCESS   5
  Ordering Change   5
  Iterative Planning   11
  The Concept of Process in Planning   14
  Iterative Planning and Disjointed Incrementalism   21
  An Example of Iterative Planning—Strategic Road
    Planning in Greater London   23

CHAPTER 2. FRAMING THE PROBLEM: TRAFFIC GROWTH,
    TOWN PLANNING AND THE CREATION OF THE
    GREATER LONDON COUNCIL   25
  London's Traffic Problem   25
  Mounting Pressure   29
  Traffic and Town Planning in Greater London   34
  Lack of Administrative Co-ordination   40
  Opportunity for Metropolitan Planning—the Creation of
    the GLC   43

viii Contents

CHAPTER 3. CONSTRUCTING A SOLUTION: A PLANNING
PRESCRIPTION FOR PHYSICALLY CONTROLLING
LONDON'S TRAFFIC   53

Abercrombie's Three Londons—an Organic View   53
The Circulatory System: Physically Canalizing Traffic   65
Abercrombie's Geometry   71
Recapitulation   83
The Buchanan Approach   86
Traditional Planning and the Tripp Connection   93

CHAPTER 4. UNWRAPPING THE BOX; RINGWAY ONE AND
THE PLANNING OF THE PRIMARY ROAD NETWORK   102

London's Long-term Strategy: the Continuing Traffic
Commitment   102
Changing the Order of Priority   105
Reinforcing—and Narrowing—the Main Road Component   111
The London Traffic Survey and its Initial Organizational
Impact   117
Unwrapping the Box   121
The Form and Function of the Primary Road Network   127

CHAPTER 5. WIDENING THE MOVEMENT PLANNING
PROCESS: THE FALL OF THE PRIMARY ROAD NETWORK   142

Redefining the Problem   142
Widening the Movement Planning Process   151
The Growth of Opposition   156
Analysing the Plan—the GLDP Inquiry   160
The Fall of the Primary Road Network   167

CHAPTER 6. ORDERING CHANGE AND CHANGING ORDERS:
AN ANALYSIS OF THE PLANNING PROCESS IN GREATER
LONDON   176

Changing Orders in the Capital   176
Cohesive Policy: Explanation and Analysis   182
Factored Policy: Explanation and Analysis   186
Diffused Policy: Explanation and Analysis   192

Policy Mode Interaction	195
Some Lessons of Strategic Planning	200
BIBLIOGRAPHY	207

Abstract

THE study is concerned with examining the on-going relationship between order and change in the urban planning process. Specifically a study of planning in Greater London is made during the period 1943–1973. The policy issue which is considered is the way in which the relationship between strategic road planning and the concept of urban order has altered during this 30-year period. It is argued that a classical approach to urban planning was put forward in 1943 which contained a set of principles for creating a coherent, convenient and compact city. It is further suggested that strategic road planning formed a key component of this approach and that interest in road building was further strengthened by the way in which Greater London's growing traffic problem was defined in the late 1950s and the early 1960s.

It is contended that a combination of concern for alleviating London's traffic congestion with designing an organization capable of undertaking strategic planning for the Capital as a whole played an important part in creating the Greater London Council in 1965. Soon after its creation the GLC proposed the construction of a Primary Road Network of urban motorways based on the initial classical approach. The physical form of London had altered significantly, however, since the classical concept of urban order was put forward and it is contended that there was a mismatch between original intent and the actual impact of the road proposals. Community concern over the proposals spread and was eventually translated into party political opposition and the Primary Road Network was abandoned in 1973.

It is argued, therefore, that *planning, although concerned with ordering change, must also continuously incorporate changing concepts of order*, because of the changing nature of the urban environment and the changing means of control available for actually implementing solutions.

Acknowledgements

TO ASSERT that planning is a process demonstrates, paraphrasing Galbraith, a reassuring grasp of the commonplace. To attempt to explain in what ways it is a process is a very much more difficult task. The work which follows is a study of a particular issue— the Primary Road Network—within the wider context of the planning process for Greater London. It has taken almost 4 years to complete and I am grateful to a number of people who provided me with information or documents during the course of this research.

I would particularly like to thank my superviser at LSE, Professor Peter Self, for three reasons. First, for teaching me a great deal about planning and about London; secondly, for willingly giving me his time to allow ideas to be developed; and finally, for initiating what promises to be a very long process—teaching me the difference between making an assertion and making a case. I would also like to thank Professor John Stewart, of the Institute of Local Government Studies, at the University of Birmingham, for his support and advice. He is one of the few people I know who is capable of being witheringly accurate in terms of criticism and at the same time of being warmly encouraging. Of the people who have read all or part of subsequent drafts, I would particularly like to express my appreciation to Mr. David Gillingwater of Loughborough University, and Mr. Derek Diamond and Dr. David Reagan, both of the LSE. The process of research is a lonely business and I suspect they little realize how dependent I was on them for their continued willingness to discuss and debate.

In addition, I would like to express my acknowledgements to Mr. David Wilcox, the Planning Correspondent of the *Evening Standard*, for allowing me to make use of his personal files and draw on the *Standard's* press library. Although I had access to a number of sources of current information the *Standard* proved to be one of the richest and most varied.

Several dozen interviews were also conducted during the course of the research. A number of individuals in the Greater London Council, in the London Boroughs, in the press and in community action groups were contacted in this way. Although it is not possible to mention all of these individuals by name, I would especially like to thank Mr. C. D. Andrews, Mr. John Blake, Mr. Tony Aldous, Miss Judy Hillman and Mr. J. Michael Thomson.

I would also like to thank the librarians at the GLC, at the Department of the Environment and, of course, at the LSE for their continued assistance. Drawings for the study were made by the drawing office of the Department of Geography at the University of Birmingham, it was patiently typed by Mrs. Gill Wise and the index was compiled by Mrs. Anne Wedgwood-Oppenheim.

At the personal level I would like to express my appreciation to both my parents and my wife's parents. Most of all, however, I would like to indicate the debt of gratitude which I owe to my wife, Barbara. Without her long-suffering support, I simply could have never undertaken, or completed, this work. I would like to dedicate it to her and to our daughter, Rebekah.

Institute of Local Government Studies   D. A. HART
University of Birmingham

Abbreviations used in the Text

BR	British Rail
BRF	British Road Federation
CLP	*County of London Plan* (1943)
DOE	Department of the Environment
GLC	Greater London Council
GLDP	*Greater London Development Plan* (1969)
GLP	*Greater London Plan* (1944)
LATA	London Amenity and Transport Association
LBA	London Boroughs Association
LCC	London County Council
LMAG	London Motorway Action Group
LT	London Transport
LTS	London Traffic Survey—later the London Transportation Study
MHLG	Ministry of Housing and Local Government
MOT	Ministry of Transport
PRN	Primary Road Network

Introduction

IT IS the grim dictum of bridge builders that they learn more from their failures than from their successes. The study which follows is in many ways a large-scale planning failure.

The issue which is analysed in this work is the attempt by the Greater London Council and the former Ministry of Transport to create a vast complex of high-speed major roads in Greater London. It was selected for study for a number of reasons. In the first place it was chosen because it represented a major planning policy for one of the world's leading urban centres. In terms of expenditure alone, for example, London's Primary Road Network was one of the largest single public projects ever put forward in the United Kingdom. Secondly, the road proposals which were developed over a lengthy period of time have generated an enormous amount of documentary material. Purely in terms of the intellectual capital involved this work deserves a systematic consideration. Few urban planning proposals can have been as lengthily and diligently researched, in technical terms, as the Primary Network.

Thirdly, quite apart from the technical aspect of the proposals this particular issue highlights several organizational and political problems of fundamental importance. For example, the problem of traffic congestion in London played an important part in shaping, and guiding the early operations of, the first of the new metropolitan authorities—the Greater London Council. Further, although the GLC played a central role in devising an urban motorway programme, several *levels* of government were actively involved in this process simultaneously. The relationship between and among these bodies merits further examination. In addition it is now part of the conventional wisdom that land-use planning is a political process. The distinction between *party* political and non-party political considerations is often, however, not made clear. The difference between the two is an important one and the Primary Road Network proposals offers the opportunity to examine this relationship in more detail.

Fourthly, the Primary System was selected for study on the grounds that it was a concrete manifestation of a concept of urban order. It is argued in the study that the road proposals physically symbolized this concept and formed the core of what could be called the classical approach to town planning. It is further held that this approach played a major part in shaping planning policy for Greater London during a 30-year period from 1943 to 1973. For reasons put forward in the text it is held that this policy has ceased to exist and the Primary Road system has now been abandoned.

Finally, although the study is an epitaph for a major policy it is also an illustration of the changing nature of the planning process. This study of the way in which a particular issue was initially framed, extended and amended over the course of time as a result of numerous technical, organizational and political influences, provides an example of the way in which the planning process in Greater London operates in practice.

The first chapter of the work suggests that one of planning's continuing tasks is to establish an effective relationship between ordering events, on one hand, and responding to changing circumstances, on the other. It is argued that the interrelationship between these two strands of activity provided an important motive force for the planning process as a whole. Two common ways of dealing with change—traditional master planning and disjointed incrementalism—are then critically examined. It is suggested that master planning is often insufficiently responsive while disjointed incrementalism is normally in the position of belatedly reacting to, rather than anticipating, events. A conceptual model based on an iterative approach to urban planning is then outlined which seeks to continuously link future commitment with actual experience as the planning process proceeds over time.

Introduction 3

As a means of applying the iterative planning approach, Chapter 2 of the study considers the way in which the problem of traffic congestion in Greater London was initially defined in the late 1950s and early 1960s. The mounting pressure for action—largely in the form of requests for large-scale road building—is examined and the traffic problem is then related to both London's public transport system and to the matter of strategic planning considerations generally. It is argued that the important relationship between traffic and strategic planning provided a substantial part of the justification for the establishment of the Greater London Council. It is further held that the GLC was given a specific and direct orientation toward major road construction from the moment of its creation and its powers and duties are briefly sketched out.

Chapter 3 contends that a long-standing pattern for the development of London was initially set out by Abercrombie almost 20 years before the GLC came into official existence. It is held that Abercrombie's concept of urban order, put forward during World War Two, was essentially organic in character and the major ordering principles underlying this "classical" approach to physical planning are set out. It is argued that the strategic road proposals were an essential component of trying to construct the kind of coherent, convenient and compact London which Abercrombie was trying to create. It is then suggested that Buchanan's approach to highway and urban planning put forward in the early 1960s played an important part in strengthening and reinforcing this set of classical ordering principles.

As the fourth chapter indicates, the basic geometric road pattern for the Capital put forward by Abercrombie was never really abandoned. Within 12 hours of beginning its official life the GLC began the attempt to implement this blueprint. Although nominally pursuing the Abercrombie–Buchanan approach to traffic canalization, however, the GLC, because of its strategic orientation and its close working relationship with the Ministry of Transport, was pursuing a policy which was in many ways a fundamental reversal of the original approach. The actual form and function of the proposed GLC–MOT Primary Network is described in some detail.

Chapter 5 points out some of the ways in which the original

definition of the traffic problem was broadened in the late 1960s and early 1970s. The importance of the relationship between public and private transport is indicated. Apart from growing concern for creating an integrated movement system for London the opposition to the Primary Road Network by many of the London Boroughs and a number of community action groups is also discussed. A shift in emphasis is noted from increasing the *supply* of road space available and reducing the *demand* for such space by suggestions for restricting the usage of the private automobile. The public examination of the road proposals at the Greater London Development Plan Inquiry is considered and the main lines of opposition to the proposals are indicated. Finally the way in which the motorway proposals at last became a party political issue is described and the manner in which they were ultimately rejected in 1973 is explained.

The last chapter is largely analytical and concentrates on the shifting nature of control mechanisms which were employed in planning during the period of the study from 1943 to 1973. It is then argued that the relationship between strategic road planning and the larger issue of the classical concept of urban order proposed by Abercrombie and Buchanan has been shattered by events. It is further held that it is possible to identify three interlocking policy "modes" which have run through the period under study and they are set out individually and then related to one another. An attempt is made to draw some lessons for the planning process based on the previous explanation and analysis. Finally, after setting out these suggestions a brief reconsideration of the nature of the planning process, initially raised in Chapter 1, is made and some of the characteristics of planning as an iterative process—in the light of the study—are put forward.

The central issue of this work—the Primary Road Network—is now history but many of the points which it has raised have not been resolved. One hopes that it is possible to learn from this experience on the grounds that history repeats itself because no one hears it the first time.

CHAPTER 1

Ordering Change: Planning as an Iterative Process

> Of special importance to the planner are the faculties of memory and association... the power to conceive new orders as the basis of planning.—
> Raymond Unwin, quoted by Walter Creese, "The planning theories of Sir Raymond Unwin, 1863–1940", *Journal of the American Institute of Planners*, Vol. XXX, No. 4, November 1964, p. 303.

ORDERING CHANGE

Establishing an effective relationship between order and change is at once planning's reason for existence and one of its most difficult problems. From a planning perspective both order and change are relative rather than absolute terms. Both levels of order and degrees of change are each partly reflected in, and a partial reflection of, the other. The level of order sought, for example, may be nothing more specific than the establishment of a broad developmental framework, or nothing more comprehensive than the design of a single project, but the conscious intent of the planner remains essentially the same: to encourage what is perceived to be benign development, and reduce the type of disbenefits normally associated with random change. Since planning must therefore *both induce and incorporate change* its commitment to the uncertain future often exhibits certain apparently paradoxical elements. The problem of urban transport provides a good illustration of many of these points and it forms the central subject of this study.

Although planning is concerned with predicting and attempting to control the future, some critics have asserted that the one thing which we know about the future with any degree of certainty is that it will not be like the past; yet, the past is the source of our knowledge about the future and it consequently provides the basis for our attempts at prediction and control.[1] Taking this argument one step further, other critics feel that broad-scale, long-term planning is not possible precisely because of the current rate of change.[2] More commonly, however, even those who acknowledge the extreme difficulty of planning for a broad area over time take the position that change indicates rather than obviates the need for long-term planning. Although plans change the environment, the environment changes both individual plans and the interrelated set of concepts underlying the whole of the planning process.[3] From this perspective, planning is something more than a simple projection of the present, and the future is something less than a completely novel and inherently unknowable set of impending conditions.

One key reason for the growth of interest in various types of planning has been the growth of uncertainty about the future.[4] Change is no longer considered to be tantamount to progress, and natural growth has a number of increasingly evident unfortunate third-party disbenefits. As the rate of social and economic change continues to increase, more rather than less planning is being attempted both as an antidote for uncertainty, and as a positive control device. Planning acts to reduce the "impending" element in the future and make the future not only more understandable, but

---

[1] See Edmund Leach, "Planning and evolution", *Journal of the Town Planning Institute*, Vol. 55, No. 1, January 1969, pp. 5–6.

[2] See, for example, Edward C. Banfield, "The uses and limitations of metropolitan planning in Massachusetts", in *Taming Megalopolis*, H. Wentworth Eldredge (Ed.), Vol. II, Garden City: Doubleday & Co., 1967, p. 712; and Constantine Doxiadis' statement regarding the need to slow change, *Ekistics*, London: Hutchinson, 1968, p. 493.

[3] On this, see also the comments of Sir Geoffrey Vickers and Colin Buchanan, *Journal of the Town Planning Institute*, Vol. 55, No. 1, January 1969, pp. 9–10.

[4] On this generally see J. K. Friend and W. N. Jessop, *Local Government and Strategic Choice*, London: Tavistock Publications, 1969.

more acceptable as well.[5] Daniel Bell has remarked about this trend that "Men will now seek to anticipate change, measure the course of its direction and its impact, control it, and even shape it for predetermined ends".[6]

Historically, at least in terms of town planning, the attempt to control change has been equated with an attempt to impose a harmonic set of relationships on the area being dealt with. This often rather holistical view has played a major part in planning thought for a good part of this century. Patrick Abercrombie remarked in 1933: "The touchstone of what constitutes a planning scheme is this matter of relationship, the accommodation of several units to make a complete but harmonious whole."[7] In a memorandum concerning the first regional plan for Greater London, published in 1929, the chief planner for the project, Raymond Unwin, wrote:

> The making of a plan for a great city region is a somewhat daunting project because two considerations which claim attention are as clearly true as they seem to be mutually paralysing. On the one hand the task as a whole is so complex that it can be comprehended only if attention be concentrated on one subject at a time; on the other hand the various aspects of the problem are so interdependent that they cannot safely be studied or handled separately; for the main purpose of the plan is to establish harmonious relations among them.[8]

Forty years later the production of the first *Greater London Development Plan* (1969)[9] indicated that the attempt to achieve a harmonious relationship between the various parts of the plan and the

---

[5] As samples of the increasing rate of change in society and its expression in public planning see, Alvin Toffler, *Future Shock*, London: The Bodley Head, 1970, pp. 397–398; and Donald Schon, *Beyond the Stable State*, London: Temple Smith, 1971, pp. 23–24.

[6] Quoted by Lloyd Rodwin, in *Nations and Cities*, Boston: Houghton, Mifflin Co., 1970, p. 286.

[7] Patrick Abercrombie, *Town and Country Planning*, 2nd ed., London: Oxford University Press, 1943, p. 11. For an even earlier example of this type of thought see a lecture given by Partick Geddes—a botanist and another of the major figures in the planning movement—at the New School for Social Research in New York City in 1923 and incorporated in the 2nd edition of his 1915 work, *Cities in Evolution*, London: Williams & Norgate Ltd., 1949, p. xvii.

[8] Memorandum No. 1, *First Report of the Greater London Regional Planning Committee*, London: Knapp, Drewitt & Sons Ltd., December 1929, p. 8.

[9] Greater London Council, *GLDP Statement*, London: GLC, 1969.

whole still occupied a position of crucial importance.[10] During the four decades which had elapsed between 1929 and 1969, however, both physical London and many of the concepts underlying the planning process as a whole had undergone a series of important changes.

One of the most important differences between the 1929 and 1969 plans was the explicit recognition in the latter that the planning subjects being dealt with were not only complex and interdependent but dynamic as well. Harmonic order had, at least in part, given way to a more dynamic conception of control, and a new synthesis between the two was beginning to emerge. The *Report of Studies* accompanying the *Greater London Development Plan* (GLDP) remarks: "Since the war social and demographic change has been rapid in large cities. The pace of such changes will undoubtedly continue and may well increase, and the planning process must take account of these trends if physical and social development are to proceed in harmony."[11] One manifestation of this new interest was a broadening of planning's scope of concern.[12] The state of constant flux also indicated that earlier plans were often cumbersome and unresponsive. The inability to accommodate change, as exemplified by the lengthy amending and modification process, threatened to overload the whole intricate planning structure.[13]

A significant body of opinion began to crystallize during the 1960s around the belief that planning, to remain effective, should operate as a reciprocal system: at the first level plans would continue to guide and control development as they had always done; but at a new second level plans were now also expected to continuously re-

[10] See, for example, GLC, *Tomorrow's London*, London: GLC, 1969, p. 44.
[11] *Report* (1969), p. 15.
[12] As Peter Self suggests this broad concern was, in itself, nothing new. Town planning has always had socio-economic objectives. What is different about current planning is the open-endedness of its future commitments. Peter J. Self, *Metropolitan Planning*, London: Weidenfeld & Nicolson, 1971, p. 3.
[13] See, for example, an early attempt to increase administrative flexibility between land and trunk road development and cut down the amount of time involved. Circular No. 82, "Town and Country Planning (General Development)", issued by the Ministry of Town and Country Planning, on 6 March 1950, para. 7. See also the diagnosis put forward in the 1967 White Paper, *Town and Country Planning*, London: HMSO, paras. 4–5.

flect change derived from monitoring new environmental circumstances. Probably the single most important exposition of this view was that of the Planning Advisory Group in their report, *The Future of Development Plans*.[14] The Planning Advisory Group (PAG) was initially appointed in 1964 to assist the Ministries of Housing and Local Government, Transportation and the Scottish Development Department in the attempt to devise a more responsive planning system. An attempt to strike a balance, it was felt had to be made between predetermined controlled change, and the ability to adapt to, and learn from, its increasingly uncertain environment.[15]

To resolve the difficulty of synthesizing flexibility and commitment the PAG suggested that plans were to be treated as strategic, decision documents rather than as detailed maps with local plans being produced at a later stage in the planning process. The documents would concern themselves with a range of activities occurring within a particular geographical area at the strategic level.[16] The approach at this level, it was felt, would help to free planning from the detailed proceduralism and excessive formalism which were often associated in the public mind with the operation of the existing machinery. By beginning at the policy formulation level, it was hoped that the plans would have a built-in measure of flexibility. The plans were to provide conceptual, "Developmental frameworks", which could be altered as proposals were made steadily more specific over time, until they at last emerged as functional programmes and operational projects. Two things are significant about the PAG recommendations: (a) the recognition of the continuous incompleteness of any given plan; and (b) partly because of this, the continuous need for up-to-date information about

[14] London: HMSO, 1965.

[15] PAG (1965), paras. 2.36 and 2.37; and *Town and Country Planning*, paras. 11 and 19; see for a professional view, J. Brian McLoughlin, "The PAG Report: background prospects", *Journal of the Town Planning Institute*, Vol. 52, No. 6, July 1965, p. 255; and D. M. Riley, "The future of development plans", *Town and Country Planning*, Vol. 34, No. 3, March 1966, p. 145.

[16] PAG (1965), paras. 1.46 and 7.11; and see also for a broad-scale American view, Harvey S. Perloff and Lowdon Wingo Jr., "Planning and development in metropolitan affairs", *Journal of the American Institute of Planners*, Vol. 28, No. 2, May 1962, pp. 70–71.

the environment.¹⁷ Government plans had long been concerned with control of directed change but only since the PAG Report have they been deliberately thought of *from the outset* as policy vehicles, continuously involved in a process of self-modification.

The attempt to achieve flexibility in planning is by no means new, however, and it has been suggested by at least one observer that it has been occurring—in practice if not in theory—for some time. Writing about planning for the London area, Foley differentiates between the earlier *unitary* approach to planning and the later *adaptive* approach which was beginning to take shape during the 1960s.¹⁸ The unitary approach was essentially design oriented and is typified by two of the Abercrombie Plans for London. "The Greater London Plan and the County of London Plan provide almost classic examples of the overwhelmingly unitary approach to planning", Foley asserts. The adaptive approach, on the other hand, is concerned with social interrelationships and the way in which the community develops over time. It is essentially evolutionary rather than deterministic and it recognizes the importance of political and economic decisions as factors in the planning process.

Foley illustrates this point clearly. He remarks regarding the *Greater London Plan* (1944) that it "despite its initial architectural-planner, unitary-character—came to be absorbed into a political and administrative process within central government that, by its very nature, was essentially adaptive in character".¹⁹ It is thus possible to convert a predominantly unitary plan into a predominantly adaptive plan through the activity of the organizational structure surrounding the planning process. As Britton Harris suggests, this type of adaptation occurs at more than one level since planning must: (1) first, modify the imperfections of the initial perception of the set of

---

¹⁷ J. Brian McLoughlin, *Urban and Regional Planning*, London: Faber & Faber, 1969, pp. 87–89.

¹⁸ Donald L. Foley, *Controlling London's Growth*, Berkeley and Los Angeles: University of California Press, 1963; for a more recent view along very similar lines see Cherry's distinction between static and adaptive planning, Gordon E. Cherry, *Town Planning in its Social Context*, London: Leonard Hill, 1970, p. 60; and see also for an operational research perspective Stafford Beer, "Planning as a process of adaptation", in *OR 69*, John Lawrence (Ed.), London: Tavistock Publications, 1970, p. 31.

¹⁹ Foley (1963), p. 173.

circumstances surrounding the problem being dealt with; and (2) second, evolve as the planning problems and the society within which they occur continue to change.[20] The extremely important but often neglected relationship between planning's conceptual intent and the way in which ideas are modified through actual governmental operation will form one of the major themes of the present study.

ITERATIVE PLANNING

The increasing consciousness of the need for adaptive planning—deliberately conceived to be so from the outset of the plan-making process rather than as an unintentional administrative effect—was finally made law through the passage of the 1968 Town and Country Planning Act.[21] Planning was forced, reflecting the new view of the city which it modelled, to become more of a broad flow and less of an intermittent series of discrete acts. Plan-making as a project, in Raymond Unwin's sense of the term, mentioned above,[22] was increasingly viewed as one important phase in—rather than the whole of—a complex process. At least in terms of the intent of the Act, planned change no longer meant an attempt to achieve a kind of static order.[23] The planning for an area such as Greater London could be neither complete nor certain, because: (a) its subject—the city region—had no finite end; and (b) perfect prediction could only be achieved through perfect knowledge or complete control. Because both of these conditions did not obtain and because speed in the modification process was essential if the public's confidence in planning was to be maintained, planning had to be made more flexible in conception and more efficient in operation. Planning became less concerned with producing and maintaining "the plan" and more interested in facilitating a wider planning process which could be used to both incorporate new information and utilize

[20] Britton Harris, "Generating projects for urban research", *Environment and Planning*, Vol. 2, No. 1, 1970, p. 2.
[21] For a parallel development in the U.S. in thought, if not in law, see Doris B. Holleb, *Social and Economic Information for Urban Planning*, Chicago: Center for Urban Studies of the University of Chicago, 1969, p. 12.
[22] See p. 7.
[23] See, for example, the comment made by Desmond Heap in *An Outline of Planning Law*, London: Sweet & Maxwell, 1969 (5th ed.), p. 33.

previous experience.[24] Or so, at any rate, the framers of the 1968 Act hoped—but, because of the recentness of the Act, it is only now becoming possible to make an analysis of its effects.

In a sense, the Town and Country Planning Acts of 1947, 1962 and 1968 have all been attempts to reduce the inflexibility caused by the increasing administrative precision with which each preceding Act had been applied. The governmental process which Foley saw as inherently adaptive often had the effect of steadily narrowing—through increasing specificity—the channels through which change was designed to flow. Adaptation became steadily slower as the channels of change began to narrow and the process of planning change became steadily more rigidly institutionalized itself.[25] In the *Explanatory Memorandum* accompanying the 1947 Act it was stated that one of the principal defects with the planning system set up under the 1932 Town and Country Planning Act was that, "(a) It is static. A planning scheme has the force of law, and can be altered only by a long and cumbersome procedure."[26] In order to avoid this difficulty, the 1947 Act proposed both that plans be broader and less detailed and that they be reviewed at 5-yearly intervals after their approval by the Minister of Town and Country planning so that they could be periodically up-dated. Unfortunately, as the new system began to function neither the intended breadth nor the quinquennial reviews[27] were capable of preventing them, in the face of accelerating change, from losing their impetus and tending, if not to inertia, at least to a kind of determined equilibrium. At least in the field of planning dynamics the interesting thing about the 1947 *Explanatory Memorandum* and the 1964 *Future of Development Plans* is the similarity of their condemnation of the systems which they replaced.

The 1968 Act differs from earlier acts in a number of important ways, it seeks to unite land use and transportation considerations; it

---

[24] See also on this, *Development Plans: a Manual on Form and Content*, Ministry of Housing and Local Government, Welsh Office, London: HMSO, 1970.

[25] See, on the relationship between institutionalized change and the urban crisis, Albert Gorvine and Samuel L. Margulies, "The urban crisis: an alternative perspective", *Urban Affairs Quarterly*, Vol. 6, No. 3, March 1971, p. 264.

[26] *Explanatory Memorandum*, Town and Country Planning Bill, Ministry of Town and Country Planning, Cmd. 7006, London: HMSO, January 1947, paras. 8–9.

[27] See, for the review provision, for instance, Town and Country Planning Act, 1947, Part II, Clause 6.

stresses the policy aspect of planning; and, it emphasizes that the planning process is both continuous and, at least in conceptual terms, capable of continuous correction.[28] All of these aspects will be examined in more detail with regard to Greater London. Although the present idea of a fluid planning operation which is constantly capable of redirecting itself has won widespread approval in governmental and professional circles, there are few examples of how such a process could be made operational.[29] On the basis of what is known about organizational theory—particularly governmental organizations—law, and the recent history of the planning process, there is good reason to believe that the shift to this type of "second generation" planning will be extremely difficult. There is also reason to believe, in view of the lack of effective guidelines, that the process of incorporating change cannot be defined but must be worked through as a kind of continuous experiment.

The Greater London Development Plan (1969) is an example of a large-scale urban plan which reflects this period of conceptual transition. "Planning on a broad scale", states the GLDP's *Report of Studies*, "is now clearly seen as a continuous process, providing a strategic framework to guide further decisions."[30] The Plan, its authors feel,

> states a set of principles for the future development of Greater London which will have to undergo a process of validation extending perhaps over several years. For the planning of London to be effective, there will have to be a sustained effort of partnership between the Council and the London Boroughs in which concepts are put forward, tested, amended, re-tested, and so on in what is commonly known these days as an "iterative process".[31]

[28] See Cullingworth's comment on the impact of the PAG proposals, J. B. Cullingworth, *Town and Country Planning in England and Wales*, London: Simon Shand Ltd., 1967 (2nd ed.), p. 297.

[29] On this see Anthony Downs, "The coming revolution in city planning", in Edward Banfield (Ed.), *Urban Government*, Glencoe: The Free Press, 1969, Revised Edition, p. 597. See also, Constance Perrin, "A noiseless secession from the comprehensive plan", *Journal of the American Institute of Planners*, Vol. 33, No. 5, September 1967, p. 340.

[30] *Report*, p. 1, and see also, *Statement*, p. 9. For an example of the process in action see the explanatory leaflet, "This Way to London—A Summary of the Greater London Development Plan", which has been revised twice and still contains an addendum. The GLC, initially issued September 1969 (revised February 1970; revised February 1971).

[31] *Statement*, p. 9, and *Tomorrow's London*, p. 49.

An empirical study of the beginning years of this iterative process with particular reference to strategic road planning will form the subject of this study.

THE CONCEPT OF PROCESS IN PLANNING

Before actually beginning the analysis, perhaps it would be worthwhile to set out a few organizing concepts and attempt to relate them to one another. The complexity of planning for an area such as Greater London necessitates that some type of coherent perspective be employed which would allow the analysis to proceed as directly and as economically as possible. Ideally, what is required is a paradigm of the planning process, but a review of the existing literature indicates that the attempt to relate planning to its environment in a systematic or diagrammatic fashion has rarely been attempted in actual field studies. There has been relatively little attention devoted to conceptually demonstrating in what sense planning is a process, and how, in fact, the process operates. While admitting the difficulties inherent in the attempt to undertake an activity of this kind its justification will have to be based on its ability to illuminate and suggest sets of relationships which help to explain why particular goals have been served in particular ways, and the consequences of serving these goals in the ways indicated, on the process of planning itself.

The concept of process plays an important, and largely unquestioned, part in planning as well as in a number of other related fields of activity.[32] Public planning, for example, takes place within a much wider network of intersecting technical, organizational and political processes.[33] Three recent works on public planning, *The City Planning Processes*, by Alan Altshuler,[34] *City Politics and Planning*, by Francine Rabinovitz,[35] and *Poverty, Planning and Politics*, by

---

[32] See for a general discussion of this problem from a wide perspective, Paul F. Kress, *Social Science and the Idea of Process*, Ill.: University of Chicago Press, Urbana, 1970.

[33] On this subject see J. K. Friend, J. M. Power and C. J. L. Yewlett, *Public Planning: the Inter-corporate Dimension*, London: Tavistock Publications, 1974.

[34] New York: Cornell University Press, Ithaca, 1965.

[35] New York: Atherton Press, 1969.

Stephan Thernstrom,[36] have all been concerned with various aspects of the planning process. It is evident however, that process in the context of these studies has more than one meaning, and that the meaning being employed at a particular time is only rarely defined in spite of its apparent importance. Normally it *appears* to mean[37] *the historical process of plan-making* and the focal point of interest is therefore on the events leading up to the adoption (or rejection) of an essentially end-state, unitary projection. The process is a finite one and there is a fairly clear division between producing the plan and causing it to be implemented. Possibly because form follows function, this projection, either a Master Plan or a plan for a particular sub-area has tended to be rather static in terms of policy and design.[38] In one influential planning text which is representative of this viewpoint, *The Urban General Plan*, by T. J. Kent, the author states simply, "To me therefore, there can be no such thing as a flexible policy in relation to physical development. A so-called 'flexible' plan is no plan at all."[39]

In all of the studies the visible, plastic element is much more the political and administrative process rather than the plan itself in spite of the fact that the books demonstrate that a plan—and a planning process—which is not capable of responding to changing interpretations of social and physical problems and alternative perceptions of the public interest must by the very nature of the complex system in which it is embedded become inoperative and ultimately irrelevant. What each of the studies does indicate is that in order for plans to succeed there must be a high degree of correspondence between: (a) the planning process and the subject system; and (b) the planning process and the system's own control devices. Planning must concern itself not only with physical reality,

[36] New York: Basic Books Inc., 1969; see especially pp. 129–162.

[37] Altshuler provides a good illustration; in *The City Planning Process*, there are eleven references to "City Planning" in the Index to the book, but there are no references at all to "Process".

[38] Henry Fagin has characterized the early attempts at this kind of architectonic control as the "one-sheet, one-shot approach"; Henry Fagin, "The evolving philosophy of urban planning", in Leo F. Schnore and Henry Fagin (Eds.), *Urban Research and Policy Planning*, Vol. I, Cal: Sage Publications, Beverley Hills, p. 318.

[39] San Francisco: Chandler Publishing Co., 1964, p. 20. Kent does, however, later concede that the plan should be reviewed from time to time, but it is a bit difficult to reconcile these two very different views.

but if it is to have an effective impact, with the means whereby reality changes. The operating control devices, most notably the political process, are continually changing and a non-flexible plan which is not capable of accommodating these sequential shifts is not a plan at all but an artefact from the moment of its creation. In a situation of limited control and manifest uncertainty such as this, the planning process as Blackman has suggested, must—if it is to effectively mesh with the wider processes surrounding it—approximate the following form:

> Planning initiates a course of action which produces events experienced by the agent, in the light of which he modifies the plan; so that in a sequence of phases, the plan is continuously initiating action or being modified by the results of action; and this modification is not merely a more efficacious employment of means to an originally intended end, (a continuous adjustment on the feedback principle), but also a modification of the end in view, a revision of intention... a development in understanding.[40]

Implicit in this definition of the planning process are two points which will now be developed and related to the paradigm: (1) that the planning process continues to occur after the initial acceptance of the strategy to be employed, and is changed because of its employment; and (2) that the traditional means-ends dichotomy, for the process as a whole, is a false one.

If this view of planning is tentatively accepted, even at the conceptual level, a problem immediately arises: if planning is conceived of as an agent initiated, continuously iterative process, in what sense does it remain planning, as the word is traditionally employed? If the planning process operates not merely through error-controlled feedback but also through a much more fundamental, successive recasting of intent, what is left of the assertion that what is taking place is in fact planning at all? To answer these questions it is essential that at least some of the assumptions upon which urban planning rests should be briefly sketched.

The concept of planning appears to concern itself, *at a minimum*, with the following types of implicit assumptions:

1. Planning presents, with varying degrees of specificity, an

---

[40] Quoted by John Dyckman in "Planning and decision theory", *Journal of the American Institute of Planners*, Vol. 17, November 1961, p. 342.

organizational perspective of a series of events or activities which have not, by definition, as yet occurred.

2. The components of the perspective, presented in statement form, numerically, or by illustration may be either: (a) predictive or, (b) prescriptive in character; normally, however, they are a combination of the two.

3. The predictive statements tend to take the form: if P^1, the initially perceived problem—which "is in fact a cluster of interlocked problems with interdependent solutions"[41]—continues to occur and nothing is done (i.e. nothing is purposively done), we can expect that by time T^n, unfavourable condition D will result.

4. The manipulative statements tend to take the form: if we wish to avoid condition D and the disadvantageous effects which it will bring in its train, we must prevent P^1 from growing steadily more unacceptable by pursuing strategy S^1, a selected line of approach or set of approaches, beginning as quickly as possible at time T^1.

5. If S^1 is adopted at T^1 not only will the disbenefits of D be avoided but a more acceptable state of affairs, condition A, will be created and maintained in a way which would not have occurred either through the operation of random chance or through the employment of any of the other strategies $(S^2 - S^N)$ considered at T^1.

6. The manipulative strategy, S^1, proposed in the plan must, to be effective, be capable of actually being implemented through the deliberate activity of some effectuating body by means of a series of operating programmes $(OP^1 - OP^n)$ derived from S^1.

7. Since the selection of a strategy relies heavily on (then) current organizational judgements of fact or value which will be shown, during the process of operating programme implementation, to be incorrect, many projected facts or values will be either modified or falsified by subsequent events or activities—*even when these events or activities are direct outgrowths of the continuing implementation of the accepted plan.*

8. Since both the perceived initial problem, P^1, and the manipulative strategy employed to resolve it, S^1, are functions of a particular

[41] David Braybrooke and Charles E. Lindblom, *A Strategy of Decision*, New York: The Free Press, 1963, p. 54.

18 Strategic Planning in London

period of time and since the relationship between P^1 and S^1 is a reciprocally changing one, operating through the elimination of observed error, EE, the more effective the operating elements of a plan are the less likely that precisely the same problem will be dealt with over a given span of time because the same problem, in precisely the same perceptual or factual terms, no longer exists.

9. Continuous planning would, therefore, more closely resemble a procedural spiral rather than the traditional closed circle.[42] From this point of view, planning would resemble a layered horizontal scanning process, with previous lines affecting the formation of each of the subsequent ones. Each scan of this process planning activity would thus help to both direct and constrain its successive iterations (see Fig. 1.1).

Since, we hinted earlier, error-elimination consists not only of marginally or fundamentally modifying the successive tentative solutions attempted, but in iteratively reshaping the perception itself. In fact this activity by a single organization is

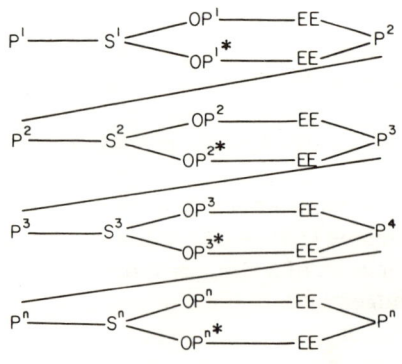

FIG. 1.1.[43]

---

[42] See for examples of the traditional view: a diagram of the planning process in Milton Keynes, Johnathan Welfare, "Programme budgeting: the experience at Milton Keynes", *Journal of the Royal Town Planning Institute*, Vol. 57, No. 8, Sept./Oct. 1971, p. 362; see also Melvin Branch's illustration, *Planning: Aspects and Applications*, New York: John Wiley & Sons, Inc., 1966, p. 305.

[43] Compare, for example, with Karl Popper's example of the way in which organisms solve problems. "Of Clouds and Clocks", The Compton Memorial Lecture, presented at Washington University, St. Louis, Mo. 1966, p. 24.

very rarely carried out in isolation. In most planning situations a core organization exists which is part of a cluster of interlinked authorities with interdependent operating procedures. Figure 1.1 serves as a useful point of departure for analysis but inter-authority considerations require that a broader focus of attention also be employed.

The import of the numbered assumptions mentioned above when considered collectively is that violence is not done to any of the traditional definitional components of planning—such as rationality-bias, policy-co-ordination, future-orientation, or breadth of focus—by maintaining that something resembling learning takes place through sequential iterations; that these iterations are an integral part of the planning process and that *the crux of the process is the interrelationship between future anticipation and experiential adaptation.*

The planning spiral is composed of two, often very closely intertwined, principal strands: commitment-anticipation and information-adaptation. The first strand is based upon a historical expectancy linked with some level of control, regarding a planned segment of the future. The second strand is composed of on-going knowledge of the recent past which will have a hithertofore unexpected or unknown effect on the unfolding present and will, therefore, modify the conceptual future. Planning occurs at the inter-face between the two, continuously combining previous commitment with present knowledge by synthesizing the two. The traditional future anticipation component of the planning process is a necessary part of that process—but it is not, in and of itself, a sufficient condition for effective implementation. Future anticipation, at the plan formulation level, can easily lend itself to deterministic planning of the architectonic kind, but this type of control is difficult to sustain for the process as a whole since there are few absolute goals in public planning.[44] Even when these goals can be ranked either cardinally or ordinally it is difficult to translate them into operating programmes without changing either their ordering or their content as implementation proceeds. A plan is a statement of

---

[44] Melvin Branch, "Goals and objectives of comprehensive planning", in John Lawrence (Ed.), *OR 69*, London: Tavistock Publications, 1970, p. 62.

conditional intent and it remains valid only as long as the conditions upon which it is based continue to maintain their projected values.

In addition, although there are many determinant elements in planning, the process in its entirety is intrinsically indeterminant[45] because: (a) of the increasing level of uncertainty—the funnel of doubt effect—as projection recedes into the distant future; and (b) because of the plasticity of the external control devices upon which intent relies for effect. In general, the level of determinancy for a particular part of a plan is a function of the extent to which commitment has been implemented. The continually spiralling planning process, however, has no concretely realizable final end. It is, more realistically, a series of means transformations extended through time. Means are converted into finite ends which are in turn fed back into the process at a new level upon their completion and become part of the means process for the realization of more temporally distant ends. In many ways planning is a search procedure which derives its value not solely through problem resolution attempts, but also through its concern with both the impact of unexpected external events and with the *ramifications* of its own resolution attempts.[46] Planning is probable rather than certain because everything affects everything else and because the intricacy of the interconnections is such that they often must be experienced to determine their nature and extent. Prediction no less than reaction is based upon historical and therefore singular change.[47] The closed-circle conception of planning indicating repetitive underlying change patterns is an appealing belief, but it is essentially an organic concept[48] which is neither an apt illustration nor an applicable ideal for something as complex, multi-directional and dynamic as a city

---

[45] Indeterminancy should not be confused with non-determinancy. Indeterminant in the sense in which it is used here simply means not strictly limited to fixed values. *Non*-determinant, on the other hand, means random, without continuity or purpose.

[46] Compare with Rabinovitz (1969): "Even decisions presumably within the planner's control can create unexpected problems", p. 79.

[47] Karl Popper, *The Poverty of Historicism*, 2nd ed., London, 1960. Although Popper stresses the tentativeness of hypotheses and the uni-directionality of change, he seems to place a good deal of faith in the relative permanence of the present.

[48] See Robert Nisbet, *Social Change and History*, New York: Oxford University Press, 1969, pp. 211–223.

such as London. This is a point which will be examined in more detail as this study proceeds.

ITERATIVE PLANNING AND DISJOINTED INCREMENTALISM

Because uncertainty in public policy-making with regard to both clientele demand and actual proposal impact is a continuing constraint on the finality of any decision, some theorists have asserted that the type of inclusive rationality which a good deal of modern planning is still nominally based upon[49] is simply not possible. They maintain instead that policy is, in fact, formulated on the basis of marginally shifting the *status quo* by utilizing limited existing knowledge to solve problems as they arise. As Etzioni observes, "Rather than attempting to foresee all of the consequences of various alternative routes, one route is tried, and the unforeseen consequences are left to be discovered and treated by subsequent increments".[50] The incrementalists regard the sin of information omission, to be preferable to the sin of confusion, and inaction.

One of the leading figures involved in this type of approach is the economist, Charles Lindblom, who calls his alternative to the classical rational-deductive method of policy making, "disjointed incrementalism".[51] In an article entitled "The Science of 'Muddling Through'", Lindblom suggests that some of the advantages of this type of "successively limited comparisons" are that they: (a) reduce the amount of information required; (b) reduce reliance upon theory; and (c) reduce the need to distinctly clarify objectives and then deduce from them empirical strategies which can be judged on the basis of the extent to which they achieve these objectives.[52] It is

---

[49] See for examples of this type of rational thinking, Donald N. Rothblatt, "Rational planning reexamined", *Journal of the American Institute of Planners*, Vol. 37, No. 1, January 1971, pp. 26–37; and Susan and Norman Fainstein, "City planning and political values", *Urban Affairs Quarterly*, Vol. 6, No. 3, March 1971, pp. 341–362.

[50] Amatai Etzioni, *The Active Society*, New York: The Free Press, 1968, p. 271.

[51] Braybrooke and Lindblom (1963), pp. 81–110; and more recently, Charles E. Lindblom, *The Intelligence of Democracy*, New York: The Free Press, 1965, pp. 143–151.

[52] Charles E. Lindblom, *Public Administration Review*, Vol. 19, No. 2, Spring 1959, p. 81.

asserted that not only is incrementalism more economical in its use of scarce resources but that it is also more effective and more likely to be employed in practice.[53] While this approach carries the concept of discrete experiential adaptation to its logical limits it is fundamentally anti-planning in terms of its basic intent since no attempt at all is made to *anticipate* a more desirable future which could be approached through a roughly *consistent* set of operating programmes.

Disjointed incrementalism's fatal flaw from the self-correcting, continuous planning standpoint is that its method of operation is also its ultimate goal. It seeks nothing less than marginal change but it also seeks nothing more. Incrementalism is, under the best possible conditions, consequential and fragmented in operation, while planning is, under the same conditions, coherent and purposeful. Incrementalism's modesty of purpose is bred of general satisfaction with the present, while planning seeks advantageous change because it is possible to imagine at least one better possible future. Incrementalism has no imagination, because imagination requires future-oriented abstraction and this type of abstraction is simply not necessary when the sole focus of concern is the present.

Continuously iterative planning differs from disjointed incrementalism in several fundamental ways: (1) it discriminatingly *creates* change in addition to merely responding to it; (2) it concerns itself with the interactional *third-party effects*, as well as the transactional two-party effects of the change "ripples" thus created; (3) it seeks to achieve a more desirable set of future states by tending asymptotically toward *optimality*; and finally, (4) it anticipates the future and on the basis of that anticipation and its on-going knowledge of the recent past co-ordinates the relevant components of the present to achieve it.[54]

In spite of the often rather black and white, Manichean character

---

[53] Lindblom (1959), p. 88.
[54] For rather different criticisms of Lindblom's thesis, see Yehezkiel Dror, "Muddling through—'Science' or Inertia?", *Public Administration Review*, Vol. 24, No. 3, September 1964, pp. 153–157; and see also Etzioni (1968), pp. 288–290. Both authors also put forward alternatives to the Lindblom model.

of the theoretical universe inhabited by both planners and their critics[55] it is possible to reject *both* the fluid approach implicit in disjointed incrementalism and the cast-iron approach symbolized by the unitary Master Plan, and assert that there is at least one other way in which it would be possible to conceive of planning as policy making. The third *logically possible* mode of planning—which has been briefly suggested in the previous few pages—views iterative planning as a spiral which seeks to serially and reciprocally relate image to reality within a context of induced, anticipated and unexpected change. Plans are necessarily probabilistic from this viewpoint because they have limited actual control over their environments and also because they are chronically short of reliable information. Even the best plans are not error-free and it is important to acknowledge from the outset that errors are inevitable and "that incorrect predictions are not accidents but are as much a part of the Predicting System as the correct predictions themselves".[56] Iterative learning makes it theoretically possible to identify and correct these errors rather than allowing them to be perpetuated as the process proceeds. The assertion that planning can, and occasionally (with varying degrees of success) does, operate through this type of mode, will be examined in detail as the analysis of empirical evidence proceeds in later chapters. There is, however, one final point which needs to be dealt with at this stage.

AN EXAMPLE OF ITERATIVE PLANNING—STRATEGIC ROAD PLANNING IN GREATER LONDON

Planning is not merely a theoretical exercise, it is also a multi-party organizational activity and the two components cannot be

---

[55] These types of either-or propositions are not limited to planning mode. Dichotomous functions within the mode also play an important part. See Britton Harris' examination of model dimensions, "Quantitative models of urban development", in *Issues In Urban Economics*, Harvey S. Perloff and Lowdon Wingo (Eds.), Baltimore, Md.: John Hopkins Press, 1968, p. 367.

[56] Irwin D. J. Bross, *Design for Decision*, Toronto: Collier–Macmillan, second printing, 1966.

safely divorced from one another. The idea that planning is a means of continuous discovery in addition to being a predictive instrument is a new concept which has received, as yet, very slender treatment in the literature.[57] To further assert that this type of activity occurs and is sustained by an *n*-organization complex of reciprocal information exchange means that there is even less in the way of potential guidance from the traditional planning literature to direct the inquiry. It seems necessary, however, to stress the importance of the planning context since plans are made, maintained and modified through the interaction of the public and private *organizations* on various levels which surround the iterative spiral.

Perhaps it would now be useful to consider an example of the way in which iterative planning operates in practice. This study would provide a useful opportunity to examine a policy issue in detail and act as a means of illustrating the way in which the planning process works. The policy issue selected for analysis is a basic planning concern in London—the relationship between strategic road planning and the concept of urban order. Organizational, technical and political factors all play a material part in shaping the relationship. Since the Greater London Council has played such a significant role in this activity perhaps it would be worth while initially considering some of the factors which underlay its creation and then to consider the way in which they have been developed and modified in practice.

---

[57] John Friedmann does provide one brief reference, see "The future of comprehensive planning: a critique", *Public Administration Review*, Vol. 31, No. 3, May/June 1971, pp. 320–321.

CHAPTER 2

Framing the Problem: Traffic Growth, Town Planning and the Creation of the Greater London Council

> The question raised by the new traffic was, in effect, the old issue which had troubled the eighteenth century, whether the traffic was to be contained to suit the road, or the road constructed to accommodate the traffic.—
> Beatrice and Sidney Webb, *The Story of the King's Highway,* London: reprinted by Frank Cass, originally published 1913, reprinted 1963, p. 242.
>
> Our problem, I submit, is not how to repress or bring under control our system and technology of transport, but rather to know how best to adapt our urban forms to it.—J. Douglas Carroll, "Adopting urban environments to travel technology or the reverse", in T. E. H. Williams (Ed.), *Urban Survival and Traffic,* London: E. J. Spon, 1962, p. 43.

LONDON'S TRAFFIC PROBLEM

Public problems have a distressing tendency to overlap traditional governmental boundaries in both spatial and functional terms. Large-scale problems of this type are not merely broad—they are protean in character and their content and ordering are steadily reshaped as a response to several mediating factors including the constant passage of time. Although organizational perception helps to define this class of problem *for* the organization, organizations are themselves defined as a result of earlier problem perceptions. The relationships between problems and organizations have, as this chapter indicates, an important effect on the planning process.

It had become increasingly evident over a period of years that London—like virtually all other large cities—faced a formidable and progressively worsening transportation problem and that no single organization existed which could resolve it. The visible effects of the problem were difficult to avoid: as Peter Hall observed in *London 2000*, "The transportation problem... is the one that strikes more of us more of the time than any other".[1] Although the problem itself was obvious enough, it was extremely difficult to put forward effective solutions. One critic argued that London was "seizing up, and the principle cause of the chaos is the... increase of motor vehicles".[2] He then went on to argue that the planners had begun to lose control of the capital.

The core of the traffic problem, it was generally agreed, was the steadily increasing level of private automobile ownership and usage in Greater London which had resulted in mounting traffic congestion, particularly in the densely packed central area;[3] it was also agreed that the problem was steadily getting worse. By the late 1950s and 1960s the problem of traffic congestion in the capital caused a great deal of concern, both publicly and privately.

It is perhaps worth while asking what the perceived nature of London's transportation problem was, in terms both of difficulty of movement and its consequent environmental impact. It is clear from comments made by observers and organizational spokesmen that no single answer could satisfactorily serve, because no single problem was collectively and uniformly perceived to exist. Most *public* problems are in fact problem complexes and the components although interrelated display varying rates of change.[4] "The problem" of traffic congestion was in fact several problems which varied in scope according to the values and interests of the labelling organizations. The London County Council, road-building interests,

---

[1] Faber & Faber Ltd., London, 2nd ed., 1969, p. 129; see also Edward Carter, *The Future of London*, Harmondsworth, Middlesex: Penguin Books, 1962, p. 134.
[2] Carter (1962), p. 152.
[3] The central area is that part of London which is bounded by the mainline railway termini: Liverpool Street, St. Pancras, King's Cross, Euston, Marylebone, Paddington, Victoria, London Bridge and Waterloo.
[4] See on this interrelationship among issues, Martin Meyerson and Edward C. Banfield, *Politics, Planning and the Public Interest*, Glencoe, Ill.: The Free Press, 1955, p. 310.

Framing the Problem 27

public transport authorities and various professional bodies all saw "the problem" in different ways.[5]

The Rt. Hon. Ernest Marples, an energetic and controversial Conservative Minister of Transport, put forward a common, if rather narrow, view in a 1963 speech. "The motor car", he maintained, "is not a problem when it is moving; it is a problem when it stops."[6] Under the terms of Mr Marples' definition, the automobile in Greater London had become a problem, first with monotonous and then with alarming, regularity. Although lost time and frayed tempers played a part in bringing the traffic problem to the fore, the real fear was that London would strangle as a result of the activities generated by its own bulk. It became fashionable in the late 1950s and early 1960s to speak of the capital suffering from a traffic thrombosis.[7]

The traffic problem, however, was not new at the turn of the century[8] and a good deal of the urgency which surrounded the problem had a chronic character. Almost 10 years before Mr Marples' speech, the recently retired Commissioner of Police for the Metropolis, Sir Harold Scott, wrote, "... as more and more cars come into use, our streets become more and more like car parks every day, and a reduced police must continue to grapple with the problem of keeping the traffic moving".[9] The Commissioner felt that although various plans had been put forward, "It is not plans, but a decision to put plans into operation that is needed, and there can be no doubt that heavy as the cost would be, it would be amply repaid by saving time in almost every aspect of London life. The alternative is a creeping paralysis which in the end must prove fatal."[10]

[5] See Raymond Bauer, "The study of policy formulation", in Raymond A. Bauer and Kenneth J. Gergen (Eds.), *The Study of Policy Formation*, New York: The Free Press, 1968, p. 14.

[6] "Opening of the conference proceedings", British Road Federation (Ed.), *People and Cities*, London: BRF, 1963, p. 11.

[7] See, for example, "Change and Challenge", Conservative Political Centre, No. 247, London, February 1962, p. 7.

[8] See the *Report of the Royal Commission on London Traffic*, London: HMSO, 1905.

[9] Sir Harold Scott, *Scotland Yard*, London: Andre Deutsch Ltd., 1954, p. 237.

[10] Scott, *Scotland Yard*, p. 239.

28 Strategic Planning in London

The Chairman of the London Transport Executive which controlled all of London's buses and underground railways also expressed grave concern regarding the paradox of urban affluence. The Chairman, Sir John Elliott, wrote in the Executive's 1958 report: "While on the one hand, transport can enable a city to thrive and prosper, traffic can increase because of that prosperity to such an extent that the streets become choked and the city stagnates."[11] During the Christmas of 1958, movement at several trouble spots was almost brought to a standstill again and again. This was felt to be "a warning of what may soon be everyday experience, unless prompt and effective measures are taken, for London is slowly throttling itself".[12]

The body officially charged with making traffic orders and advising the Minister of Transport regarding road conditions in Greater London, the forty-six member London and Home Counties Traffic Advisory Committee was even more concerned.[13] As the *Evening News* noted, London has "Been told by the London and Home Counties Traffic Advisory Committee that unless radical action is taken traffic will come to a standstill in this (the Central) area within five years".[14] According to the Road Research Laboratory, during peak times the average speed in Central London was about 11 miles per hour in 1953. By 1959 the traffic speed had fallen to almost 8 miles per hour.[15]

---

[11] Sir John Elliott, "Forward", *London Transport in 1958*, London: London Transport, 1959, p. 7.

[12] *London Transport in 1958*, p. 14.

[13] The LHCTAC, with members from all the governmental bodies with a traffic concern in Greater London, attempted to take the broadest possible view of affected interests. One member, for example, was specifically appointed "to represent the interests of persons using bicycles and tricycles, not being motor cycles, within the London Traffic Area". The Area, established under the London Traffic Act of 1924, consisted of a circle 25 miles in circumference centering on Charing Cross.

[14] Felix Barker, *Riverside Highway—The Evening News Plan*, St. Albans: Associated Newspapers, 1956, p. 3.

[15] P. F. Scott, "Structure and management", *Traffic Engineering and Control*, Vol. 9, No. 1, May 1967, p. 39.

MOUNTING PRESSURE

The belief that road-building was an essential component in preventing ultimate traffic strangulation seemed to most observers to be axiomatic. The British Road Federation, composed of a large number of commercial interests, argued, for comprehensible reasons, "London's needs are many—the most pressing is a solution to its traffic problems".[16] "Conditions are worsening so rapidly", the report continued, "that a coherent and imaginative road programme for London must be undertaken swiftly."[17]

Although most parties agreed that the main cause of congestion was "insufficient road space to carry the volume of present day traffic",[18] no major new roads were initiated as time passed. Roads were difficult to construct in London—particularly Central London—for three main reasons: (a) the number of administrative agencies involved; (b) the cost of construction, specially with regard to compensation; and, finally, (c) the short-term method of making grants then in existence which militated against the long-range planning necessary for major projects. On the evening of 28 October 1965 matters had reached the point that the Speaker of the House of Commons agreed to allow a 3-hour emergency parliamentary debate to take place whose sole topic of concern was the essentially local problem of London's traffic congestion.

Mr. R. Gresham Cooke (Twickenham), opening the debate for the Opposition, asserted that as a former director of the Society of Motor Manufacturers he was gravely concerned:

> In several parts of London traffic has been brought to a complete standstill in the last week. On the anniversary of the coming to power of the Labour Government London traffic has never been worse than it is now. There is a complete standstill. On Monday evening there was a standstill lasting about an hour in Parliament Square. On Tuesday or Wednesday of this week there was one in Knightsbridge for about one and a quarter hours.[19]

[16] British Road Federation, *London Needs*, London: BRF Ltd., 1960, p. 1.
[17] BRF, *London Needs*, p. 7.
[18] LHCTAC Report to the Ministry of Transport, *London Traffic Congestion*, London: HMSO, 1951, p. 11.
[19] *Parliamentary Debates*, Fifth Series, Vol. 718, cols. 431–432.

"For too long", another speaker in the debate, Sir Clive Bossom (Leominster), argued, "the Government have marked time with a completely negative policy on traffic congestion in London. It is a vast and growing problem... which has really become ugly and terrifying. Time is no longer on our side....".[20]

Speaker after speaker rose to attack the Minister of Transport for what they considered to be his non-constructive policies and his slow rate of implementation; few co-ordinated solutions were advanced, however, as alternatives. Mr. Geoffrey Howe (Bebington) commented acidly that the previous Minister, Ernest Marples, had made mistakes but that he "was out and about doing and trying and introducing solutions... but of the present Minister the most that can be said is, 'For God's sake say something even if its only "Goodbye"'".[21]

On the day of the debate the *Evening Standard* maintained in a leading article that

> the Ministry of Transport awaits the reports of a study group. The Ministry assures us that it is studying the problem. But London's traffic chaos has been the subject of continuous study for years. It is not an over-night revolution and it is about time that the Minister of Transport came up with some concrete suggestions.

The *Evening News* was equally critical: "In the last few days the evening rush hour has given London a sharp foretaste of the complete traffic paralysis which has been threatening for years and looms nearer every week." Critics of the Government were not slow to point out these opinions to the House.

Patience had given way to frustration and frustration to a growing fear about the seeming inevitability of mounting congestion. "We want action from the Minister now", argued Mr Dudley Smith (Brentford and Chiswick), "we have said this a number of times before. We shall repeat it and go on repeating it until we get action."[22] Concern by this point was no longer publicly confined to the Opposition. Even the Government spokesman, the Ministry of Transport's joint Secretary for Parliamentary Affairs, Mr. Stephen

---

[20] *Parliamentary Debates*, Fifth Series, Vol. 718, col. 439.
[21] *Parliamentary Debates*, Fifth Series, Vol. 718, col. 461.
[22] *Parliamentary Debates*, Fifth Series, Vol. 718, col. 437.

Framing the Problem   31

Swingler, tersely agreed that "The situation is known to be urgent".[23] Mr. Swingler also maintained that the Government was spending more on road construction than had ever been spent before and that the problem which had taken some time to assume its present form would take some time to cure.

As the Greater London Council indicated several years later:

> By 1960 the great fear was upon us: how much longer could we go on? When would traffic come to a total standstill? The planners responded to the increasing chaos in the only way they could, at first: by traffic management and minor improvements in lay-out. There was no hope that we could afford really major schemes. One-way systems multiplied. Parking was restricted. Right-turns and U-turns were progressively prohibited. A few major schemes were squeezed in with difficulty, like the Hyde Park Corner underpass.... But these smaller schemes were slow in bearing fruit... the pressure on the roads seemed so strong that the planners thought more and more about American experience with the freeways and enormous parking lots. But whereas the Americans planned in terms of ever greater urban sprawl with central area workers travelling in regularly by car, train and even plane from as far as 100 miles away, British planning has been in terms of containment, not sprawl; Green Belts not ribbon development; New Towns not Satellites. And when it became apparent that there was a yearning across the Atlantic for their vanished public transport it became clear that London demanded a special solution of its own.[24]

The underlying difficulty was essentially a planning problem which turned on the idea of what kind of London *should* be created. The traffic solution could only be approached as a complementary solution to the normative London which was put forward.

One of the difficulties with regard to the traffic problem—like many other aspects of London life—was both where to start and where to end. Many areas cried out for attention but how could they be effectively limited and practically related to one another? However unwillingly, the sheer increase in the number of automobiles per annum within London had a kind of compulsive fascination. This grim interest had a narrowing effect on perspective breadth as the immediate threat filled the foreground. Traffic was not equivalent to transportation but it did represent one of transportation's major failings.

---

[23] *Parliamentary Debates*, Fifth Series, Vol. 718, col. 438.
[24] GLC, *Tomorrow's London*, pp. 63–64.

A few numerical examples will help to demonstrate the magnitude of the problem and the rate at which it was growing during the late 1950s and early 1960s. These examples also indicate that the traffic problem was a problem primarily for, and increasingly affected by, a single mode of transport—the private passenger-carrying vehicle. A study of Central London in 1965 by Munt and Webster revealed that during the morning peak inbound *79 per cent* of the traffic which passed through the cordons consisted of private cars, taxis or motor-cycles. Only 3 per cent of the total of traffic surveyed were buses in spite of the fact that the buses carried more than half of the people entering Central London by road.[25] The predominance of the automobile was not limited to the central area although its effects were perhaps most apparent there. Throughout the London area both automobile ownership and automobile usage showed a steep raise with a predictable increase in the competition for the relatively scarce road space available.

One of the most ominous things about the traffic problem *was* its predictability. The problem had broached certain thresholds of attention with regard to its unpleasantness and inefficiency and it was evident that it would be a very long time before it would even begin to reach its peak. The tunnel became progressively blacker: (a) between 1952 and 1960 the number of private cars checked in annual traffic census counts throughout the administrative county of London rose from roughly 563,000 to over 1,000,000;[26] (b) as a percentage of total traffic automobiles increased during the 8-year period from 32 per cent to 44 per cent; (c) heavy commercial vehicles—operating primarily outside of the central area—grew in percentage terms even faster than the automobile, by more than 100 per cent, during the survey period; and (d) all of these trends showed no signs of abating. What could be done?

---

[25] R. N. Hunt and F. V. Webster, "A study of road traffic crossing the cordons round the central areas of eight towns with populations ranging from 18,000 to 8 million", *Road Research Laboratory Report*, LR 209, Crowthorne, Berkshire, 1968, pp. 35 and 56.

[26] See Table 2.1 for a more detailed disaggregation.

TABLE 2.1. Traffic Numbers at Sixty-four Comparable Points within the Administrative County of London: 1952, 1954, 1956, 1958 and 1960

Type of vehicle	Number of vehicles recorded					Increase(+) or Decrease(−) compared with 1952	
	1952	1954	1956	1958	1960	Number	%
Private cars	563,000[a]	673,000	804,000	893,000	1,045,000	+483,000	+85.8
Taxi cabs	175,000	178,000	182,000	186,000	197,000	+22,000	+12.6
Commercial vehicles:							
Light	437,000	469,000	494,000	485,000	475,000	+38,000	+8.8
Heavy	74,000	85,000	99,000	119,000	155,000	+81,000	+110.1
Locomotives and tractors	1000	2000	1000	1000	2000	[b]	+43.4
Omnibuses	185,000	175,000	159,000	149,000	125,000	−60,000	−32.6
Coaches	15,000	17,000	16,000	16,000	17,000	+1000	+6.6
Tram cars or trolley buses	24,000	25,000	21,000	19,000	12,000	−12,000	−49.1
Private motor-cycles	79,000	89,000	119,000	149,000	191,000	+19,000	+21.3
Pedal cycles	182,000	147,000	144,000	134,000	106,000	−76,000	−41.8
Horse-drawn vehicles and barrows	4000	4000	2000	2000	2000	−2000	−61.3
Motor-assisted pedal cycles	13,000	14,000	22,000	20,000	34,000	+21,000	+179.9
TOTAL: All vehicles:	1,752,000	1,878,000	2,062,000	2,191,000	2,361,000	+609,000	+34.8

[a] All figures have been rounded to the nearest thousand—totals therefore may not agree.
[b] Less than 1000.
SOURCE: Metropolitan Census of Traffic.

The authorities were very concerned indeed; the motorists were incensed; and the public transport authorities were dismayed.[27] If there are any inexorable laws in post-war planning it is that the automobile and related vehicles will steadily increase in number and consume the space which is available and that the demand for such space will constantly exceed the supply.[28] There was, in the 1950s, little chance that the *demand* could be effectively reduced; *the only alternative available was to increase the level of supply*. As Dahl suggests, considerations of broad policies are influenced by a number of related factors:

1. The alternatives "open" or "available" to you.
2. The likely consequences of each alternative.
3. The value to you of each set of consequences.
4. Your estimate of the relative probability of the consequences.
5. Your attitudes toward risk and uncertainty.[29]

On all of these dimensions a massive increase in road space seemed essential for the projected traffic increase. The automobile was not just highly valued—it was inevitable from almost any perspective—and the question became one of how best to cooperate.

TRAFFIC AND TOWN PLANNING IN GREATER LONDON

Two basic issues were raised by the growing volume of traffic: (1) How could traffic best be related to general transportation considerations?; and (2) How could both be related to a desirable form for London? As the traffic problem grew the danger increased that the normative component for planning a future London—or a set of futures for London—would be successively narrowed and heavily weighted in favour of what *must be*. Normative London was, at least in terms of the magnitude of the threat posed, increasingly subjected

---

[27] During the 8-year period the number of buses in service declined by 60,000—almost one-third of the total number of buses in operation.

[28] See on this, for example, Sir Robert Hall (*et al.*), *The Transport Needs of Great Britain in the next Twenty Years*, Report to the Ministry of Transport, London: HMSO, 1963, para. 66.

[29] Robert A. Dahl, *Modern Political Analysis*, Englewood Cliffs, New Jersey: Prentice-Hall, Inc., 1965, p. 97.

Framing the Problem 35

to constraints which consumed enormous amounts of resources—not least of these was the focusing of attention. Alternative Londons were slowly being compressed into an Inevitable London and that London would be chaotic without rapid corrective action.

Two aspects of the traffic problem became steadily more clear as automobile numbers increased and speed decreased: first the problem was growing increasingly urgent; and secondly, as indicated above, that the problem appeared to be inevitable.[30] One critic suggested that the automobile was an irresistible force which was threatening to become an immovable object and destroy the city in the process.[31]

At the same time, however, it should be noted that London possessed an extensive public transport network; although the private automobile was an important component of movement in London it was only one part. Some urban areas are wholly dependent on road-related modes but London was served by an intricate linkage of transportation types.[32] The transportation modes available included all surface and sub-surface road and rail vehicles used within Greater London and reflected the problems and opportunities which they cumulatively created. From a functional point of view, British Rail trains, London Transport underground railways and buses, private passenger vehicles, lorries, bicycles and people on foot are all substantive components of the same problem.

The attempt to come to grips with the problem was additionally complicated by the fact that although modal transportation systems and their relationships with one another were extremely important considerations, even they did not constitute the problem in its entirety since: *it is extremely difficult conceptually or practically to disengage the movement process represented by a particular mode from the structure of an urban area within which the mode functions.*

---

[30] On this see, for example, Joan V. Aucott, "Planning and the motor vehicle", *Town and Country Planning*, Vol. XXVIII, No. 12, December 1960, p. 413.

[31] Wilfred Owen, *The Accessible City*, Washington: The Brooking Institute, 1972, p. 1.

[32] According to a study less than 6 per cent of London's population is more than a mile away from either a London Transport Underground station or a British Rail station or both. GLC, *Greater London Development Plan—Report of Studies*, London: GLC, 1969, p. 147.

There are no perfect transportation patterns because this presupposes a level of uniformity among cities which does not in fact exist. The tension between movement process and structural pattern in the sense of achieving an efficient and agreeable match between the two is a very difficult one, particularly since both components change at different speeds. The transportation problem is a problem in the dynamics of land-use change as well as in the applicability of a particular type of vehicular mode.[33]

The transportation problem is in fact a political, economic and social land-use problem as well. Planning for the resolution, or at least the diminution, of one set of difficulties on this scale necessarily involves impinging on a number of other areas of activity as well. Land-use and transportation planning have an intimate and direct, if a not always intended, impact on one another.[34] As Kirwan suggests within the urban setting—particularly in terms of transportation planning—"everything affects everything else".[35] Since planning necessarily, as Chapter 1 suggested, *deals with both inducing and incorporating change*, transportation planning must be doubly concerned with *impact as well as intent* because of the breadth of its range of influence.

The increasing lack of ease of traffic movement in Greater London had a number of far-reaching planning effects. The Ministry of Housing and Local Government in their submission of evidence in 1959 to the Royal Commission on Local Government in Greater London stated flatly:

> The major failure of planning in Greater London has been dealing with the problem of traffic congestion. Many of the big road proposals in the Abercrombie Plans[36] were abandoned and nothing has taken their place. This is no doubt a

---

[33] On this see, Albert Guttenberg, "Urban structure and urban growth", *Journal of the American Institute of Planners*, Vol. XXVI, No. 2, May 1960, p. 109.

[34] See, for example, Frederick Gutheim, "The future city and its transportation", *Planning Outlook*, New Series, Vol. 7, Autumn 1969, p. 12.

[35] R. M. Kirwan, "Economics and methodology in urban transport planning", in J. B. Cullingworth and S. C. Orr (Eds.), *Regional and Urban Studies*, London: George Allen & Unwin Ltd., 1969, p. 194.

[36] See pp. 74–75 below.

Framing the Problem 37

matter on which the Ministry of Transport will comment. It does illustrate the difficulties which arise out of the existing local government organization when it comes to the really big problems of the region.[37]

It is impossible, and unnecessary, to isolate transportation from its urban context. Even when transportation is considered within its context its importance derives from its ability to *facilitate* activity rather than from its own inherent satisfaction yielding capability.[38] This type of activity facilitation often acts as a spur for geographical growth and London—once again like most major cities—has shown a persistent historical tendency to outgrow its nominal administrative boundaries.[39]

"The first problem with London", as Peter Hall has remarked, "is to define it."[40] This is so not so much because of the present inadequacies of the transportation system but because of their previous success. In the nineteenth century, an early attempt to administratively define the capital resulted in the establishment of the London County Council (LCC) under the provisions of the London Government Act of 1888. The LCC was a political compromise with regard to land area—too large to be a county borough and too small to be a county as they have been traditionally conceived—and even at the time of its creation the *administrative* county did not include the entirety of the fast growing built-up area.

As public transport—particularly motorized transport—grew, London spread. The area governed by the LCC, for example, included a number of competing private and public modes composed of omnibuses, tramways and various underground lines. This fragmented and incomplete transportation complex was drawn together in 1933 and placed under the control of a public body—the London Passenger Transport Board—which was made statutorily responsible for co-ordinating their activities.[41] Among other reasons,

---

[37] Ministry of Housing and Local Government, "Memorandum of evidence", in Royal Commission of Local Government in Greater London, *Memoranda of Evidence from Governmental Departments*, London: HMSO, p. 120. Italics added.
[38] Israel Stollman, "Getting from here to there", *Planning*, Vol. 37, No. 10, November 1971, p. 161.
[39] See, on this, *H. of C. Debates*, Vol. 654, cols. 101–102, 19 February 1962.
[40] Hall, *London 2000*, p. 17.
[41] The creation of the Board was largely due to the suggestion of the London and Home Counties Traffic Advisory Committee and Herbert Morrison who had earlier recommended its creation to the Labour Government.

the largely independent board was established because of the early recognition of the growing level of traffic on the streets and also because no single London government authority including the LCC had a wide enough area of jurisdiction to justify its acting as the Greater London agent for public transport purposes.[42]

The LCC embraced an area of 117 square miles while the London Passenger Transport Area covered nearly 2000 square miles. This mismatch of jurisdictional boundaries had the important effect (in conjunction with the operation of the mainline railways which later became British Rail in 1947) of giving London a public transport system which not only exceeded both its administrative boundaries and its continuously built-up area, but which—partly as a result of historical private enterprise decisions and partly as a result of LPTB policy—systematically funnelled traffic into a relatively tiny 10-square-mile Central Area. Central London which covers roughly one-sixtieth of the built-up area had approximately 30 per cent of the total employment.[43] London was thus a classic representation of what could be called a nuclear city which spread outward in irregular concentric rings from a small and tightly packed centre.[44] The main surface and sub-surface and rail lines radiated in all directions from this single centre and thus reflected and reinforced its primacy. The natural—probably inevitable—result was that in spite of various policies for controlling London's growth including the Green Belt, London continued to expand, and the principal areas of expansion were those which paralleled the main radial lines of communication.[45] London grew throughout the 1950s and its Central Area served not only as the major retail trade market for the South-east, but also as a major public and private employment centre and central area workers took advantage of the existing facilities for rail travel to move progressively further from their place of work. In terms of passenger flows during this period,

[42] See Gerald Rhodes and S. K. Ruck, *The Government of Greater London*, London: George Allen & Unwin Ltd., 1970, p. 159.

[43] GLC, *Movement in London*, London: GLC, 1969, p. 7.

[44] See, for example, an application of von Thunen's rings to an urban setting in Ernest W. Burgess' "Growth of the city", in R. E. Park *et al.* (Eds.), *The City*, Chicago, 1925.

[45] See also for a description, London County Council, *Administrative County of London Development Plan 1951—Analysis*, London: LCC, 1951, p. 142.

Framing the Problem 39

London was centripetal by day and centrifugal by night. In Central London well over a million people entered the area to work every morning and left again every evening.[46] When Duncan Sandys was Minister of Housing and Local Government he remarked, "at the root of almost all London's planning problems is the evil of congestion and its effects on living, working, and travelling conditions".[47]

Increasing automobile usage and ownership during the 10 to 15 years following World War Two created a number of new factors which affected the city's life in addition to the obvious problem of vehicular congestion. A more subtle but no less important change was the slowly evolving effect of a high degree of automobile ownership of the radial and concentric ring configuration of physical London. Rail networks by their nature tend to focus on a single or a small number of points along an essentially linear pattern rather than act as uniform distributors throughout a given area and London until some time after World War Two was an archetypal rail oriented city which bore on a single point.[48] Schematically Greater London resembled a roughly circular target overlaid by a complex network of rail lines bearing on the dense nucleus.[49] Raymond Unwin, the planner mentioned in the first chapter, who played an extremely important part in drawing up a strategy for London suggested that the capital most closely resembled a spider web.[50] Clearly the automobile could have an important impact on city *structure* as well as influencing movement *processes*. One observer has suggested that "the transportation system is at once an essential service and a powerful agent in modifying the land use structure and the spatial organization of the city".[51]

---

[46] GLC, *GLDP Report* (1969), para. 6.57.
[47] LCC, *Minutes 1955*, London: LCC, 1956, p. 130.
[48] See also on this topic, Patrick Abercrombie, *Town and Country Planning*, first published in 1933, London: Oxford University Press, 1959, p. 119.
[49] See for an examination of concentric London, Maurice Ash, *A Guide to the Structure of London*, Bath: Adams & Dart, 1972, pp. 14–30.
[50] Raymond Unwin, *Town Planning in Practice*, 2nd ed., London: T. Fisher Unwin, 1911, pp. 235–236.
[51] Norman Pearson, "Land use and transport systems", *Planning Outlook*, Vol. IV, No. 1, 1956, p. 45.

40 Strategic Planning in London

LACK OF ADMINISTRATIVE CO-ORDINATION

Although, as we have suggested, the urban transportation problem is not merely geographical in nature, the geographical boundary of a city is fundamental. In most studies it provides both a basic term of reference and one of the principle regulating ideas as well. One prevalent concept in transportation planning is that urban areas should be encouraged "to deal with transportation problems on an overall integrated basis to attack problems which spill over the boundaries of individual governmental units".[52]

Within the geographical area of Greater London two very different administrative methods for dealing with public and private movement had evolved, however. In the public sphere the highly centralized London Passenger Transport Board[53] played an active part in providing London (once again in conjunction with British Rail) with a vast infrastructural network which, whatever its geometrical or interchange shortcomings, could be favourably compared with any other world capital in terms of density and extensiveness. Underground lines were extended by the Board as much as 20 miles from Central London.[54] The Board did not, however, closely integrate its activities with any kind of overall plan for London. One critic suggested that "the London Passenger Board, now pioneer, now camp follower, plays a vigorous if sometimes uncertain role. It creates new suburbs and then finds itself unable to cope with traffic: extensions in other directions aim at a further spread of the population."[55]

At the same time, the road system authorities were, by comparison, extremely restricted and fragmented.[56] The mosaic of road

[52] Lyce C. Fitch and associates, *Urban Transportation and Public Policy*, San Francisco: Chandler Publishing Co., 1964, p. 5.

[53] Later the London Transport Executive.

[54] See John Tetlow and Anthony Goss, *Homes, Towns and Traffic*, London: Faber & Faber, 2nd ed., 1968, pp. 29–30.

[55] Patrick Abercrombie, *Greater London Plan 1944*, London: HMSO, 1945, p. 3; see also on this topic C. B. Purdom, *How Shall We Rebuild London?*, London: J. M. Dent, 1945, p. 115.

[56] It should be remembered that one very important public carrier, the bus, is a road user. The difficulties posed by public and private transport cannot simply be resolved into a road–rail split. It is also interesting to note that in terms of passengers carried the bus is the public mode which is experiencing the most difficulty.

Framing the Problem 41

authorities assumed the following pattern in the late 1950s and early 1960s: within Greater London responsibilities for roads were divided among 109 different highway authorities. These included:

    The Ministry of Transport
    6 County Councils
    3 County Borough Councils
    29 Metropolitan Borough Councils (including the City of London Corporation)
    41 Municipal Boroughs
    29 Urban District Councils[57]

There were—to further complicate matters—several classes of road and jurisdiction was divided between the Ministry of Transport and the local authorities.

The LCC, the largest of the governmental units wholly within the built-up area, did not except in a very limited way even possess highway authority powers, or any direct control over road traffic and parking.[58] With the exception of bridges and tunnels, the LCC was compelled after undertaking major projects to return them upon completion to one of the twenty-nine Metropolitan Borough Councils which shared its area of jurisdiction.[59] In general the LCC confined its activities to road widening rather than road building.[60]

London's road pattern was a complex and irregular cobweb of routes which had slowly evolved—with significantly few exceptions—over a period of several centuries. Although physical London had been largely destroyed by the Great Fire of 1666 the road pattern remained substantially unaltered because the rebuilding which occurred after the fire took place, to Wren's annoyance, along almost exactly the same routes which had previously existed.

[57] Ministry of Transport, "Memorandum of Evidence", Royal Commission on Local Government in Greater London, *Memoranda of Evidence of Government Departments*, London: HMSO, 1959, p. 162.
[58] See LCC *Minutes*, 1957, p. 654.
[59] LCC, "Written evidence", Royal Commission, *Written Evidence from Local Authorities, Miscellaneous Bodies and Private Individuals*, London: HMSO, 1962, p. 3.
[60] See, for example, LCC, *Administrative Development Plan Statement 1951*, London: LCC, 1951, p. 8.

Physical Central London is therefore mostly Stuart in terms of its oldest buildings; the *pattern of access*, however, dates well back into the Middle Ages and some of the most important routes are Roman in origin. Attempts were made again and again[61] to build major roads within and around Greater London but the sheer size of the problem coupled with the existing financial and administrative difficulties made rapid or extensive solutions extremely difficult to achieve. With very few exceptions such as the North Circular, major new road projects were simply not undertaken. In the twentieth century as road traffic began its phenomenal increase no major central road project had been completed for over 50 years since the opening of Kingsway in 1905.[62] Few things are more permanent, or for that matter as recent events have shown, more difficult to initiate than major road construction within the inner area.[63]

For some time the amount spent on roads had been extremely limited. One authority, Professor William Robson, argued that the amount spent on roads remained almost constant between 1889 and 1935. During this period the LCC spent approximately £320,000 per annum. Between 1855 and 1889, however, when roads were under the control of the Metropolitan Board of Works, the average annual amount spent was £400,000.[64] After World War Two although road spending began to slowly increase many felt that it was not keeping pace with traffic increase.

The irresistible momentum of traffic increase caused continuing pressure at the point where it met the apparently immovable quantity of road space available within the city core. Throughout the 1950s the distribution of traffic by mode entering the Central area had been changing: during the 10-year period while the number of

---

[61] See, for example, The Board of Trade, *Reports of the London Traffic Branch*, London: HMSO, prior to World War One; or, the Bressey Report, Ministry of Transport, *Highway Development Survey (Greater London)*, London: HMSO, 1937.

[62] Kingsway is a good illustration of the type of difficulties involved—it had taken more than 30 years to complete and had displaced many inner city poor in the process. See Percy Johnson-Marshall, *Rebuilding Cities*, Edinburgh: Edinburgh University Press, 1966, p. 177.

[63] Inner London includes that area which fell under the jurisdiction of the LCC, some 117 square miles in area.

[64] William A. Robson, *The Government and Misgovernment of London*, London: Allen & Unwin, 2nd ed., 1948, p. 196.

Framing the Problem 43

public transport passengers had increased fractionally the number of private transport passengers had more than doubled (see Table 2.2). The following table also indicates that the biggest absolute gain was scored by British Rail while buses lost over 70,000 passengers during the survey period. The number of automobiles had increased by more than 100 per cent and were continuing to grow rapidly. The local authorities were unwilling or more commonly simply unable to meet the demands which this travel shift implied. Space was the key and space was both expensive and limited at the centre. The LCC, although excellent in many other respects, was both too small and too functionally narrow to solve the growing congestion problem.

In December 1957 a Royal Commission was appointed under the chairmanship of Sir Edwin Herbert to investigate town planning, traffic and a number of related matters under the general heading of the effectiveness and convenience of local government in Greater London.

OPPORTUNITY FOR METROPOLITAN PLANNING — THE CREATION OF THE GLC

One of the things the Herbert Commission were most concerned with was the idea of London: what kind of shape it should have assumed and how London had actually for a variety of reasons failed to achieve it. In practice the Commission tended to concentrate on the divergences from a particular strategy and as a result of these divergences to put forward a programme for reform which allowed at least the potential for achieving a closer fit between government scope and activities with the reality of Greater London. The strategy for London was largely based, as the next chapter indicates, on two plans produced during World War Two by Patrick Abercrombie: the *County of London Plan* (1943) and the *Greater London Plan* (1944). One particularly grave flaw which the Commission indicated was the continuing divergence between transportation and strategic planning.[65] Under the terms of the *Greater London*

---

[65] This separation occurred in other geographical areas as well, see Donald L. Foley, "British town planning: one ideology or three?", *British Journal of Sociology*, Vol. II, No. 3, September 1960, p. 229.

TABLE 2.2. PASSENGERS DAILY ENTERING CENTRAL LONDON DURING MORNING PEAK 7–10 A.M. 1950–9

Year	Main Line RR	London Transport RR	London trams, buses	Total public[a]	Private car	Motor-cycles[b]	Pedal cycles	Total private
1950	381,000	461,000	295,000	1,137,000	[c]	[c]	[c]	[c]
1951	375,000	448,000	291,000	1,115,000	40,000	6000	14,000	60,000
1952	382,000	453,000	286,000	1,121,000	45,000	8000	16,000	69,000
1953	373,000	450,000	281,000	1,105,000	50,000	9000	14,000	73,000
1954	396,000	459,000	269,000	1,124,000	55,000	10,000	13,000	78,000
1955	400,000	472,000	271,000	1,143,000	60,000	11,000	13,000	84,000
1956	413,000	469,000	259,000	1,142,000	65,000	11,000	13,000	89,000
1957	426,000	460,000	258,000	1,144,000	69,000	11,000	9000	89,000
1958	441,000	474,000	234,000	1,148,000	79,000	17,000	14,000	110,000
1959	438,000	489,000[d]	222,000	1,149,000	85,000	19,000	12,000	116,000

[a]Public figures have been rounded to the nearest thousand to make them comparable with private figures.
[b]Includes motor scooters.
[c]Figures not available.
[d]Includes for the first time passengers from Knightsbridge and Sloane Square Stations.
SOURCE: *London Statistics 1950–1959.*

Plan 1944, "the planning and construction of highways: improvement of facilities for London Transport, particularly tubes; and suburban railway development" were all to be co-ordinated over a wide area. But over time, partly because of the number of public authorities, "The matter of tubes and suburban railways disappeared entirely and the matter of highway construction very largely".[66] The Commission continued:

> a consequence of this divorce between transport and planning has been the grave increase in congestion on roads, railways and underground railways... it will be far more expensive to provide an adequate road system now than it would have been fifteen years ago, and in the meantime the already intolerable travel conditions... are likely to get worse.[67]

Several interesting points emerge from this section of the Report. The first is that the planning function was considered to be of fundamental importance *for the area as a whole* and formed one of the principal rationales for administrative reform. In 1959 to guide the region's development nine separate County Council and County Borough Plans, all loosely based on the Abercrombie Plans, were in effect[68] and each of them had come into force at different points in time and reflected marginally different perspectives and intentions. Long term co-ordination was exceedingly difficult to achieve.[69] According to one critic, Greater London was

> a bewildering myriad of quasi-independent, and often competing local units—urban districts, metropolitan boroughs, municipal boroughs, county boroughs, administrative counties, special boards, special authorities and special commissions—which were expected to be guided... in a manner that would enable them to plan and implement a coherent, comprehensive and unified public policy for the entire Greater London metropolis.[70]

---

[66] Herbert Commission, *Report*, pp. 87–88. See also the Memorandum by the Minister of Town and Country Planning on the *Report of the Advisory Committee for London Regional Planning*, London: HMSO, 1947.

[67] Herbert Commission, *Report*, pp. 88–89.

[68] Even this was an improvement. Before the 1947 Town and Country Planning Act there were 136 planning authorities in the Greater London Area. See Minister of Local Government and Planning, *Town and Country Planning 1943–51*, London: HMSO, 1951, p. 73.

[69] Frank Smallwood, *Greater London*, Indianapolis: Bobbs-Merrill, 1965, p. 74.

[70] Smallwood (1965) and see William A. Robson (1948), p. 142.

One observer stated in fact that

> It is not an exaggeration to say that the need for an area-wide planning authority is the crux of the case for the reorganization of London Government. Although there were undoubtedly other highly important considerations underpinning the arguments put by the Commission, notably the co-ordination of planning with highways, traffic and housing... had there not been an overwhelming case for a "permanent Abercrombie" for London, it is doubtful whether the Herbert Report could have taken the far reaching form that it did.[71]

The second point is that in spite of the quite explicit criticism levelled by the Commission of previous failures to consider transportation and planning under a single head, they themselves had been placed in exactly the same position. The consideration of public transport was specifically excluded from their terms of reference by the Government before their deliberations had even begun. As the Prime Minister explained to the House of Commons it was felt that the Herbert Commission had a difficult enough job to do and that "to have given them further tasks such as looking at public transport would have been a very big undertaking".[72] The exclusion of public transport meant that the administrative idea which was to become the GLC was given a particular type of orientation with regard to movement in London 7 years before it came into legal existence. Finally, another type of administrative orientation was provided by the Commission's overt recognition of the need "to provide an adequate road system", concluding with the warning that *until* it was constructed "travel conditions... are likely to get worse".

One revealing theme which runs through the *Report*'s 9th chapter is the divisibility of the traffic sub-component. Just as the traffic problem was a sub-set of the transport problem so traffic itself could be divided into a number of major sub-components. Among other things, the Herbert Commission included under the title "traffic" three "separate though related subjects": traffic management (including parking), highway planning and highway construction. The

---

[71] L. J. Sharpe, "Research in local government", The London School of Economics, Greater London Papers No. 10, 1965, pp. 8–9.
[72] Quoted by Gerald Rhodes, *The Government of London: The Struggle for Reform*, London: Weidenfeld & Nicolson, 1970, pp. 22–23.

Commission agreed with the Ministry of Transport that "the machinery of administration of road traffic in London is at present unsatisfactory".[73] One of the Commission's most important findings in this field was that *"while improvement of administrative machinery will not of itself solve London's traffic problem, that problem is insoluble under the present machinery"*.[74] The Commission recommended that a single authority should be established to control traffic for the whole of the Greater London area.

It is interesting to note in the Ministry of Transport's evidence to the Commission that it was extremely concerned with *through* traffic. It was stated for example that "... the Ministry, in the interests of through traffic, must think in terms of length of road and not in terms of local authority boundaries enclosing blocks of population".[75] The MOT therefore indicated that it favoured a reduction in highway authorities, at the same time, however, it became increasingly evident that the Ministry would play a very strong part in traffic matters in the capital even after reorganization.[76]

At least in the short term the transportation problem became one of traffic management—of moving people and vehicles expeditiously through the streets.[77] Traffic concerns and roads bulk large in the Commission's conclusions but no mention was made either of the environment through which the traffic passed or of transportation generally. Logically there was unanimous agreement that various transport modes were part of a seamless whole; in practice an important rent had been once again identified and once again regretfully perpetuated. A *geographical* limit to the scope of the problem had been suggested, however, and a *functional* administrative basic minimum requirement—a single authority—had been put forward as an essential condition for the problem's ultimate resolution. The Herbert Commission reported in 1960 and the mass of

---

[73] Ministry of Transport, "Evidence" (1959), p. 169.
[74] Herbert Commission, *Report* (1959), p. 119. Italics added.
[75] Ministry of Transport, "Evidence" (1959), p. 165.
[76] See Michael Goldrick, "The administration of transportation in Greater London", unpublished Ph.D. Thesis, London School of Economics, 1967, p. 155.
[77] A London Traffic Management Unit was set up by the MOT in 1960 to speed the traffic flow. See Rhodes and Ruck (1970), p. 98.

48 Strategic Planning in London

evidence from various authorities, and individuals, persuaded them that the establishment of a Council for Greater London was not only desirable but imperative if Central Government control was to be avoided, and London's growth-related problems were to be effectively tackled.[78]

The Government indicated in their 1961 White Paper, *London Government: Government Proposals for Reorganisation*,[79] a broad acceptance of the Herbert Commission's recommendations, although they did favour making the boroughs larger and more powerful than did the Commission.[80] The White paper noted

> London has clearly outgrown the system of local government devised to meet the vastly different physical and social conditions of the last century. This great town now faces immense problems of congestion, of traffic, of land shortage and of major redevelopment.[81]

In November of the 1962–3 Session of Parliament a lengthy and complicated London Government Act was introduced. The Act was vigorously and sometimes bitterly opposed both in the House of Commons and in the House of Lords by the Labour Opposition and by some Home County Tories. The Government was accused of offences ranging from unnecessary disturbance to blatant gerrymandering. The Deputy Leader of the Labour Party, George Brown, called it a "crack-pot plan" in January 1962, and Hugh Gaitskell, the Opposition Leader, referred to the Act 5 months later as "a squalid attempt on the part of the Tory Party to snatch the banner of London for itself by altering the boundaries because they cannot get the votes".[82]

Resistance was extremely stiff in both Houses: about 1500 amend-

---

[78] The suggestion that a Ministry of London be created was generally regarded with distaste by most observers as being inimical to local democracy, see "A Council for Greater London?", *Labour Research*, Vol. 49, No. 12, December 1960, pp. 204–205.

[79] Cmnd. 1562, London: HMSO, 1961.

[80] The Commission recommended the creation of fifty-one boroughs while the Government suggested that the figure should be put at thirty-two (including the City of London) and this is the figure which was eventually adopted.

[81] Cmnd. 1562, p. 4.

[82] Quoted by F. Smallwood (1965), p. 261.

Framing the Problem   49

ments[83] were introduced and the Opposition vowed to fight the Bill line by line and repeal it if they were elected within the year. During the passage of the Bill the unpopular guillotine—the Allocation of Time order—was used twice: once with regard to the original proposal and again to take cognizance of the Lords' amendments. The House of Lords was subjected to the longest single sitting in its long history.[84] Even with these expedients, however, the Act took 7 months to progress through both Houses and it was not until July 1963 that the royal assent was given.

Under the terms of the Act a metropolitan Greater London Council was established which came into official existence on 1st April 1965. A good deal of the manifest concern with traffic is actually built into the structure of the Bill. This "parent statute" revealed many of the basic policy considerations which were to play so large a part in governing subsequent strategic planning for the London area. Briefly, the Act stipulated:

(A) *Area and Composition.*[85] Greater London was to be 620 square miles in area[86] with a two-tier governmental structure consisting of: (1) a top tier Greater London Council which undertook the strategic function required by its 7,850,000 inhabitants; and (2) 32 Greater London "most-purpose" Boroughs (plus the City of London) each with an approximate population of 250,000.[87]

(B) *Strategic Planning Powers.*[87] (1) An important guiding principle in determining the complicated relationship between the GLC and the powerful

[83] Some parliamentarians feel that this probable record was due as much to the complexity of the Bill as to the Opposition's attempt to weaken it since many of the amendments were government initiated.

[84] In the Lords' debate, the former Leader of the LCC, Lord Morrison, argued that the attempt to create a GLC was merely an example of the passion for superficial tidiness which bedevilled the higher civil service. See William A. Robson, "The reform of London Government", *Public Administration*, Vol. 39, Spring 1961, p. 66. There is a certain historical irony in this contention since it was Morrison who was responsible, as a former Minister of Transport, for tidying up privately owned public transport and creating the London Passenger Transport Board in 1933.

[85] London Government Bill, Part I, Clauses 1 and 2 and schedule 1.

[86] Which roughly coincided with the inner edge of the Green Belt and was a compromise between the LCC's 117 square mile area and the Royal Commission's review area of 845 square miles.

[87] Once again this was a compromise between the twenty-nine old London Boroughs and the Herbert Commission's recommended fifty-two boroughs. For an example of the GLC's view of current powers and functions see GLC, *Greater London Services*, London, 1970–1971, pp. 11–12.

Strategic Planning in London

Boroughs was the Government's contention that the GLC was not a "higher" but a "wider authority";[88] (2) the GLC was to be the planning authority, in consultation with the boroughs, for the whole of its area with the GLC producing a broad strategic plan—the Greater London Development Plan (GLDP)—and the boroughs fitting in more detailed local structure plans and local action plans after ministerial approval of the GLC's plan; (3) The Greater London Development Plan "*shall lay down considerations of general Policy with respect to the use of land in the various parts of Greater London, including in particular guidance as to the future road system...*"[89] (4) In general development control was to be undertaken by the boroughs with the GLC acting as a reviewing authority without veto powers. There are certain important exceptions however including those developments which are deemed to have strategic importance, and which are therefore dealt with directly by the GLC.[90]

(C) *Highway Powers.*[91] As in strategic planning a complex division of labour obtains among the various levels of government involved. In this case an additional complicating factor is the active part played by the Ministry of Transport, which has a number of concurrent administrative powers[92] exercised in conjunction with the GLC. A tripartite division of roads was established: (1) Trunk Roads, one hundred and fifty miles in length, were the responsibility of the Ministry; (2) Metropolitan Roads[93] five hundred and fifty miles in length, were the responsibility of the GLC and; (3) the remaining Local Roads within the area, some seven thousand miles in length, were the responsibility of the boroughs through which they pass.[94] (The metropolitan road designation has important planning implications because the GLC has been given development control—220 feet—on either side of this type of main road.) Finally under the terms of the Bill[95] the boroughs could be named as the agents of the GLC with regard to road construction, but—particularly with regard to Metropolitan Roads—the

---

[88] The phrase is Sir Keith Joseph's. See for additional information on strategic planning Peter Self, *Metropolitan Planning*, 1971, pp. 12–14.

[89] Bill, Part II, 25(3). Italics added.

[90] See The Town and Country Planning (Local Planning Authorities in Greater London) Regulations, 1965. Statutory Instruments 1965, No. 679, reg. 4, and see also (C)(3).

[91] Bill, Part II, clauses 16–18, and schedule 7.

[92] As opposed, for example, to the financial powers exercised through its principle road grant-making powers. The original bill which the Government drafted contained an even larger role for the MOT but this was diminished by subsequent amendments. See *Parliamentary Papers 1961–62*, Vol. 2, HMSO: London. It does serve to indicate the reluctance with which the Ministry relinquished its powers and the implicit belief that the untried GLC was not capable of mastering its own traffic matters.

[93] See Schedule 8 of the Bill. Although these roads were listed they were not *defined* and no criteria for their selection was indicated except that their importance was of a "metropolitan" character.

[94] See the London Boroughs Association, *LBA Handbook*, London: GLC, 1970, p. 17.

[95] Part II, clause 18.

Framing the Problem 51

GLC chose to create its own large construction section.
(D) *Traffic Management Powers*.[96] The GLC was responsible for making traffic orders in consultation with the boroughs, the Metropolitan Police and the Ministry of Transport.[97] These orders included such schemes as one-way systems, the banning of right-hand turns and the creation of urban clearways. In the first draft of the Bill a Director of Traffic position was created to help carry these schemes into operation, it was later deleted as being too restrictive, however. In spite of reservations on the part of the Ministry—a provision was written into the Act requiring the GLC to inform the MOT of the administrative machinery it proposed to establish to discharge its traffic powers before 1st April 1965[98]—the GLC assumed the work of the Ministry's London Traffic Management Unit. There were, however, a number of concurrent powers still remaining. Finally, the GLC shared power with the boroughs in the provision of off-street parking facilities. Again the GLC was limited in its latitude and could only undertake the provision of this type of parking with the prior consent of the borough involved.[99] Matters were later clarified to a certain extent by the Transport (London) 1969 Act.

In summary the GLC became the strategic planning for the whole area[100] the highway authority for the Metropolitan Roads, and the traffic management authority for all of the roads within the area.[101] The powers, however, were subject to a complex division of responsibilities among the various governmental tiers and a number of potential difficulties existed. Matters were particularly complicated by the interlocking powers possessed by the Ministry of Transport, the GLC and the London Boroughs with regard to highways and planning. As the following chapters indicate because their respective responsibilities were not clearly spelled out, interauthority problems played a central part in Greater London's

[96] Bill, Part II, clauses 9–11.
[97] One important limitation on the GLC's powers in this regard is that the GLC was not allowed to make traffic orders affecting the Ministry's trunk roads without the prior consent of the Minister. Clause 10(3).
[98] Part II, clause 9.
[99] For a general consideration of the 1963 Act see Rhodes and Ruck (1970), pp. 45–69.
[100] Even at the time of the White Paper the Town Planning Institute and the Royal Institute of Chartered Surveyors expressed the opinion that the GLC would not be large enough or have enough effective planning control to act as a truly metropolitan authority. See Rhodes (1970), p. 138.
[101] See "The work of the Highways and Traffic Committees 1966–67", London: GLC, typewritten, April 1967, p. 1.

52 Strategic Planning in London

planning process.[102] As one senior GLC Officer noted, "Whatever divinity shaped the London Government Act of 1963 left the ends a little rough-hewn".[103]

The creation of the GLC was an important step in the attempt to define London's transportation problem through the establishment of an expanded boundary and an increase in administrative powers. As two commentators noted:

> Looked at from the angle of the GLC...it is useful to consider planning, highways and traffic together, not only because of the links between them but also because, apart from housing, most other functions of the GLC although important in themselves, do not add up to an argument for a large authority of this type. The GLC is a strategic planning authority, taken in the widest sense, or it is nothing.[104]

After having considered some of the factors—such as the perceived importance of the traffic problem—which played a part in shaping the GLC perhaps it would be worth while going on to consider the basic planning strategy which underlay the attempt to control London's growth. As Chapter 3 indicates a blueprint for the capital was already in existence which the GLC faithfully followed during its first years of life. The nature of the blueprint and the way in which the GLC applied it had an important effect on the planning process and on the way in which the traffic problem has been successively modified over time.

---

[102] See on the division of functions, Greater London Group, "The lessons of the London Government reforms", *Royal Commission on Local Government in England*, London: HMSO, p. 31.

[103] C. D. Andrews, "The GLC as a transportation authority", *Journal of the Greenlands Association*, Vol. 3, No. 7, Spring 1970, p. 234.

[104] Rhodes and Ruck (1970), p. 96.

CHAPTER 3

Constructing a Solution: A Planning Prescription for Physically Controlling London's Traffic

> Make no little plans; they have no magic to stir men's blood, and probably themselves will not be realized. Make big plans: aim high in hope and work, remembering that a noble, logical diagram, once recorded, will never die, but long after we are gone will be a living thing, asserting itself with ever growing insistency.—Daniel Burnham.
>
> Although the larger scale thinking made possible by the huge area of the GLC changed the picture, much of what is happening now had its foundations laid before 1965.—John Craig, GLC Chief Developments Planner (December 1970).

ABERCROMBIE'S THREE LONDONS—AN ORGANIC VIEW

The shaping of the Greater London Council was a rational attempt, tempered by political modifications, to create an organizational structure which would be capable of freshly and vigorously tackling the London area's growing planning and traffic problems. The new administrative instrument was guided, however, from the moment of its creation by several on-going strands of thought indicating a desirable relationship between London's overall form and traffic's place within that basic framework. Few organizations, however, now are in fact completely free from either their predecessor's personnel or the major operating strategies which gave meaning to their previous activities. Most "new" administrative units do in practice exhibit a high level of continuity since they inherit large measures of both. But if the GLC was not a complete *tabula rasa* it did at least provide the *opportunity* for a fundamental reassessment of London's planning problems. Many critics felt that such a re-examination was long overdue.[1] Although London had changed dramatically since World War Two in a variety of ways the capital continued to be guided by a body of officially accepted assumptions and prescriptions which were in large measure more than 20 years old before the GLC had even begun its official existence.

The principle source of suggestions for dealing with the London region at the most fundamental level were contained in two documents: the *County of London Plan (1943)*[2] prepared by Professor Patrick Abercrombie and J. H. Forshaw for the London County Council, which covered the LCC's 117-square-mile area;[3] and Abercrombie's much larger *Greater London Plan 1944*,[4] covering almost 2600 square miles, prepared for the Ministry of Works and Planning[5] at the request of Lord Reith. Both plans were advisory in character and were expressly designed to give guidance to governmental policy makers.

The influence of the plans has been so pervasive that it is difficult to discuss planning London without agreeing with—or reacting against—Patrick Abercrombie's view of the city. An understanding of conceptual development of a proposed solution for that apparently most intractable of urban difficulties—traffic congestion—is simply not possible without at least a general consideration of Abercrombie's perspective. Although Abercrombie's views are interesting for purely historical reasons they also are even more significant because of the extent of their actual influence on subsequent local and national government decisions. As Wyndham Thomas wrote, of the many advisory plans produced during World War Two, "none achieved greater publicity, was bolder in its proposals, or has come nearer to fulfilment than Abercrombie's

---

[1] Peter Self, "Town planning in Greater London", Greater London Papers No. 7, London School of Economics, 1962, p. 11; and see the Herbert Commission *Report* (1960), pp. 80–93.
[2] Known hereafter as *CLP (1943)*.
[3] Macmillan & Co. Ltd., London, 1943.
[4] Known hereafter as *GLP (1944)*.
[5] HMSO: London, 1945.

Constructing a Solution 55

Greater London Plan of 1944".[6] The plans were initially well received[7] and a former member of the staff which prepared the 1943 Plan under Abercrombie's direction, Alec Bellamy, could still remark many years later: "On reflection I retain the conviction that this contribution to London has fully measured up over the passage of time to the acclaim it was first accorded."[8] One of the top GLC planners, John Craig, simply and approvingly noted in 1970 that the *County of London Plan* was "the biggest landmark in urban planning".[9]

In the late 1950s the Ministry of Housing and Local Government explained that

> The Abercrombie–Forshaw County of London Plan (1943) and the Greater London Plan (1944) by Sir Patrick Abercrombie form the basis for policy and assumptions regarding the development of the Greater London Area. The plans were endorsed by the planning authorities concerned and although there have been amendments they still provide the background against which Development Plans are prepared under the 1947 Town and Country Planning Act.[10]

At the local government level the County of Kent asserted that the Greater London Plan "has virtually been written into..." the various development plans for the London area and the two most affected counties—London and Middlesex—echoed these views in their own official statements.[11]

Given this enduring influence, what precisely—particularly with regard to traffic—did Abercrombie (a) perceive to be, and (b)

---

[6] "The growth of the London Region", *Town and Country Planning*, Vol. 29, No. 5, May 1961, p. 185.

[7] They were also quickly put into use. See the Minister of Town and Country Planning's 1946 Memorandum to planning authorities indicating that the *GLP (1944)* would serve as the interim development guide for the region. Reproduced in *The Journal of the Town Planning Institute*, Vol. XXXII, No. 2, January–February 1946, p. 69.

[8] Quoted by John Craig, "The 1943 London Plan: a perspective", *Official Architecture and Planning*, Vol. 33, No. 12, December 1970, p. 1076.

[9] Craig (1970), p. 1075.

[10] Ministry of Housing and Local Government, "Written evidence", Herbert Commission, p. 119. See also on this topic Chapter 4, pp. 104–105.

[11] See LCC *Minutes 1950*, p. 473; and Middlesex, "Written evidence", Herbert Commission, p. 248; and see also Peter Shepeard *et al.*, "The New London", text of a BBC radio broadcast which took place on the Third Programme, 28 March 1950, typescript, p. 8.

prescribe for London's principal defects? One of the keys to understanding Abercrombie's proposals was the fact that although he was a brilliant synthesizer with a concern for the whole of the planning sphere, he was also, partly because of his breadth of vision, relatively unconcerned either with the resource cost of the plans or with the impact of unforeseen change on the solutions which he advanced.[12] Although he carefully drew together several disparate threads and created an intelligible and attractive London his vision of the future was largely a static one.[13] By pursuing the proposals outlined in the plans, often worked out in considerable detail, a corrective process was to be initiated, it was hoped, which would lead ultimately to the realization and maintenance of a stable state for the entire area.[14] Through planned development Greater London was to achieve an essentially changless equilibrium.

Paradoxically in many ways the plans were based on an organic concept of the city. Although London had grown naturally a conscious development policy was required it was argued if it were to achieve its full potential and a balanced maturity. As Abercrombie wrote in 1933 regarding his theory of the role of planning:

> Town and Country Planning seeks to proffer a guiding hand to the trend of natural evolution as a result of careful study of the place itself and its external relationships. The result is to be more than a piece of skilful engineering or satisfactory hygiene or successful economics; it should be a *social organism* and a work of art.[15]

This blending of the natural and the artificial constituted the essence of good planning for Abercrombie and it was clear that the purposeful intervention on the part of the planner from a design point of

---

[12] See for costs and priorities, for example, the *CLP (1943)*, pp. 18–20, or the *GLP (1944)*, pp. 185–186.

[13] See for a contemporary criticism along these lines, Prof. Gordon Stephenson's address to the Town and Country Planning Association, "Hopes and fears for the London plans", 5 October 1951, typescript, p. 4; and see also for a more recent criticism, Herbert Gans' analysis of the impact of this type of approach in the U.S., "City planning in America: a sociological analysis", in *People and Plans*, Harmondsworth, Middlesex: Penguin Books, 1972, pp. 78–79.

[14] *CLP (1943)*, p. 3 and see also p. 121.

[15] Patrick Abercrombie, *Town and Country Planning*, London: Oxford University Press, 1933, 3rd edition revised by D. Rigby Childs (1959), p. 27, italics added; and see also *CLP (1943)*, p. 145.

Constructing a Solution   57

view was to be subservient to the needs of the city as a coherent and unified whole.[16] Thus though Abercrombie felt that design considerations should play an important part in the building of the new London[17] they should only be employed to the extent that they strengthened the perceived underlying order. London was to be *corrected* through a set of interlocking proposals rather than transformed.[18] Before turning to these proposals, however, it would be useful to briefly attempt two things: first to sketch the main lines of thought which influenced Abercrombie's conception of a desirable order for the city; and secondly to examine the other half of the equation: the nature of London's perceived defects.

To argue that the London Plans attempted to reaffirm an existing order which had somehow been blurred or distorted by excessive growth and overcrowding begged the fundamental question of the *nature* of the order sought. In his planning synthesis for London, Abercrombie carried on what could almost be called a classical view of the city and of planning's purpose within it. In terms of thoroughness and comprehensiveness the plans went further than any previous documents dealing with London had done but few of the actual ideas which they advanced were new. Abercrombie's formulations were firmly in the main stream of British planning and he borrowed extensively from the work of the early leaders of the planning movement—Howard, Geddes and Unwin.[19]

The thread which knitted these various contributions together was

[16] For a purely architectural treatment of London see the Royal Academy's Plan which was also produced during World War Two under the direction of Sir Edwin Lutyens and Sir Charles Bressey. The Academy's planning committee stated explicitly that their "principle concern is with good architectural planning and design...", Royal Academy Planning Committee, "London replanned" (interim report), *County Life*, 1942, p. 15.

[17] *GLP (1944)*, p. 180.

[18] See for an example of a proposed transformation the MARS Plan, also produced during World War Two, A. Korn and F. J. A. Samuely, "A master plan for London" (Modern Architectural Research Group), *Architectural Forum*, Vol. XCI, No. 546, June 1942, pp. 143–150; and see also C. M. Buchanan, *London Road Plans 1900–1970*, Research Report No. 11, Greater London Council, London, December 1970, p. 23.

[19] "Oscar Wilde said he went to the first night of his own plays to see if the audience was a success. The publication of the County of London Plan by Sir Patrick Abercrombie and J. H. Forshaw was in some ways a Geddes' first night"—T. Findlay Lyon, "After Geddes", *Planning Outlook*, Vol. 1, No. 1, July 1948, p. 15.

the description of London as an organic complex. Patrick Geddes, for example, a botanist, compared urban areas in his 1915 work, *Cities in Evolution*, with a coral-reef complex.[20] The most powerful of these biological analogies, however, was probably also the most familiar: that of the city as a garden. Ebenezer Howard was particularly concerned in his influential *Garden Cities of Tomorrow* (1902) with securing an actual increase in green space by constructing purpose-built new communities.[21] Two changes occurred, however, as time passed to give Howard's intent a rather wider meaning. First, the garden concept began to be employed as an analogy for the functioning of the city as well as a prescriptive device for increasing a particular type of land use.[22] In this vein, Raymond Unwin, remarked that although men could not create natural beauty the gardener's art allowed him to construct a frame for nature.[23] He then went on to examine "the strong analogy between the landscape school of gardening and the informal system of town planning" and concluded that in England at any rate, "there is a direct historical connection...".[24]

Secondly, as Abercrombie showed, it was possible to apply Garden City principles to an existing community—even one as vast and amorphous as London.[25] One of the leaders of the Garden City movement, Sir Frederick Osborn, wrote in 1945 that the *Greater London Plan of 1944* was "the most fully worked out Garden City plan for a great metropolis".[26] Sir William Holford who played an

---

[20] New Edition with an Introduction by Percy Johnson-Marshall, Ernest Benn Ltd., London, 1968, p. 142.

[21] Faber & Faber Ltd., London, New Edition, 1946, pp. 51–53.

[22] This view of the city organic is still a persuasive one. Amos Hawley has written of the city that it is "...a whole which is something different from the sum of its parts, possesses powers and potentialities not present in any of its components. If not an organism it is at least a super-organism." Quoted by Leo T. Schnore, "The city as a social organism", in Larry S. Bourne (Ed.), *Internal Structure of the City*, New York: Oxford University Press, 1971, p. 34.

[23] *Town Planning in Practice*, 2nd ed., London: T. Fisher Unwin, 1911, p. 120.

[24] Unwin (1911), p. 126.

[25] This was one of Howard's long-range intentions and he briefly considered this problem in the 13th chapter of *Garden Cities*, "The future of London", pp. 151–159. From this perspective the County of London Plan was as much a Howard first night as it was Geddes'.

[26] Osborn, "The Garden City Movement: a revaluation", *The Journal of the Town Planning Institute*, Vol. XXXI, No. 6, September–October 1945, p. 204.

Constructing a Solution 59

important part in planning the reconstruction of the City of London stated that the Abercrombie Plans, "are attempts to continue London's long tradition of distinction. It is still possible as Unwin and Abercrombie believed for it to open up into an *organic* pattern in spite of its size and disorder".[27]

Gradually the organic analogy[28] was extended, formalized and accepted as a conceptual model for the way in which London *should* develop. The continuing fundamental assumption which ran through the work of Abercrombie and his predecessors was that a natural order for London existed and that the planner's initial function was as Herbert Simon has remarked in another context, "to show that complexity, correctly viewed is only a mask for simplicity", and that there is in fact "a pattern hidden in apparent chaos".[29] This is partly because "Chaos is only the absence of order and order is nothing but the understanding of structure".[30] The planner's task was, by means of analysis, to discern London's hidden structure and then act to reduce the chaotic element which manifested itself in perceived defects by means of structural corrections.

According to the biological perspective employed by Abercrombie, London's principal defects arose not from its essential structure but precisely because this basic form had never been properly realized. Excessive growth of population, employment, and travel provided the key disruptive influences and each of these factors had a mutually reinforcing effect on the others in preventing a desirable order from being achieved.[31] Four specific defects were identified: (i) *"The most obvious and ubiquitous defect in pre-war London was that of traffic, both the congestion in the streets and the strap-*

---

[27] "The Plans for London", text of a BBC radio programme broadcast on the 3rd Programme on 5 April 1950, typescript, p. 2.

[28] See again Schnore (1971), p. 34; and for a wider view, Gilbert Herbert, "The organic analogy in town planning", *Journal of the American Institute of Planners*, Vol. XXIX, No. 3, August 1963, p. 200.

[29] *The Sciences of the Artificial*, Cambridge, Mass.: MIT Press, 1969, p. 1.

[30] William Alonso, "Cities and city planners", in H. Wentworth Eldredge (Ed.), *Taming Megalopolis*, Doubleday & Co. Inc., Garden City, New York, Vol. II, 1967, p. 587.

[31] Form, from this perspective, was conceived of in an almost Aristotelian sense as "the organization of a certain structure to achieve a certain end", where the end was taken as given. See Herbert (1963), p. 200, for a defence of this perspective.

60   Strategic Planning in London

hanging in tubes."[32] (ii) A second defect was that of depressed residential areas particularly in the East End.[33] (iii) Thirdly, there was an inadequate and uneven distribution of parks and open spaces.[34] (iv) Finally, there was "an apparent haphazard mixing up of industry and housing...".[35] Although these shortcomings could be conceived of as at least analytically separable they were in fact according to the plans closely related and the problem of unrestricted growth played a major part in the creation of each. It was at this point that planning could begin to play a constructive role. In London, "There is no coherence, no compactness, no convenience", Abercrombie wrote, "Can the designer bring order into this disorderly medly? Something must be attempted."[36]

In many ways the Abercrombie Plans were an attempt to achieve development through redistribution rather than growth in the hope that decentralization would ultimately mean decongestion.[37] The central prescriptive belief which Abercrombie held with regard to London was that it was too large, and that although population was declining within the LCC area the downward trend was both too disorderly and too slow. He further held, based on the Barlow Commission Report[38] and discernible natural trends, that within the

---

[32] *CLP (1943)*, p. 3, italics added.
[33] *CLP (1943)*, p. 4.
[34] *CLP (1943)*, p. 4.
[35] *CLP (1943)*, p. 5.
[36] *GLP (1944)*, p. 82.
[37] See, for a criticism of the decentralizing school in America, Jane Jacobs, *The Death and Life of Great American Cities*, New York: Random House, 1961, pp. 29–30. With regard to much of the Garden City movement's development Mrs. Jacobs' criticisms are fundamentally misconceived. Two general points may be made: first, the Garden City proponents are in no sense "anti-city", as Mrs. Jacobs charges, rather they are against the symptoms of a certain city *type* arising from overcrowding. From Howard on, the attempt has not been to destroy a place like London but to revive it *internally*, as well as decanting population externally. The first half of this consideration is largely neglected in *Death and Life*. Secondly, it is simply not true that decentrists like Abercrombie have made no attempt to understand how a large city works; clearly he did, as his plans demonstrate. Unfortunately Abercrombie, one of the most important planning figures of the twentieth century and the leading practitioner of how Garden City concepts may be employed in a world city, is not even considered by Mrs. Jacobs.
[38] *Report of the Royal Commission on the Distribution of the Industrial Population*, Cmd. 6153, London: HMSO, 1940. Abercrombie was a member of the Commission.

Greater London area (as well as the nation as a whole)[39] "the total population will not increase, but on the contrary, will be somewhat reduced".[40] Given a relatively constant level of population *and a powerful planning co-ordinating agency*[41] it would thus be possible to *plan for stability* within the Greater London area by reducing congestion through density controls and the removal of industrial concerns; altogether the plans proposed that well over a million people were to leave the built-up area to allow the desired equilibrium to be achieved. Decongestion within the city was thus to be achieved through an external decentralization of both workers and their jobs in a concentrated pattern of dispersement outside of London's boundary. Continuously built-up London was to be *contained*[42] by the long-advocated Green Belt[43] thus allowing a clear distinction to be drawn between town and countryside.[44] Within the area surrounding London, New Towns, expanded existing towns and satellites were to receive the population overflow and function as complete communities rather than as mere dormitories. Greater London was to become an ordered set of communities—in one case created afresh and in the other renewed and revived—on the basis of the same fundamental principals.[45] These measures—basically a vast pruning exercise—would allow natural boundaries to be more "sharply defined instead of blurred as in an image of an out-of-focus photograph".[46]

Within London the natural boundaries had two principal lines of demarcation: (a) the *functional* and (b) the *spatial*. In terms of

---

[39] At least one major demographical work produced during this period, *The Population Problem*, felt that the *problem* was the *lack* of population growth. T. H. Marshall (Ed.), London: Allen & Unwin, 1938.
[40] *GLP (1944)*, p. 5.
[41] The Greater London Plan proposed the establishment of a regional planning board with executive powers.
[42] See on the containment philosophy, M. L. Harrison, "Development control", in *Town Planning Review*, Vol. 43, No. 3, July 1972; and Foley (1963), pp. 54–55.
[43] See, for example, Raymond Unwin's 1933 Memorandum to the London Regional Planning Committee in their *Second Report*, London: Knapp, Drewitt & Sons Ltd., 1933, p. 48.
[44] Abercrombie (1933), p. 19.
[45] See the Cohesive Mode prescriptions on p. 101.
[46] *GLP (1944)*, p. 7.

function organic London divided into three different but basically complementary components: (i) first, London consisted of a complex of *communities* where people lived, worked and participated in social activities but which had been marred by excessive densities or by mixed land use;[47] (ii) secondly, London also had a *monumental* character which was typified by a number of geographical precincts—often of aesthetic and historical value—which were directly related to its size and status as a great commercial and culture centre of world standard, and which were damaged by the constant, and largely unnecessary, intrusion of through traffic;[48] (iii) finally, London had a *mechanistic* component—particularly with regard to traffic movement—which was performing inefficiently because of "the amount of diurnal travel to and from work".[49] Each of these interlocking components appear again and again in the plans' proposals and form one of the major bases for making Greater London environmentally more attractive, structurally more ordered and functionally more efficient.

It is important to remember that Abercrombie's three functional Londons, Community London, Monumental London, and Mechanistic London interacted with one another continuously and the proposals put forward in the plans turned on the concept of improving *all* of the components embraced simultaneously. Trade-off considerations were minimized by the essentially complementary nature of the functional sub-units. The real problem was thus not that of devising appropriate alternative solutions for London but of synthesizing the various components involved and establishing an order of priority for that unique solution which grew logically out of the organic analysis.

It is interesting to note that the three functional Londons taken collectively helped to emphasize the importance of the central area. From the monumental standpoint most public structures which symbolized London as the Empire's hub could be found within the area bounded by the mainline railway termini. Almost by definition,

---

[47] *CLP (1943)*, p. 7.
[48] *CLP (1943)*, p. 10.
[49] *CLP (1943)*, p. 13.

mechanistic London was both extremely important and extremely visible in the central area where a high proportion of journeys either began or ended, or both. Mechanistic London also served as the link between monumental and community London. Although most of the residential communities were located outside of the central area many of the most important examples of working precincts, such as the Temple and the Inns of Court, could be found within it.[50]

The second major line of demarcation for organic London—the *spatial*—also revealed three complementary Londons within the Green Belt. Structurally the capital could be divided into sets of concentric annular rings,[51] which consisted of: (i) the Inner Urban Ring centring on Charing Cross and roughly covering the LCC's area; (ii) the Suburban Ring roughly corresponding to the area which is now under the control of the GLC: (iii) the proposed Green Belt where extensive building would be prohibited; and (iv) on the other side of the Green Belt, the Outer Country Ring which extended to a distance of 30 miles from Charing Cross.[52] In diagrammatic form (Fig. 3.1) the three *spatial* Londons could be conceived of as a set which was both nested and symmetrical in character.

The rings were based on the level of existing urbanization and pre-war residential density figures. Using lowered figures progressively extending away from the centre, it was calculated that the

[50] See on this subject Geddes' concept of a "Biological Triad"—Environment, Function and Organism, or Work, Place and Folk—which he borrowed from Le Play (Geddes (1915), p. 392); and Abercrombie, *Planning in Town and Country*, An Inaugural Lecture at University College, London: Hodder & Stoughton, 1937, p. 13.

[51] These rings show a marked similarity with Unwin's much earlier "A" ring, "B" ring, "C" ring and "D" ring analysis of London. Raymond Unwin, "Memorandum No. 1", *First Report of the Greater London Regional Planning Committee*, Knapp, Drewitt & Sons Ltd.: London, December 1929, p. 10; and see also for a similar spatial analysis put forward 4 years earlier, Ernest W. Burgess, "The growth of the City", in Robert E. Park, Ernest W. Burgess and Roderick D. McKenzie, *The City*, Chicago: The University of Chicago Press, 1925, pp. 54–56.

[52] *GLP (1944)*, p. 22. The vital central area within the Inner Urban Ring was not dealt with in more detail by Abercrombie since a major section, the one square mile City of London, had been "punched out" and was the subject of a separate plan. C. H. Holden and W. G. Holford, *Reconstruction in the City of London* (Report by the Consultants), London, 1947. This area nevertheless formed an integral part of Abercrombie's framework for London as a whole in spite of its special historical character.

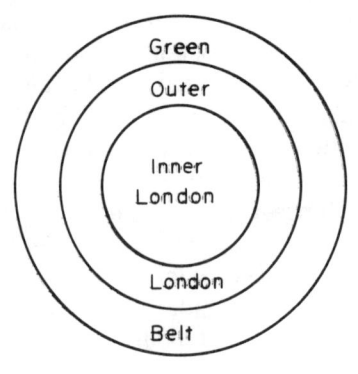

FIG. 3.1. The three spatial Londons within the Green Belt—nested symmetry.

innermost ring would lose a substantial amount of population and industry and that the population level of the Suburban Ring and Green Belt would remain substantially unchanged. The Outer Country Ring would operate as the primary reception area for the population thus decanted.[53] As decentralization occurred, physical redevelopment would renew the outworn and badly bombed inner area fabric and the central area could be raised to the architectural level which accorded with its status as the focal point of one of the leading world cities and the centre of a vast Empire. The intent of Abercrombie was less to turn London inside out than to sharpen the focus on the vital central area and order the informality which had continuingly characterized London. This attempt to reinforce a classical monocentric pattern was designed to make London the gravitational centre of a co-ordinated functional and spatial universe.[54] Thus, "The natural evolution of disorderly growth can be shaped into some semblance of ordered design, both for population grouping, land use, transportation and public services".[55]

Abercrombie's concern with rationalization of existing patterns to improve London's fundamental order often led him to express his

---

[53] *GLP (1944)*, pp. 37–38.
[54] See also Howard's diagrams in *Garden Cities* (1902), pp. 52–53.
[55] *GLP (1944)*, p. 7; and see also *CLP (1943)*, p. 21.

Constructing a Solution 65

proposed remedies in geometrical or symmetrical terms;[56] *not, however, because he felt that these shapes had an intrinsic value*[57] *but because he felt that these prescriptions grew logically out of both the city's spatial arrangement and its major functions and satisfied the safety,*[58] *amenity and efficiency criteria which he felt to be essential principals of good town planning.* A classic example of the integration of a large-scale architectonic design with London's organic order was Abercrombie's proposals for a ring-radial-cross system of roads to serve the fundamental requirements of the city *in its entirety*.

THE CIRCULATORY SYSTEM: PHYSICALLY CANALIZING TRAFFIC

Abercrombie was clearly aware of the difficulties of uniting road planning with the other planning requirements, in such a way that a balance could be achieved and maintained. He remarked in 1937, well before either of the London plans had been initiated,

> The transport problem is so insistent—so dinned into our brains and ears, that it may seem superfluous to describe its dominating effect upon planning. Indeed, the Road plan—the most easily grasped manifestation of the Town plan—is too much stressed, and Town planning is in danger of becoming road planning.[59]

At the same time, however, he was equally aware of the need for a solution for the problem of traffic congestion. As he wrote in the *County of London Plan (1943):*

---

[56] J. Michael Thomson, *A Transportation Strategy for London*, GLDP (1969), Inquiry Proof E12/20, London, January 1971, typescript, p. 150; and for an explicit condemnation of this type of approach, Colin Buchanan, *Traffic in Towns* (1963), pp. 42–43.
[57] See Abercrombie's condemnation of "drawing-board planning" in Sidcup, Kent, in *GLP (1944)*, picture between pp. 22–23; and the remark made by Abercrombie's collaborator, J. H. Forshaw in his 1943 Chadwick Lecture, *Town Planning and Health*, delivered on 11 November 1943, Westminster: P. S. King & Staples Ltd., picture between pp. 4–5.
[58] Forshaw (1943), p. 3.
[59] Abercrombie (1937), p. 41; compare with Peter Hall's and Edward Carter's comments on p. 26. Italics added.

66   Strategic Planning in London

The need for improved traffic facilities in and around London has become so acute that unless drastic measures are taken to relieve a large number of thoroughfares, crossing and junctions of their present congestion, there will be a grave danger that the whole traffic system will, before long, be slowed down to an intolerable degree.[60]

In attempting to resolve these two points of view four objectives were put forward:

(i) The improvement of traffic circulation.
(ii) The segregation of fast long-distance traffic from traffic of a purely local nature.
(iii) A reduction in the number of accidents.
(iv) The maintenance of existing communities free of through traffic or, where such roads already pass through them, the provision of alternative routes between communities.[61]

In order to achieve these goals several far-reaching changes in the way in which London functioned were necessitated.

The initial step in achieving these aims—particularly the first—had no actual connection with road planning itself. This fundamental step, already alluded to, was that of attempting to move a large number of workers and industrial employment out of London and by so doing reducing the *total amount of travel* which took place. This corrective surgery was justified: (a) on the grounds that the opportunity to improve the local environment would be created through lower densities; and (b) because only by so doing could the underlying cause of the traffic *symptom*—overcrowding—be tackled at its source.[62] From this perspective the twice daily *journey to and from work* was the principal offender since it determined the capacity of the transport system and, by its very nature, was easily the most important trip generator which had the added disadvantage of occurring at regular and predictable peak periods.[63] By simultane-

[60] Page 48 and see p. 53.
[61] *CLP (1943)*, p. 49; and see also Unwin (1933), p. 62.
[62] *CLP (1943)*, p. 13; and J. M. Richards, "London plans", *The Geographical Magazine*, Vol. XVI, No. 1, May 1943, p. 1.
[63] The evening peak was, however, larger, probably because of shoppers and miscellaneous journeys. See for a more recent view of this problem John Meyer, "Urban transportation", in James Q. Wilson (Ed.), *The Metropolitan Enigma*, Cambridge, Mass.: Harvard University Press, Revised Ed., 1968, p. 47.

Constructing a Solution 67

ously moving population and industry out of London the concentrated pressure of the peak should have been proportionately reduced. An attempt has been made, *The County of London Plan* explained, to "achieve a balanced community in which home and work will not be unduly separated—or for which, at any rate, provision is made that diurnal travel is reduced as much as possible".[64] To lessen this strain on existing resources was not, however, enough for a complete solution to the problem. Once the attempt to reduce total travel through external decentralization had been taken additional corrective action was required if all of the traffic objectives were to be completely realized, and London was to be freed to function in the manner indicated by Abercrombie's concept of city order.

The policy which Abercrombie advocated with regard to travel, in addition to diminishing the *level* of daily work journeys, was one of *canalizing vehicular flows* on the basis of length, purpose and speed.[65] The process of canalization had two distinct elements which were directly related to the level of analysis. At the upper, city-wide level, canalization meant that new primary roads would be constructed which would attract rapid traffic away from community areas and at the same time at the lower, precinctal level, it would be possible to so arrange the areas' physical design that long distance traffic was discouraged from making use of the existing street network.[66] This combination of primary network "pull" and precinctal area "push" meant that traffic could at last be so ordered *through physical structures* that the higher the traffic's speed the less in the way of obstructions it would encounter and the more it would be insulated from people conducting their ordinary domestic and working lives. "The essence of good road planning", Abercrombie maintained in his Inaugural Lecture, "is to canalize main streams of traffic; it is a confession of failure to widen indiscriminately."[67]

[64] Page 34; and *GLP (1944)*, p. 50; and see also Owen (1972). "One solution for the urban problem is to attempt to reduce the total volume of movement...", Wilfred Owen, *The Accessible City*, The Brookings Institute, Washington D.C., 1972, p. 88.
[65] See Unwin (1933), p. 64.
[66] See for similar suggestions, Clarence Perry, *Housing for the Machine Age*, Russell Sage Foundation, New York, 1939.
[67] Abercrombie (1937), p. 43.

Basically there were two different *kinds* of traffic within a city and it was argued that it was the failure to distinguish between them which had led to the present unsatisfactory state of affairs with mounting traffic congestion, high road accidents, and deteriorating community area amenities. Roads, as Unwin had noted before World War One, served as both highways for traffic movement and as sites for buildings.[68] Traffic, therefore, should be divided "into different classes (a) those which are primarily required to provide movement from place to place, and (b) those which are intended to afford access to individual buildings".[69] The existing "nondescript" road could not be allowed to remain: lacking any clear and single purpose, cluttered with different types of vehicles, and providing frontage access to the buildings which lined its route, it positively invited accidents and congestion. In fact the two defects were closely related and unless some type of purposeful intervention on the part of the planner occurred both were likely to become progressively worse.

Once again a rational analysis of the problem allowed Abercrombie to *deduce* from his conceptual model *the* correct order for vehicular movement in an almost *a priori* fashion. Although organic London had evolved continuously over a period of several centuries its road network had remained curiously stunted and was therefore structurally inadequate to meet the modern demands made upon it. The blend of description and prescription which characterized the biological model not only revealed current defects—they also indicated the way in which these difficulties should be resolved; two very different matters in the absence of an underlying organizing concept.[70] Given this implicit order, however, the answer to London's traffic defects was not only clear but inescapable: London's traffic defects both could and must be remedied through the creation

---

[68] Raymond Unwin, *Town Planning in Practice*, London: T. Fisher Unwin, 2nd ed., 1911, p. 235; compare this with the assertion in the *GLP (1944)*, p. 63, that the distinction between the two different kinds of traffic had only recently been made.

[69] Unwin (1933), p. 75.

[70] This model continues to exercise an important degree of influence. See, for example, Victor Gruen, *The Heart of Our Cities*, London: Thames & Hudson, 1965, pp. 271–273.

Constructing a Solution 69

of a hierarchical "circulatory system".[71] Corrective surgery was required and would necessitate the insertion of artificial channels, or canals, to drain away traffic from areas where it was both unnecessary and unwanted. The central area was, as usual, the principal case in point: a good deal of the traffic which entered it, it was felt, had no real business for being within its limited spatial compass since it neither began nor ended its journey there. On a smaller level all over London neighbourhoods—potential precincts—were being disrupted in a miniature repetition of the central area's dilemma. At both the centre and the periphery a basic difficulty was that the motorist had *no real choice* as to road speed—primarily because of the lack of road *types*[72]—and was often compelled to follow the route which he felt to be the quickest—regardless of the nature of the area through which it passed. The proposed new channels would, however, offer a choice of both speed and area based on the road's main function. The proposed road hierarchy fell into three distinct tiers and was based on the categories originally developed by the Assistant Commissioner of Metropolitan Police, H. Alker Tripp.[73] (a) The top tier was composed of *Arterial Roads* exclusively for fast, through traffic which were to have no direct building frontage, no side street access and which had parallel service roads at long intervals; (b) the intermediate tier consisted of *Sub-arterial Roads* which were a combination of the main existing roads' traffic roads in the built-up area and new purpose-built roads designed to carry slower traffic—direct frontages along these routes were not

---

[71] See one of Abercrombie's contemporaries, C. B. Purdom, for a detailed simile, "Transport in all its forms is a system of arteries and veins through which the blood stream of the city carries oxygen to the brain and nourishment to every part of the organism", *How Shall We Rebuild London?*, London: J. M. Dent & Sons, 1945, p. 122.

[72] With the *possible* exception of the major radial trunk roads. Most of these, however, also suffered from the same defects which beset the "nondescript road" on a larger scale.

[73] In view of Tripp's importance in this field it is a bit surprising to note that little explicit reference was made to him in the plans for London. Abercrombie did, however, write in the Introduction to Tripp's 1942 work, *Town Planning and Road Traffic*, "I can speak personally for one town and country planner who had benefited enormously from Mr Tripp's accurate and, may I add, intrepid thinking on the subject of Road Design for the Motor Age", London: Edward Arnold & Co., 1942, p. 8.

forbidden although service roads were to be provided when possible; and (c) finally, the bottom tier of the hierarchy was to consist of the already constructed *Approach or Local Road* network which contained both slow building-seeking traffic and vehicles which were parked at their destination (or point of departure).[74] The interrelationship of the three tiers provided a fully articulated system of movement for motor vehicles while at the same time affording maximum protection to the inhabitants of the precincts which the main roads bounded and the local roads serviced through a controlled flow of traffic.

The "mix-up of all forms of traffic on all roads, consequent upon an inadequate policy of distinguishing between through and...local traffic",[75] could at last be ended. Within the precincts it would only become necessary to encounter through traffic when a vehicular journey was to be undertaken.[76] "The ordinary daily life in the town...", Tripp wrote, "can be *completely* separated from the lethal through traffic; daily life can carry on as if the through traffic did not exist."[77]

Through traffic which was to become both rapid and orderly[78] was to be carried not merely on new roads but on a new *kind* of road: a grade-separated, limited access, multi-lane highway, similar in form to the newly constructed Italian Autostrada or the German Reichsautobahn.[79] The concept of order which was being employed meant

---

[74] *CLP (1943)*, p. 50, the lower tier could be further subdivided according to major precinctal purpose; see also Tripp (1942), p. 42.

[75] *GLP (1944)*, p. 65.

[76] It is instructive to notice that the basic dichotomy between through and local traffic had given rise to a trichotomy with regard to the road system because of the *relationship* between the various traffic streams. This distinction has had a profound impact on planning thought—particularly with regard to the problem of relationships between and among highway components. It is only necessary to briefly raise this matter at this point, it will be considered in more detail later in the thesis. See Tripp (1942), p. 112, and for a rather different way of making a triple distinction, Hall (1963), p. 112.

[77] Tripp (1942), p. 112, author's italics.

[78] Tripp remarked that "those two problems are in fact one" (1942), p. 17; see also Hall (1963), p. 28.

[79] This type of road had also been considered by the authors of a long-term highway plan undertaken before the London plans had been initiated. See Sir Charles Bressey and Sir Edwin Lutyens, *Highway Development Survey 1937 (Greater London)*,

Constructing a Solution 71

not only that pedestrians and fast traffic should be separated by the new roads and hence kept in their "proper" places[80] but that on a larger scale the new roads themselves should be so arranged that there was a correct fit between them and the many other facets of urban life which occurred within the built-up area and gave London its structure. Order was thus to be both preserved from the community standpoint and enhanced from the traffic point of view through the deft surgical insertion of an artificial system of "canals"; a single means to unite what had previously been perceived as an insoluble conflict between two apparently incompatible ends: motion and statics—mobility and community.

ABERCROMBIE'S GEOMETRY

The problem remained, however, at the strategic level of actually siting the new arterial and sub-arterial roads in such a way that community disruption was minimized, and of determining the most effective design for the new roads to follow. Once again the synoptic perspective of London as both a coherent and a living whole was employed so that, according to Abercrombie, the arterial road pattern grew naturally out of the earlier triple functional and spatial analysis of the city.[81] *The road plan was according to Abercrombie, to be subservient to the needs of London as a whole and it possessed value only to the extent to which it contributed to the progressive realization of London's ultimate order and form.* The road plan was thus one integrated part of the many prescriptive organizing devices which Abercrombie put forward to achieve his rationally deter-

---

London: HMSO, 1938, p. 28. It is interesting to note that one of the reasons why Abercrombie favoured this type of highway was that he felt that they would be *narrower* than the conventional parkway. They "would require no footpaths or cycle-tracks and would only have connections with the country at appropriate intervals like stations on a railway", Abercrombie (1937), pp. 20–21.
[80] Tripp referred to this as "place segregation" (1942), p. 26.
[81] *GLP (1944)*, p. 9. Compare this with Tripp's (1942) assertion regarding the *dominant* effect of road planning on town planning: "Any town plan is on inspection found to be defined mainly in terms of road layout. The road layout becomes—so to speak—the skeleton of the body", p. 37.

mined aims for London of increased safety, enhanced amenity and strengthened efficiency.

Before considering Abercrombie's siting solution—his planning geometry—in detail it would perhaps be useful to consider two related points: (a) the *direction* of traffic flow and (b) the relationship between the road plan and the activities conducted within the central area. Taking the second point first, it was recognized that London's core was composed of a number of interrelated functions. It was asserted that "the central area as such should be recognized and its limits should be defined". This could be achieved by the provision of an inner ring road "on a scale necessary for it (i.e. the city centre) to function properly...".[82] The importance of *the* central area was thus to be both clarified and underlined by means of a functional and spatial boundary: the inner ring road. No other major centres for business, shopping or cultural pursuits were even considered in the plans: the central area was felt to be not merely important but deservedly unique and its special status was to be further strengthened by means of the road proposals. This monocentralization tendency was to be continued and no rival centres were proposed for construction basically because they were simply unnecessary. The central area's West End, for example, it was argued "is adequate in size to meet all the business, amusement and other centralized requirements of London for a long time to come".[83] In Abercrombie's London the massive *external decentralization* previously mentioned was to be matched in a mirror image way by a vigorous reinforcement of an *internal reconcentration* of activities, particularly those which took place in the central area.

This concern with the relationship between traffic and the primacy of the city centre was also evident in a more subtle way with regard to the *direction* of traffic. The highest road tier—the arteries—were so named not merely because they were designed to canalize traffic but because they were, in the manner of a living organism's corresponding component, to carry this flow *away* from the city's heart, and more generally, to distribute it in such a way that the

[82] *CLP (1943)*, p. 22.
[83] *CLP (1943)*, p. 23.

Constructing a Solution   73

centre did not become choked. The core traffic problem thus had two major parts according to Abercrombie: (a) traffic was forced into the centre by the existing radial system even though a good deal of it simply wished to pass *through* the centre since there was no means whereby it could conveniently move *around* it; and, further, (b) once this traffic had gained access to this area there was no rapid means by which either it or the traffic which had actual business within the area could exit and thus each contributed to the congestion experienced by the other. According to the *County of London Plan*, a major provision of the road plan should be "the imposition; on the present network of thoroughfares of a properly co-ordinated system of road communications, in the form of a ring-radial-cross system, incorporating *a ring-road for fast traffic and facilities for quick egress from the congested centre*".[84] This draining away of extraneous traffic—extraneous in the double sense of drivers only using the existing local street pattern because they had no alternative and of residents also being inconvenienced by what they saw as a traffic invasion—would ultimately mean a better environment for both.

After considering these largely implicit factors in Abercrombie's thinking it is now possible to examine the most visible but in a curious way one of the least important aspects of his road plan: its physical geometry. This particular facet was one of the least important aspects of the plan *because according to Abercrombie the geometric pattern was completely dominated by contextual considerations such as spatial and functional relationships and grew logically from them: the physical form of the primary road network had no inherent value in and of itself.* The purpose-dependent nature of Abercrombie's road plan was another indication of his conception of the extremely close relationship between form and substance in organic London and of the necessity to reflect this in his prescriptions to improve it. It was for this reason that he modified, where necessary, a highway survey which had been undertaken in 1937 by Sir Charles Bressey and Sir Edwin Lutyens to provide a 30-year

---

[84] Page 50, italics added.

74 Strategic Planning in London

plan for the improvement of London's road system.[85] The Bressey Report encompassed a large *spatial* area but suffered from a certain *functional* narrowness in its lack of concern with wider urban relationships.[86] As the *County of London Plan* discreetly inquired, "The Highway Development Survey 1937, was clearly a piece of planning on the strategic scale but was it sufficiently comprehensive in character, in dealing with planning as a road matter alone?"[87] The tactful conclusion was that it was not and that Bressey would have to be modified in the light of community requirements.

Basically the top-tier road plan was an extremely simple one: five ring roads were to be constructed at varying distances from the centre and were to be linked with eleven radial roads; within the centre itself two major "X" and "Y" shaped roads would be constructed, partially in tunnels, and would connect both the inner ring (the "A" Ring) and the innermost parts of the main radials.[88] The inner "A" Ring was designated originally as a sub-arterial road[89] and was to link the mainline railway termini in the central area. The "B" Ring was to be located at a distance of approximately 3 miles from the centre and formed a roughly box-shaped internal by-pass for the traffic wishing to avoid the central area entirely.[90] The "C" Ring was to consist of the completed North and South Circular Roads which had been proposed well before the beginning of World War One, and parts of which had already been constructed. At the leading edge of the Green Belt, approximately 12 miles from the centre, a "D" Ring was to be built which would completely surround the built-up area and act as the principal external by-pass for the capital. Finally, on the opposite side of the expanded Green Belt its limits would be clearly marked by the last major circular—the "E" Ring.[91] The

[85] See the *Bressey Report* (1938).
[86] See, in this regard, William A. Robson, *The Government and Misgovernment of London*, London: George Allen & Unwin, 2nd ed., 1948, p. 154.
[87] *CLP (1943)*, p. 2.
[88] *GLP*, pp. 61–63; and *CLP*, p. 67.
[89] For a brief history of the various modifications which government policy dictated before the GLC began operation with particular regard to the "A" Ring see Chapter 4.
[90] *CLP (1943)*, p. 55.
[91] On this see Unwin; a distinct separation should be made between town and countryside, he contended. This could be achieved "by wide boulevards, avenues or belts of park land..." (1911), p. 154.

Constructing a Solution 75

radials would both relate the London Road System to the national network and allow that traffic *which wished to do so* to quickly penetrate to the centre—in some ways even more importantly it would allow the traffic generated there by central area activities to freely exit. The "X" and "Y" roads were particularly important in facilitating the unrestricted flow of traffic in this regard and both were to be of arterial standard.[92]

Having considered all of these factors, the actual part to be played by the ring roads at the strategic level can now be indicated in outline.[93] Abercrombie had long been an admirer of a ring-road system of urban communication which he saw as a device helping to reduce the strong radial tendency of most historical road patterns. Ten years before the publication of the London plans he remarked in an analysis of the concentric rings which had developed in fortified continental towns, that Moscow, Paris and Vienna all made use of "ring streets". He regretted that English towns "have never had the chance of creating these superb rings".[94] By 1943 the long-awaited chance had come. His proposed ring system, he contended, had not been designed to achieve the obvious purpose of furthering "... continuous gyratory traffic; it is to be viewed more in the light of the linking up of a series of cross-routes connecting the radial roads. Another way of regarding the ring was as a magnified by-pass, enabling traffic entering the area to avoid passing through and adding to the congestion of the centre."[95] At this level the rings could be conceived of as a *supplementary* device for making the best use of the existing radial network by increasing the ability of traffic to move freely from one radial to another without entering the traditional "switching area" at the city's centre.

[92] See Fig. 3.2 for a map of the most important aspects of the communication system.
[93] See for previous ring road proposals for London: Niven and Pepler's plans made before World War One, in Foley (1963), p. 151. The North and South Circular was proposed about this time as well and was originally designed as an external by-pass. Because of London's growth however, by the time that the Abercrombie plans were drawn up the North and South Circular—newly designated as the "C" Ring—was firmly embedded within the built-up area of the capital and thus could no longer serve its original purpose as an *external* by-pass.
[94] Abercrombie (1933), p. 64; or as the *GLP (1944)* sadly observed, "There is not a single complete Ring Road in the County or Region of London", p. 65.
[95] *GLP (1944)*, p. 67.

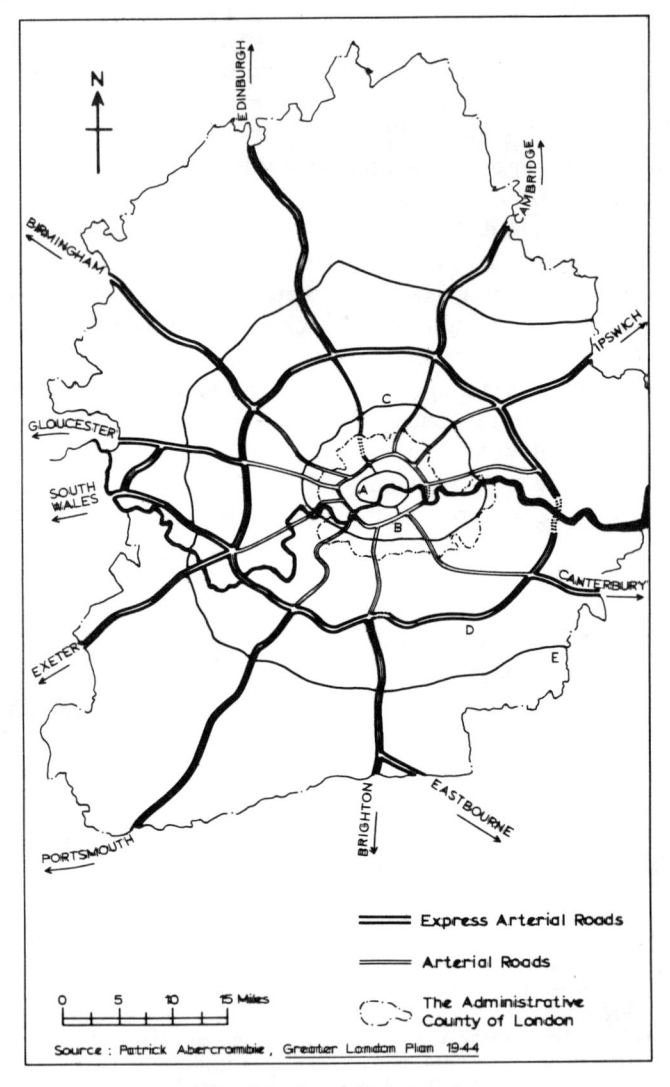

FIG. 3.2. Greater London plan.

Constructing a Solution   77

In addition to acting as a *by-pass* and radial switching device the ring roads, in keeping with Abercrombie's rather static view of the capital, performed two additional major functions. Although both have already been touched upon it would, perhaps, be useful to place them within the broader geometric context now being considered. In the first place, the rings were to act as valves for bleeding off internal traffic generated within each of the zones which the rings encompassed—once again with particular regard to Central London. In the second place the circular roads located at varying distances from the centre would serve as *boundaries*—and in the case of the "A" and "E" Rings as almost *defensive barriers* to prevent further growth and to stabilize certain broad types of land use.[96]

Returning to the concept of the Three Spatial Londons, by means of the concentric ring system, each London could be demarked, controlled and internal traffic pressure reduced through the relief action provided by the three sub-arterial rings: the "A", "C", and "E". At the same time the "B" and "D" Rings were to function as the main inner and outer by-passes for the areas which they contained, either allowing traffic to switch from one radial to another or to

[96] See Table 3.1.

TABLE 3.1. LONDON'S RING SYSTEM: ABERCROMBIE'S GEOMETRY

Ring	Standard	Distance from centre (miles)	Principal purpose
"A"	Sub-arterial	1	Central area barrier, pressure valve for central area activities
"B"	Arterial	3	Main internal by-pass, inner radial switching device
"C"	Sub-arterial	7	Rough LCC boundary, pressure valve for inner area activities
"D"	Arterial	12	Main external by-pass, outer radial switching device
"E"	Sub-arterial	18	built-up area barrier, pressure valve for outer area activities

completely skirt the encircled area.[97] In what could be called a "horizontal" differentiation, Abercrombie's geometry was manifested through a complex interrelationship of boundary, pressure valve, barrier and by-pass activities and gave actual effect to the previous analytical identification of the Three Spatial Londons.[98]

Establishing a Cellular Structure

If the geometric form of the proposed road system could be used to horizontally differentiate between the various spatial Londons at the strategic level, its hierarchical nature could also be employed with effect at the local level to relate the Functional Londons to one another. Monumental, Community and Mechanistic London could all be served "vertically" by means of the triple-tiered road hierarchy which would allow traffic to move upwards from one level to another thus servicing and at the same time protecting the character of London's numerous communities and the central area itself. This superimposition of a ring-radial-cross system overlaying the existing road network meant that a traffic hierarchy would be created which would ultimately achieve the plans' complete traffic and land use objectives.[99]

Nor were the proposals mere "top-down" planning. At least an equal amount of attention was devoted to the functional "cellular structure" of proposed community neighbourhoods and precincts to ensure that the best possible results were obtained at the local level as well so that the strategic and the tactical solutions could be fused with one another. One of the prime functions of the proposed road system was to give meaning to this cellular concept.

---

[97] See how closely the internal and external by-pass idea accords with Tripp's thinking (1942), p. 61.
[98] This explanation helps, perhaps, to indicate the reason why the rings were arranged in their particular configurative pattern. This pattern has puzzled more than one observer, see, for example, Stephen Plowden, *Towns Against Traffic*, London: Andre Deutsch Ltd., 1972, p. 83.
[99] *GLP (1944)*, p. 9.

The roads... would canalize the main through traffic and split up the area into a series of cells. By the closing of side streets entering the arterial roads and of some entering the sub-arterial roads, or by the provision of service roads where the latter proves to be impossible, these cells would be free from through traffic.[100]

The nature and substance of this type of phraseology indicates the extent to which the implicit organic order could be carried without doing violence to its basic premises: at each step from the level of the city as a complex whole, to the requirements of its proposed "circulatory system", and finally culminating in the attempt to sustain and protect the smallest units of planning concern—the "cellular" neighbourhoods, or precincts—the conceptual order employed remained remarkably consistent. At each level the model employed suggested a remedy which would logically relate to the demands arising out of the needs of the levels above or below it. Paraphrasing Maitland, the road system in its entirety allowed a seamless web of planning proposals to be put forward which could not only benefit almost every sphere of city life *but which could only be achieved through the agency of the road network.*

The top-down planning of the form and function of the new roads was thus matched by the "bottom-up" concern for the primacy of the central area and the integrity of the communities which the roads served:

> In the preparation of the Plan, the maintenance and development of the community structure of London has been one of the first considerations. In the road plan, for instance, care has been taken to avoid new routes cutting across the centres of communities.[101]

In order to achieve this aim existing seams in London's fabric were to be utilized for road construction to the maximum extent possible. The co-author of the *County of London Plan*, Forshaw, maintained in a 1943 lecture that "Roads should be constructed along the side of existing railways with open space being provided on either side".[102]

---

[100] *CLP (1943)*, p. 50, italics added.
[101] *CLP (1943)*, p. 29.
[102] Forshaw (1943), p. 13; and see also the *Bressey Report* (1938), p. 29. In this regard little seems to have changed over the past 30 years, see Walter Bor and John Roberts, "Urban motorways impact", *Town Planning Review*, Vol. 43, No. 4, October 1972, p. 317.

80 Strategic Planning in London

Canals, industrial estates and areas which had been badly bombed could all be used in this attempt to achieve a network not just of new roads but of redeveloped "corridors" both insulated from and at the same time insulating the major communities.

The communities in turn would be subdivided into neighbourhoods of between 5000 and 10,000 people, each whose major focus would be the local primary school.[103] These communities, which were based on the villages from which London had grown and which still remained in varying degrees recognizable entities, gave London, according to earlier commentators, its unique character.[104] London could in fact be conceived of as a set of distinct geographical units and the plans sought to define, complete and reclaim them—through physical separation and the canalization of activities. A diagrammatic representation of the Functional Londons, on their various levels, and their relationship with the triple-tiered hierarchy of the

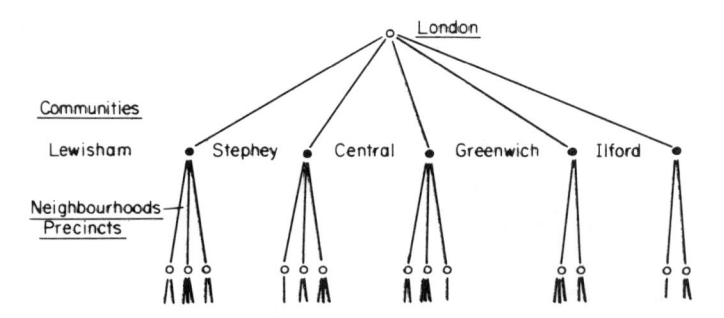

FIG. 3.3. Defining the functional Londons—relating community London and the road system.

---

[103] *CLP (1943)*, p. 9. The development of the neighbourhood unit is an important study in its own right as a major planning concept. Although it is still an important influence on current planning a detailed examination of this topic is beyond the scope of the present study. See, however, James Dahir, *The Neighbourhood Unit: its Spread and Acceptance*, New York: Russell Sage Foundation, 1947; and for a more recent example, Nathan Glazer, "The School as an instrument of planning", *Journal of the American Institute of Planners*, Vol. XXV, No. 4, November 1959, pp. 191–196.

[104] See Steen Rasmussen, *London: The Unique City*, London: Cape, 1937; and see also Lewis Mumford, "Address to the Town Planning Institute", *Journal of the Town Planning Institute*, Vol. XXXII, No. 5, August 1946, p. 178.

highway network appears in Fig. 3.3. This attempt to delineate these sub-components of the city was felt to be necessary since London had lost one of the most vital components of urban life: a sense of social well-being arising from belonging to an identifiable spatial community.[105] It was contended that although many existing communities retained their names, they had in many cases lost their earlier distinctiveness.[106]

This sense of community was to be re-created by means of the establishment of a series of traffic controlled precincts which were to be bounded by sub-arterial roads thus simultaneously freeing them from extraneous traffic and linking them with the primary road system.[107] An existing example of this kind of arrangement, according to Alker Tripp, was the collegiate layout of the Inns of Court[108] and Abercrombie also proposed that new precincts should be created in which buildings "turned their backs" on the main streams of traffic; specifically he suggested, in some architectural detail, how this might be accomplished in the Bloomsbury and Westminster Areas.[109]

At both the bottom and the top levels the road system would be almost wholly beneficial. By means of this *system* overlap could be eliminated and order restored as the major units—the communities—and the sub-units—the neighbourhoods or precincts—were isolated related to larger sets, and systematically reinforced.[110] Not only would the three Functional Londons be separated "verti-

---

[105] See on this type of internal decentralization, Svend Riemer, "The nucleated city", *The British Journal of Sociology*, Vol. 22, No. 3, September 1971, p. 234.

[106] See, for example, Carter (1962), p. 69; one contemporary critic, C. B. Purdom, argued, however, that the plans were merely giving old names to new centres (1945), p. 170.

[107] See Fig. 3.3.

[108] (1942), p. 76.

[109] See Fig. 3.4 and see also Forshaw (1943), p. 13.

[110] See for an important theoretical contribution on this subject, Christopher Alexander, "A city is not a tree", in Gwen Bell and Jacqueline Tyrwhitt (Eds.), *Human Identity in the Urban Environment*, Harmondsworth, Middlesex; Penguin Books, 1972, p. 407. Compare Alexander's diagram on that page with the diagram on the previous page of the text. Note that: (a) Alexander views London as only a two-tiered hierarchy; and (b) no indication is given of the way in which the road system may serve as a device for creating the various distinct sub-components which Alexander is concerned with.

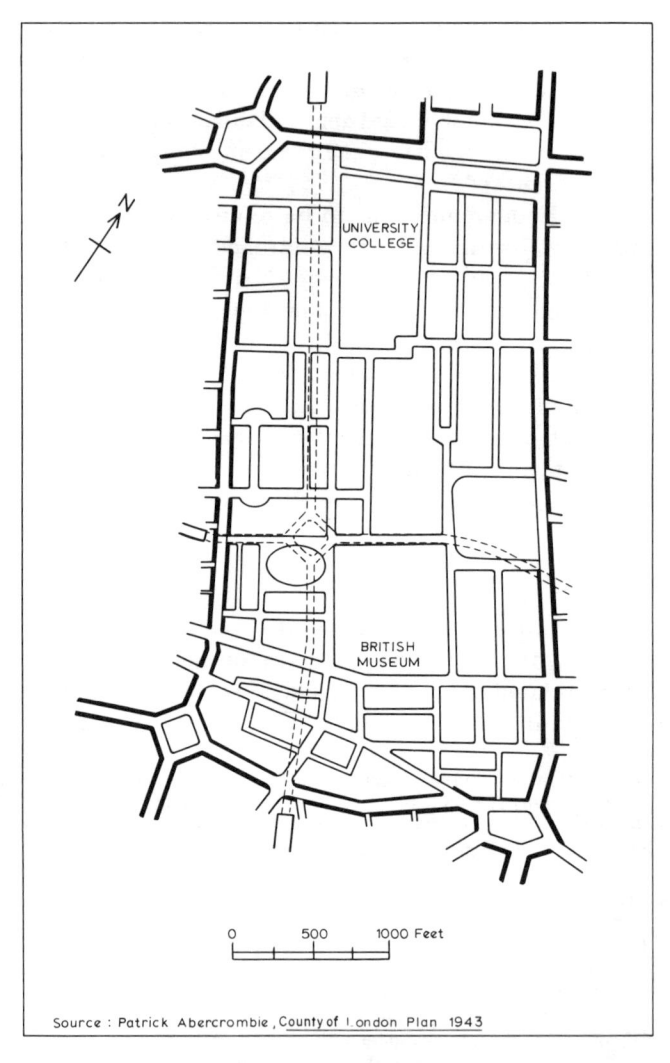

FIG. 3.4. University precinct: Bloomsbury.

cally by the road system *hierarchy*, but the three Spatial Londons would be "horizontally" differentiated by the network's *geometric symmetry*. Once again the stress on hierarchical and symmetrical relationships among parts and the way in which they combine to form a unified whole is indicative of an organic order. By means of a complex symbiotic relationship, each of the various Londons would be assisted individually and all would benefit collectively through the holistical value conferred by the highway network. As well as providing the *sine qua non* for the progressive realization of London's ultimate strategic form the road system had substantial internal value purely with regard to traffic matters. "We put forward the road scheme with confidence", the authors of the *County of London Plan* wrote, "as we believe it provides a basis for the satisfactory solution of London's traffic problems".[111]

RECAPITULATION

It might be useful at this point to briefly review Abercrombie's major suggestions for the development of the London Region. London was to be replanned from both top and bottom *simultaneously* along basically conservative lines with regard to its underlying structure in the belief, in Burk's phrase, that it was sometimes necessary to "reform in order to preserve" and that London was simply incapable of reforming itself. To use a simplified form of the organic concept of order: London was overgrown and although certain areas of decay existed the organism—or more properly, the organic complex occupying a given territory, for example a park or garden—was continuing to increase outwards at such a rate that it needed to be fenced off, pruned and reshaped, and the prunings replanted at the periphery in New Towns based on the same essential principles so that a desirable equilibrium could be achieved. In outline, the policy mode employed at this stage of the analysis yielded the following prescriptions with regard to strategic physical structure.

[111] *CLP (1943)*, p. 63; and *GLP (1944)*, p. 113.

(i) *Horizontal Containment*

London's growth was to be halted and a distinct separation drawn between town and country by means of: (a) the expanded Green Belt; and (b) the "D" ring which was to run along the inner edge of the Belt and the "E" ring which was to mark its outer edge.

(ii) *Concentrated External Dispersal*

A number of compact New Towns would be established in the Outer Country ring which would receive London's decanted population and provide them with employment and thus help to reduce the *overall* travel volume. "Blobs rather than smudges" was to be the guiding philosophy for the shape of dispersal; in many ways these blobs would be scaled-down replicas of the central city at least as far as general form was concerned and again virtually all of the same policy prescriptions would apply equally to both.

(iii) *Mono-centralization*

The central area's governmental, commercial and entertainment dominance was to be maintained and even improved: (a) *positively*, by the arrangement of the proposed road system; and (b) *permissively*, by the lack of any proposals for sub- or competing centres within the built-up area.

(iv) *Concentric Configurative Pattern*

London's target-like spatial pattern was to be enhanced by means of the proposed ring-radial road system which was to sharpen this concentric pattern, define the rings and at the same time provide a major internal and external by-pass for the bounded urban area.

(v) *Cellular Delineation*

Within the built-up area "cells" based on the control of traffic thus making it subservient to the major activities carried on within each of the sub-components would be established by means of the road system and through the architectural modification of buildings in relation to roads where necessary.[112]

(vi) *Hierarchical Traffic Canalization*

Three basic types of road were proposed with regard to London's "circulatory system"; arterial, sub-arterial and approach roads would automatically differentiate between through and local traffic, link them and physically canalize them into streams.

(vii) *Strengthening the Centre–Periphery Relationship*

Because London was the product of a long, unbroken history, it was in essence a collection of villages and these cellular groupings which had long been linked to the centre by radial rail and road connections would have the latter linkage improved by means of the proposed up-grading of the road network and the already strong centre–periphery relationship would thus be further strengthened.

(viii) *Urban Completeness*

One of the reflections of Abercrombie's end-state view of the city was particularly evident with regard to the approach to the problems

---

[112] On the architectural means of dealing with the problem of traffic see Clarence Stein, discussing the planning of Radburn, New Jersey, as a deliberate attempt to modify Garden City principles and place them within an automotive context. "Radburn planning: an American Experiment", *Official Architecture and Planning*, Vol. 29, No. 3, March 1966, p. 370.

arising from the journey to work. In the first place, by means of density controls the number of inhabitants would be limited absolutely. In the second place the Green Belt was to act as a physical barrier to growth while the internal cellular rearrangement within the area would allow work and residences to be moved more closely together given the limits imposed by safety and amenity considerations. These limiting internal and external measures taken together would have the effect of increasing self-sufficiency within the major communities and the city as a whole and hence of reducing total travel distance.

(ix) *Creating a Regional Development Authority*

Obviously the completion of changes of this magnitude would require a long period of time (Abercrombie's assumption was roughly the turn of this century) and throughout this period continued technical control would be required or the opportunity would be lost through piece-meal in-filling of an unplanned nature. In order to have the plans' various components properly co-ordinated and related to each other during the process of implementation a regional planning authority centering on the metropolitan area would be required.

(x) *On-going Political Consensus*

In addition to technical control in order for the large-scale proposals to be put into effect a high level of political consensus would also be required. Because of their scope not only would many separate local authorities be required to actively co-operate, but both of the major political parties would also have to agree in principle to allow the proposals to be executed, and in each case this is broadly what transpired.[113]

In an important sense these prescriptions form a basis for the

---

[113] See on this subject Chapter 3, pp. 99–100.

traditional approach to town planning and the road proposals run like an unbroken thread weaving them together. This consideration does not exhaust the breadth or depth of the "classical" approach; it does, however, indicate an important and largely accepted core of planning thought which has been modified over the passage of time but which largely retains its basic integrity, and which has shown a surprising persistence.

THE BUCHANAN APPROACH

It is to a specific aspect of the development of this theme that we may now briefly turn. Exactly 20 years after the publication of the *County of London Plan* a second major conceptual influence on post-war planning in London appeared in the form of a report to the Ministry of Transport, entitled *Traffic in Towns*.[114] During the interim little in the way of fresh governmental thinking about a desirable relationship between traffic and urban structure over the long term had taken place.[115] Most of the Abercrombie proposals had been accepted by the LCC[116] and with rather less enthusiasm and more modification of components by the Central Government.[117] Implementation, particularly with regard to new roads, was, however, far from rapid and the question dealing with "the extent to which society is prepared to go with the motor vehicle", as J. Alan

---

[114] London: HMSO, 1963.

[115] See, for example, *Design and Layout of Roads in Built-up Areas*, London: HMSO, 1946, for the approach adopted by the Ministry of Transport.

[116] Lewis Silkin served as Chairman of the Town Planning Committee which endorsed the proposals. *LCC Minutes*, June 1945, p. 8.

[117] See the provisional acceptance of the principles of the Abercrombie plans by the Minister of Town and Country Planning in December 1945; the Advisory Committee for London Regional Planning and Technical Sub-Committee, *Report to the Minister of Town and Country Planning*, London: HMSO, 1946, p. 25; the Advisory Committee "Memorandum", p. 9; and the *Memorandum by the Minister of Town and Country Planning on the Report of the Advisory Committee*, London: HMSO, 1947, all had the effect of supporting the initial acceptance. See also the *Clement Davies Report*, London: HMSO, 1949.

Proudlove noted,[118] had lost none of its importance during the intervening years. As the number of vehicles in cities continued to mount alarmingly (see chapter 2), a Working Party headed by Colin Buchanan was formed by the Government in 1961 and asked to consider precisely the question posed by Proudlove; specifically, their terms of reference were "to study the long-term development of roads and traffic in urban areas and their influence on the urban environment".[119]

Like the *County of London Plan* the Buchanan Report was to be a long-term aid to policy makers of a purely advisory nature. Unlike the County of London Plan, however, Buchanan was not asked to produce a plan for any specific place within the UK as he went to some effort to indicate—"least of all for London".[120] In spite of this caveat, *Traffic in Towns* has had a profound impact on thinking about the way in which London could approach its traffic problem and Buchanan and his consulting firm, Colin Buchanan and Partners, have subsequently developed and elaborated "Buchananism" with regard to the capital in their role as consultants to the Greater London Council.[121]

At its most basic the problem outlined in *Traffic in Towns* was that of an irresistible force—the increasing flow of motor vehicles—meeting an immovable object—the traditional pattern of buildings and the existing road system. This conflict resulted in a steady fall in environmental standards as attempts to increase *accessibility* by both governmental authorities and individual motorists had an unintended combined impact of a detrimental nature: in spite of roads constantly being widened by public action, private drivers continued to invade areas of high amenity value in the attempt to

---

[118] "Traffic in towns: a review", *The Town Planning Review*, Vol. XXXIV, No. 4, January 1964, p. 261.
[119] *Traffic in Towns* (1963), p. 7.
[120] Page 7.
[121] In this role a number of documents have been produced. See, for example, Colin Buchanan and Partners, *North East London: Some Implications of the Greater London Development Plan*, a Report to the GLC, London, June 1970; Colin Buchanan and Partners, *Greenwich and Blackheath Study*, a Report to the GLC, London, April 1971; and Colin Buchanan and Partners, *Greenwich and Deptford Management Study*, a Report to the GLC, London, July 1972.

Constructing a Solution 89

avoid increasing congestion. There was every reason to believe that matters would get steadily worse. In 1942 at the time the *County of London Plan* was being prepared there were 1,840,400 vehicles in the United Kingdom. Abercrombie estimated that during the 50-year course of the Plan the number of vehicles would double or possibly triple.[122] By 1962 the number of vehicles had grown to 10,500,000.[123] An increase in 20 years by a factor of 5. In addition, during the decade from 1963 to 1973 the number of vehicles was expected to double[124]—road space and associated facilities would have to be found in the crowded cities for a total of more than 21 million vehicles.

As an engineer by training, Buchanan approached the problem as one of design. The basic problem complex was felt to be how to "*contrive the efficient distribution, or accessibility, of large numbers of vehicles to large numbers of buildings, and to do it in such a way that a satisfactory standard of environment is achieved*".[125] The point to begin in this war of each against all, Buchanan felt, was by the subdivision of the city into convenient units. These units which Buchanan called "environmental areas" were, like Abercrombie's neighbourhoods (or precincts), to provide the primary focus for planning attention; unlike Abercrombie's sub-divisions, however, the environmental areas were to be based neither on social nor on homogenous land-use considerations. Environmental areas would be based instead exclusively on the achievement of a satisfactory relationship between traffic, both moving and at rest, and environmental standards. The problem complex mentioned above could then be conceived of as falling into four major sub-components—all concerned with the basic problem of design. The *initial* design problem was of necessity the formulation of standards which would allow environmental quality to be determined and related to the demands imposed by traffic.[126] These standards which were to be

[122] *CLP (1943)*, p. 49.
[123] *Traffic in Towns*, p. 11.
[124] *Traffic in Towns*, p. 11.
[125] Proudlove (1964), p. 260.
[126] See both the first Appendix to *Traffic in Towns*, pp. 203–213; and the approach adopted in *North East London* (1970).

90 Strategic Planning in London

primarily physical and quantitative in character would be measurable by independent observers. Precision would be substituted for what had previously been an intuitive operation: quantification could then be used to assess quality.

It was emphasized that the environmental areas would differ a great deal from one another depending on the physical arrangement which they possessed and would therefore also differ with regard to the total amount of traffic they could contain. This "crude capacity" gave rise to the *second* major design sub-component: an application of the previously determined amenity standards meant that an effort would be required to exclude inessential traffic and thus establish the "environmental capacity" for the areas which were thus delineated. Essential traffic was defined by the Report as "The business, commercial and industrial traffic which is necessary to service and maintain the life of a community".[127] Optional traffic—the use of cars for private pleasure and convenience[128]—could then be squeezed out by means of road closures, structural alterations, and the provision of a suitable alternative road network. Clearly within some of the environmental areas a considerable amount of traffic could be accommodated provided that it satisfied the previously mentioned amenity standards and the traffic was essential to the functioning of the area.[129] Equally clearly the *total amount of traffic movement within the city as a whole* could not be realistically dealt with *solely* by means of structural alterations because of the enormous cost and disruption involved. One of the lessons which the Working Party drew from their case studies of various sized towns was that there were *absolute* limits to the amount of vehicles which could be accommodated in towns in a satisfactory manner.[130] The study of a central area block, for example, convinced them that the provision for unrestricted use of the automobile in Central

---

[127] *Traffic in Towns*, Appendix 3, p. 222.
[128] *Traffic in Towns*, p. 34. In fact the breakdown is more complex than this and involves *mode, purpose* and *time of journey* considerations. See p. 222.
[129] See the statement regarding the failure of traffic studies to relate land-use considerations and traffic flows by the Research Committee of the Town Planning Institute, "Urban traffic problems", *Journal of the Town Planning Institute*, Vol. XLVI, No. 2, January 1960.
[130] *Traffic in Towns*, p. 191.

Constructing a Solution   91

London would cause design problems that would be impossibly large and complicated. Within any *given area*, however, the amount of traffic which could be suitably provided for was not unalterably fixed. Three variables were involved: the environmental standards, the level of accessibility and the amount of resources which could be expended on modification. Using these variables Buchanan formulated his now famous law, *"within any urban area as it stands the establishment of environmental standards automatically determines the accessibility, but the latter can be increased according to the amount of money that can be spent on physical alterations"*.[131]

One of the most important of the physical alterations at this micro-area level was the suggested conception of buildings and streets as related parts of a single structure. The *third* major task of design was thus the integration of traffic and architectural considerations so that a coherent approach to the problem in its entirety could be undertaken. Buchanan called the arranging of buildings for efficient circulation *and* good environment "traffic architecture"[132] and noted that where this comprehensive architectural approach had been adopted as in the case of the New Town at Cumbernauld a significant advance in urban design had been achieved. Since as Louis Kahn had earlier remarked, "the street wants to be a building"[133] a number of design considerations could apply equally to both. The concept of traffic architecture might mean that in a densely developed centre like London it might be necessary to develop central areas on several decks: one for parking, one for shopping and so on.[134] Pedestrians and vehicles would thus be clearly separated vertically and both could proceed in an unimpeded manner in the pursuit of their respective activities.[135]

These three design problems: (a) the establishment of environ-

---

[131] *Traffic in Towns*, p. 45, italics in original.
[132] Colin Buchanan, "Comprehensive redevelopment—the opportunity for traffic", in T. E. H. Williams (Ed.), *Urban Survival and Traffic*, London: E. & F. N. Spon Ltd., 1962, p. 8.
[133] Quoted by David A. Crane, "The city symbolic", *Journal of the American Institute of Planners*, Vol. XXVI, No. 4, November 1960, p. 288.
[134] See for a similar proposal for New York's Fifth Avenue, Paul and Percy Goodman, *Communitas*, New York: Vintage Books, 1947, 2nd ed., 1960, pp. 236–237.
[135] *Traffic in Towns*, p. 46.

92 Strategic Planning in London

mental standards; (b) the separation of essential and optional traffic within the delineated environmental areas through physical means; and (c) the application of traffic architecture principles to separate vehicles and those on foot, horizontally, and when necessary, vertically, all gave rise to the *fourth* and last problem: the establishment of a road system for the entire city which would suitably facilitate both movement and accessibility. At a 1960 Town and Country Planning Conference, Buchanan argued that it was the *penetrating* power of the private automobile which people most valued and it was therefore of little use to merely build a few main arteries.[136] Something more than the traditional top-down approach to major highway planning was patently required if the roads were to serve the needs of the people who lived *beside* as well as those who travelled *along* them.

The key to approaching this macro-problem, according to Buchanan, turned on *first* establishing the numerous "urban rooms" which his environmental approach necessitated for the entire built-up area under consideration; the *next* step would then be the designation and construction of a by now familiar solution: a road hierarchy which would be divided into two basic types: distributors designed for movement and access roads designed to serve buildings.[137] In practice, however, in a large city such as London an additional link would be required. The "primary" distributors would be linked to the "local" distributors by means of an intermediate tier at the district level. "The system", according to *Traffic in Towns*, "may be likened to the trunk, limbs, branches and finally the twigs (corresponding to the access roads) of a tree".[138] The shape of the road hierarchy would thus grow logically from the collective requirements of the individual environmental areas.

---

[136] Joan V. Aucott, "Planning and the motor vehicle", *Town and County Planning*, Vol. XXVIII, No. 12, December 1960, p. 408.
[137] Compare with Unwin's 1911 distinction on p. 68.
[138] Page 44; and see also S. Wood's suggestion that a *street* should be considered a stem linking buildings and therefore a place as distinguished from a *road* whose only purpose would be to facilitate movement. Team 10, The role of the architect in community building", in Gwen Bell and Jacqueline Tyrwhitt (Eds.), *Human Identity in the Urban Environment*, Harmondsworth, Middlesex: Penguin Books, 1972, p. 387.

In an echo of the Abercrombie organic model Buchanan remarked that the city could then begin "taking on a cellular structure consisting of environmental areas set within an interlacing network of distributory highways".[139] It was, however, contended by Buchanan that he deliberately avoided preconceived geometric notions about the correct shape of the road network. He remarked that *Traffic in Towns* differed from earlier studies in that

> Attention is first turned to the environment to delineating the areas within which life is led and activities conducted. Gradually, for the whole town working outwards from a large number of points, the cellular structure takes shape, and as it does so, by a complementary process, the pattern of the network declares itself. This, we submit, is the right ... place—the place of service, no more, to the buildings and the activities therein.[140]

At first glance this deliberate eschewing of the geometric approach to highway planning coupled with Buchanan's previously mentioned lack of explicit concern with *social* as opposed to amenity considerations would seem to provide two major points of contrast between Abercrombie's and Buchanan's approach. In fact the differences are not as sharply defined as they first appear even at the theoretical level and as Buchanan's thought has been subsequently developed in London through actual application a surprisingly high degree of convergence has occurred between the two schools. In spite of the fact that *Traffic in Towns* was additive and concentrated on the lower tier of the city while the *County of London Plan* was largely deductive and concentrated on the top and bottom levels of the city simultaneously, the Buchanan approach could be viewed less as a new departure and more as a logical extension of long dominant traditional planning principles given the changed traffic context of the 1960s.

TRADITIONAL PLANNING AND THE TRIPP CONNECTION

In a sense Buchanan provided a bridge between Abercrombie's organic view of the city and the functionally narrower and more

[139] *Traffic in Towns*, p. 42.
[140] Page 52.

specific approach which characterized the contributions made by the various specialists involved in the actual process of implementing the London plans. It was necessary to reverse this trend toward increasing compartmentalization of the city based on divergent professional perspectives Buchanan held[141] because the character of the traditional city could only be preserved in the face of a massive automobile onslaught by a *comprehensive approach to the problem of traffic.*[142] In terms of form and structure, however, in the broadest sense Buchanan's analysis of the mechanism of movement within the city in no way invalidated Abercrombie's broader organic framework; *rather it would have been at least theoretically possible to achieve Abercrombie's traffic strategy for London through Buchanan's tactics.* Further, it may also be contended that not only could the latter approach be conveniently superimposed on the former without doing violence to either set of ideas, but far more importantly, *Traffic in Towns* provided one of the few possible courses which would allow the type of city that Abercrombie had done so much to shape and maintain to be preserved in the face of growing personal vehicular mobility. The Buchanan Report could almost be read as a blueprint for survival for existing London as it attempted to come to terms with the automobile age, while retaining its basic form.

Just as Abercrombie could be viewed as providing a working context for Buchanan to be applied to a specific geographical area so Buchanan could be conceived of as supplying an intellectual matrix to unite various professional interests[143] in the attainment of that context through a revived interest in planning's basic sphere of concern: the primacy of the urban environment. Although Abercrombie had shown a high degree of concern with the quality of the urban environment in its entirety, and hence had displayed a

---

[141] *Traffic in Towns*, p. 7, and see also the comments of the Steering Group chaired by Sir Geoffrey Crowther, para. 55.

[142] See, for example, the condemnation of the separation of traffic and land-use studies in *Traffic in Towns*, p. 193.

[143] See, on the continuing problem of the relationships between planning and other professions in the urban sphere, J. Brian McLoughlin, "The changing state of British practice", *Journal of the American Institute of Planners*, Vol. XXXII, No. 6, November 1966, p. 353.

considerable "breadth" of physical and functional comprehensiveness in the London plans as his cohesive vision of the city was sub-divided and allocated to operating departments during the process of implementation, a number of problems arose. In the transition from conceptualizing to controlling London the environment was seen from a variety of specialist perspectives and at least part of Buchanan's purpose was to achieve a higher degree of coherence in their cumulative view of the city with regard to the traffic problem.

The initial constraint which Abercrombie faced in extending his general aims was *spatial* and could be seen in his analysis of the three geographical Londons within the Green Belt mentioned earlier.[144] As he remarked his intent was to enlarge his basic model of planned order until it covered the region which his studies dealt with.

> The County of London Plan proposed the gradual completion of an organic community pattern which was closely related to the communications, open space and industrial proposals. The regional outline plan of community development shown in the Master Plan is conceived of as a continuation of this Organic pattern.[145]

Buchanan, however, took the overall shape, boundaries and major land-use patterns in the existing city as largely given, and essentially desirable.[146] He contended that it was reasonable to assume that at least until the turn of the century, *"towns and cities will continue to exist broadly in their present form"*[147] and that land-use rearrangements were therefore likely to be both slow and marginal in character.

---

[144] Page 64.
[145] *GLP (1944)*, p. 111.
[146] See, for example, Colin Buchanan, *Transport and the community*, an Inaugural Lecture delivered at the Imperial College of the University of London, 18 February 1964, p. 186; and see also the defence put forward in *Traffic in Towns*, p. 31, on city "compactness".
[147] *Traffic in Towns*, p. 30, italics added, and see D. J. Reynolds, *Economics, Town Planning and Traffic*, London: Institute of Economic Affairs, 1966, p. 68.

96 Strategic Planning in London

The initial constraint which concerned Buchanan was therefore less the general internal spatial arrangements and sub-divisions of the city and more the nature of the defects arising from the way in which *the city worked at the local level*. Because of this *functional* constraint with particular regard to the problem of vehicular movement, *Traffic in Towns*, in keeping with a major strand of traditional planning thought for most of this century, concluded that the city performed inefficiently because of the difficulties which arose from an inherited road system characterized by poor alignments, frequent intersections, irregular street widths and buildings fronting directly onto main roads.[148]

These manifest defects in London's physical arrangements in this vital sphere of city life meant that the organic order's continued viability was put at risk as traffic steadily increased. Unless protective steps were taken by planners and allied professions, Abercrombie and Buchanan both maintained, cities would be faced by a slow strangulation of their circulatory systems and an equally disastrous accompanying breakdown of the boundaries surrounding their cellular subdivisions. Apparently only one course remained open as Abercrombie had indicated in his discussion of the Mechanistic component of the three functional Londons[149] and as Buchanan had contended with regard to the trade-off between amenity and accessibility[150] traffic must be physically canalized. Without canalization it would simply not be possible to relegate traffic to its proper service role and prevent it from progressively undermining the wider environmental considerations which collectively constituted some of the most desirable aspects of urban life.[151]

If progressive strangulation were to be averted the real question was not whether canalization should be employed but how it could best be achieved. It was evident to both men that at least two distinct factors needed to be related to one another in controlling

---

[148] Page 38 and p. 191; see for an early example of the traditional view, *Report of the Royal Commission on London Traffic*, London: HMSO, 1905; and Robson (1948), p. 146.

[149] Page 81.

[150] Page 91.

[151] See for a similar American view F. Stuart Chapin, *Urban Land Use Planning*, Urbana; University of Illinois Press, 2nd ed., 1965, p. 47.

traffic flows. On the one hand, there must be a positive force such as Abercrombie's arterial roads or Buchanan's primary distributors to attract high-speed, through traffic away from the existing street system. On the other hand, continuing the magnetic analogy, there must also be a repelling force such as the physical arrangement of Abercrombie's neighbourhoods or Buchanan's environmental areas which would exclude traffic that did not terminate within them.[152] Without a *combination* of tactical area "push" and circulatory system "pull" the policy for ordering traffic simply could not be made to work with any degree of effectiveness.

The entire attempt to control traffic and protect the quality of the micro-areas of social and environmental cohesion advocated by the *County of London Plan* and *Traffic in Towns* thus turned on the pivot of, *at a basic minimum*, successfully differentiating between through and local traffic.[153] In both studies a broadly similar way of conceiving of the city and of the traffic problem within it is evident—culminating in each case with the advocacy of a multi-tiered hierarchy. The concept of modifying or constructing physical means for achieving the community push–motorway pull effect is clearly evident in the writings of Sir Alker Tripp and it is he who provides an important connection between Abercrombie and Buchanan.[154]

Tripp, the Assistant Commissioner of Metropolitan Police,[155] was particularly concerned with traffic safety and he maintained that "The whole trouble originates in unsuitable lay-out; the problem is fundamentally one of design and planning".[156] With regard to canalization, Tripp indicated that it would be possible to deal with traffic either by restriction or by construction. The latter method was felt to be more effective and therefore preferable. "Nothing", Tripp wrote, "should ever be done by means of legal restrictions which it

---

[152] See, for example, Buchanan (1964), *Inaugural*, p. 184, on this idea.

[153] See on this *CLP (1943)*, p. 55; and *Traffic in Towns* (1963), p. 34 and p. 222. On Buchanan's addition distinction between essential and optional traffic and the way in which this distinction relates to the basic through-local dichotomy, see Chapter 5.

[154] See, for example, Buchanan's brief acknowledgement to Tripp and the *County of London Plan*, *Traffic in Towns* (1963), p. 42.

[155] See p. 69.

[156] Tripp (1942), p. 16.

is practicable to effect by layout; this principle must be regarded as an axiom of traffic science."[157]

To achieve this end, Tripp designated basic planning units which he called "precincts"[158] and employed a proposed graded road system called "conduits"[159] which, when linked with one another, would segregate fast traffic, slow traffic, and those on foot, spatially. His basic intent was of creating, "...an ordered series of safe and sequestered precincts wherein every avocation is peacefully pursued in safety..."[160] by means of traffic streaming through the combined agency of local area redesign and the operation of a triple-tiered road hierarchy. This ultimate aim was also close to the heart of Buchanan and Abercrombie's traffic proposals. For example, Buchanan maintained that "...the freedom with which a person can walk about and look around is a useful guide to the civilized quality of an urban area".[161] The key to civilizing the city, therefore, rested on controlling the automobile and this was one of Buchanan's basic purposes in writing *Traffic in Towns*. Abercrombie similarly felt that if control could be accomplished within the proposed precincts they would then be "free from noise, dirt and the dangers of through traffic, people should be able to spend their working hours and city dwellers their lives" in this healthier and less harried atmosphere.[162]

In spite of the fact that Tripp, Abercrombie and Buchanan approached the problem of formulating a strategic traffic policy from different directions, reflecting in part their differing backgrounds, and in spite of the fact that their work was separated by a time span of more than 20 years a remarkably high level of conceptual continuity can be discerned. Nor was this continuity of policy confined to the problem of traffic alone since each author contended that the traffic problem was merely one facet of a much

---

[157] Tripp (1942), p. 21; on the actual layout of town roads see Alker Tripp, *Road Traffic and its Control*, London: Edward Arnold & Co., 1938, pp. 328–329.
[158] Tripp (1942), p. 75, and see Fig. 3.4.
[159] See Tripp (1938), pp. 292–293.
[160] Tripp (1942), p. 85.
[161] *Traffic* (1963), p. 39.
[162] *CLP (1943)*, p. 51.

Constructing a Solution 99

wider difficulty: the outmoded physical structure of the city at both the strategic and tactical levels. In each of the suggested strategies for attempting to control traffic, however, it was recognized that unless traffic was dealt with a desirable city order and a satisfactory urban environment could not be achieved.

It is important to note that the purpose-built road system "principle" which Buchanan had accepted and advocated was accompanied by an acceptance of a number of related traditional planning principles as well. In almost all matters of substance Buchanan did not differ significantly from the basic planning propositions put forward by Abercrombie.[163] The interrelated and internally consistent bundle of traditional planning prescriptions which Abercrombie had put forward during World War Two[164] and which had done so much to influence governmental thinking regarding a suitable strategy for London could be found in a marginally revised, but essentially complete form in Buchanan's policy formulations. For example, Buchanan held:

(a) that the city should continue to be horizontally contained by a combination of Green Belt and development controls;[165]
(b) that overcrowding should be relieved through external dispersal of people and their employment and relocated in compact New Towns;[166]
(c) that the city should continue to be serviced by a concentrated central area;[167]
(d) that traffic should be streamed on specially constructed and designed roads arranged to provide a hierarchy of accessibility;[168]
(e) that care should be taken to ensure the primacy of amenity concerns by delineating a complex set of micro-areas which

---

[163] See Fig. 3.2, p. 101.
[164] See the summary on pp. 83–86.
[165] *Traffic* (1963), p. 30.
[166] See Colin Buchanan, *Mixed Blessing*, London: Leonard Hill, 1958, pp. 154–155; and *Traffic* (1963), p. 31 and p. 165.
[167] *Inaugural* (1964), p. 183; and see also *Traffic* (1963), p. 165.
[168] *Traffic* (1963), pp. 43–44; and *Inaugural* (1964), pp. 186–187.

100 Strategic Planning in London

would exclude undesirable traffic and at the same time relate to the proposed urban road system;[169]

(f) that within existing cities historical areas of high environmental value should be protected by "environmental management" and thus protected be then linked to other major points including the city centre;[170]

(g) that in so far as possible urban areas are compact and complete in themselves to help reduce both the need for, and the distance of, travel;[171]

(h) that long-term technical control should be exercised by a regional agency so that opportunities for a comprehensive treatment of the traffic problem are not lost through the "piecemeal replacement of individual buildings..." and the failure to take a co-ordinated professional approach;[172]

(i) that a high degree of consensus either existed or could be created with regard to the proposed physical controls for the traffic problem and that political will needed to be mobilized so that continuing support for the lengthy construction period required could be provided.[173]

In addition to accepting and readvocating this set of measures in a rather more developed but clearly recognizable form Buchanan also held that major land-use changes *within* the city were unlikely to occur. In realistic terms, he asserted, that over the next few decades "our towns will continue to exist more or less as we know them",[174] and he also indicated that his studies "have revolved around a somewhat static concept of the size of towns".[175] Thus in this final regard, Buchanan, once again like Abercrombie, sought to achieve an eventual equilibrium between motion and statics, in large meas-

---

[169] *Traffic* (1963), pp. 44–45; and *Inaugural* (1964), p. 184.
[170] *Traffic* (1963), pp. 197 and 222; and *Mixed Blessing* (1958), pp. 199–200.
[171] *Inaugural* (1964), p. 186; and *Traffic* (1963), p. 31.
[172] *Traffic* (1963), p. 198; and *Inaugural* (1964), pp. 191–192.
[173] See *Traffic* (1963), p. 201, and the Steering Committee Report under Geoffrey Crowther, paras. 3 and 55. See also Geoffrey Vickers, *The Art of Judgement*, London: Methuen, 1965, p. 52, on the public education aspect of the Buchanan Report.
[174] *Inaugural* (1964), p. 192.
[175] *Traffic* (1963), p. 192.

ure through Tripp's canalization methods,[176] based on an essentially static view of city size.[177]

TABLE 3.2. A COHESIVE SET OF PHYSICAL PLANNING PRESCRIPTIONS

Major prescription	Level of continuity	
	A	B
1. Horizontal containment	+	+
2. Concentrated external dispersal	+	+
3. Mono-centralization	+	+
4. Concentric configurative pattern	+	−
5. Hierarchical traffic canalization	+	+
6. Cellular delineation	+	+
7. Strengthening the centre–periphery relationship	+	+
8. Urban completeness	+	+
9. Creating a regional development authority	+	+
10. On-going political consensus	+	+

A = Abercrombie; B = Buchanan; + = Explicit acceptance; − = Little explicit positive or negative comment.

Again, through planned change it was hoped that a stable state for the city could be achieved and maintained. Because of spatial and functional interrelationships the way in which the traffic problem was dealt with played no small part in determining to what extent the basic planning principles for traditional London could be sustained. As Buchanan asserted. "It is not traffic movement but civilized town life that is at stake".[178]

---

[176] Buchanan held, for example, that in a restructured town "all longer movements would be canalized *without choice*". *Traffic* (1963), p. 42; author's italics.
[177] See on a criticism of Buchanan in this regard Reynolds (1966), *Economics*, p. 67.
[178] *Mixed Blessing* (1958), p. 210.

CHAPTER 4

Unwrapping the Box: Ringway One and the Planning of the Primary Road Network

> The cars will keep on coming, not because of some horrid conspiracy but because we the people want them. They will clog our already overburdened streets more and more until economic and social strangulation results, unless someone does something about it. Who? It has to be the highway planner.... He must assess the traffic demand—he *must* plan capacious traffic arteries to accommodate it—he simply has no choice.—R. I. Wolf, "Letter to the Editor", *Journal of the American Institute of Planners*, Vol. XXVII, No. 1, February 1961, p. 75. Italics in original.
>
> In the long run, the action, which is desired and may be possible, depends on the interplay of complex social and economic forces. These lie behind and all around the ostensibly simpler concepts which planners represent by their words and drawings... there is of course the character and quality of *government: the will of the powers-that-be to direct and control*....— Edward Carter, *The Future of London*, 1962, p. 191. Italics added.

LONDON'S LONG-TERM STRATEGY: THE CONTINUING TRAFFIC COMMITMENT

Within 12 hours of beginning its official life the Greater London Council announced a major construction project to help alleviate London's traffic congestion. At a meeting held on 1 April 1965 and attended by representatives from the thirty-two London Boroughs and the Press an inner ring road costing an estimated £450 million was unveiled. It was asserted at the meeting by the Council that the greatest return to the community would be realized by an "Urban Motorway Box" of high-speed, limited access roads forming a rough rectangle 4 to 6 miles from central London which would link the existing radials and the new intercity roads then being constructed as part of the emerging national motorway network[1] Mr. Christopher Higgins, Chairman of the Planning and Communication Committee, which supervised the project bluntly underlined its perceived importance to the new Council by announcing that unless the GLC put forward its road intentions it would be failing in the major purpose for which it had been established.[2]

Three interlocking factors played an important part in bringing the Motorway Box into being. *First,* as indicated above the GLC possessed a strategic orientation and an actual construction capability which gave major road planning for the Capital as a whole a new level of importance. Once again according to the London Government Act (1963) which created the GLC the Council was explicitly required to lay down "considerations of general policy with respect to the use of land in the various parts of Greater London, *including in particular guidance as to the future road system*".[3] Although a good deal of the planning of the Motorway Box had, of course, taken place under the GLC's predecessor, the London County Council, the Box also served as the first step in fulfilling this important component of the GLC's legal reason for existence.[4]

Secondly, a long-held and widely shared perception of the nature of the traffic problem existed which turned on the idea that the *central difficulty in the Capital was a deficiency in the supply of road space available.* One observer wrote before World War One with regard to this problem,

> In London we are woefully wanting in space. This handicaps everything we wish to do. How can it be provided? We can steal it from some other use, such as a public garden or a park; we can purchase at great cost land and houses, sweep them away and spread out on the level; or we can burrow or go aloft.[5]

During World War Two the *Greater London Plan 1944* succinctly

[1] Greater London Council, *Minutes 1965*, London: GLC, 1965, p. 348. A map of the Box was first revealed in *New Society* on 25 March 1965 by Peter Hall, a week before the official announcement was made. Vol. 5, No. 139, pp. 18–19.
[2] See, Michael F. King, "50 motorway miles for London", the *Evening Standard*, 1 April 1965, p. 15.
[3] Part III, 25(3), italics added.
[4] See on the GLC's organizational structure generally, Chapter 2 pp. 49–51.
[5] Captain G. S. C. Swinton, "London traffic", *Journal of the Society of Arts*, 2 March 1906, p. 439. See also for a similar view Patrick Balfour, "Times change, why not the roads?", London: British Road Federation, 1938, unpaginated.

observed the automobile "....has suddenly and completely overgrown the static surface upon which movement takes place. Cars have changed; roads have remained."[6]

Finally, the cohesive bundle of planning principles initially put forward by Abercrombie and later reinforced by Buchanan for creating an almost classical form of urban order for London had been broadly accepted as government policy and was in the process of slowly and selectively being implemented. The eventual construction of a fully articulated road network was seen by both men as an essential component in the development of London and a necessary instrument for the achievement of its ultimate form. The tenacity with which the classical compact city philosophy and its associated road pattern was maintained over a lengthy period of time is evident at both the national and the local planning levels.[7] A joint statement was made, for example, by the Minister of Town and Country Planning and the Minister of Transport in 1947 indicating that a central feature of long-term government policy for London would be to divide the London Region into four geographical rings largely by means of a ring-road system based on the original Abercrombie proposals.[8] The ring and radial hierarchy of roads was also accepted by the LCC in principle for its own area and significant elements of this type of thinking can be found in the 1951 *Administrative County of London Development Plan* which was officially approved in 1955 and in the Plan's *First Review* which appeared 5 years later.[9] In each of these documents, for example, a continuing commitment to establishing cellular neighbourhoods and central area precincts at the local level *by means* of a hierarchical road system was also

---

[6] Patrick Abercrombie (1945), London: HMSO, p. 63. During an LCC debate it was argued that London's traffic was 50 years in advance of the capacity of its street system. London County Council, *Minutes 1956*, London: Staples Press Ltd., 1957, p. 716. See also on this topic generally, Chapter 2, pp. 27–28.

[7] On the advantages of city compactness see, for example, Colin Buchanan, *Traffic in Towns*, London: HMSO, 1963, p. 31.

[8] See on the level of informal co-operation growing out of this particular proposal at the regional level, Ministry of Housing and Local Government, *Memorandum of Evidence*, Royal Commission on Local Government in Greater London, London: HMSO, 1959, p. 119.

[9] LCC, *Administrative County of London Development Plan 1951—Statement*, London: LCC, 1951, p. 1; and LCC, *Administrative County of London Development Plan—First Review*, London: LCC, 1960, pp. 2–4.

Unwrapping the Box 105

clearly evident. In the 1960 *Review* the Chairman of the Town and Country Planning Committee, Richard Edmonds, explicitly acknowledged that in the Capital "Planning continuity derives from the aims so ably set out by Abercrombie and Forshaw in 1943, in whose work lay vital guiding principles for the ever developing metropolis".[10] One of the most basic of these principles held that if the desired physical form for London were to be realized a necessary precondition was the segregation and physical canalization of traffic.[11]

Given: (a) the *perceived problem*, (b) the accepted *planning prescription* to control it, and (c) the *powers* possessed by the GLC to put it into effect, the Box appeared to be both an essential step in controlling traffic congestion in the short run and a necessary precondition for allowing London's ultimate form to be progressively realized in the long term. Each of these factors individually pointed to a pressing need for new roads to be constructed— considered collectively the case for concrete action seemed irrefutable.

CHANGING THE ORDER OF PRIORITY

The concrete action symbolized by the Box also indicated an important reordering of organizational and resource priorities. For several years after World War Two attempts both inside and outside of the LCC to secure an increase in the amount of funds available spent on roads in London had met with little success. On 14 May 1946, for example, the Conservative opposition on the Council proposed that £100,000 should be put aside for the safeguarding of land required for the development of the ring roads and the radials put forward in the *County of London Plan (1943)*. Even this

[10] Richard Edmonds, "Introduction", *Review* (1960), p. vi. See in addition on this topic the comments made by the Chief Planner of the Ministry of Housing and Local Government on the need to relate the desired compact city form to the problem of growing automobile usage and hence the importance of adopting "Buchanan-style" planning tactics. J. R. James, "The next fifty years", *Journal of the Town Planning Institute*, Vol. 50, No. 1, January 1964, pp. 9–10. For an amplification of the Abercrombie–Buchanan ordering principles see Chapter 3, pp. 99–101.

[11] See, for example, on the continuing interest in this idea, the joint circular issued by the Ministry of Housing and Local Government and the Ministry of Transport, "The Buchanan Report: Traffic in Towns", Circular 1/64, London: HMSO, 1964, pp. 2–3, for an indication of its impact on public policy.

relatively small amount was, however, promptly defeated on the grounds of financial stringency.[12] The Central Government also adopted much the same approach. When a delegation from the LCC attempted to meet with the Minister of Transport to discuss the widening of heavily travelled Finchley Road they were rather curtly informed by letter that in view of the extremely limited amount of funds available the Minister "considered that in the circumstances there was no point in discussing the matter".[13]

Throughout this period although Abercrombie's strategic road network was delayed in execution, largely because of financial stringency and the lack of a co-ordinating agency for the whole of the Greater London area, a good deal of construction was undertaken at the local level as a result of the Council's major activity: the provision of public housing. Housing's pre-eminence and a related concern with planning the new estates as physical neighbourhoods were both virtually unquestioned objectives for most of the LCC's postwar life.[14] As time passed, however, an interest in top-tier highway construction began occupying an increasingly important— if still very much less urgent—position in the order of Council priorities. Apart from any other consideration it became evident that in spite of the massive resource expenditure on housing that unless parallel work on the strategic road system was brought forward it would simply not be possible to create the type of formal structure for London which had so long been accepted as desirable from a public policy standpoint.[15] The gradual rebuilding of London from

[12] LCC, *Minutes 1946*, London: Staples Press Ltd., 1947, p. 252. The same amendment was raised again and again in 1947, 1948 and 1949 and was rejected each time for the same reason.

[13] Quoted in LCC, *Minutes 1953*, p. 62. See in addition on this subject, a comment by Peter Hall, "The importance of Finchley Road", *Socialist Commentary*, June 1961.

[14] See, for example, W. Eric Jackson, *Achievement: A Short History of the LCC*, London: Longmans, Green & Co., Ltd., 1965, pp. 93–97. See for a detailed example of neighbourhood planning, Abercrombie's proposal for Stepney, *CLP (1943)*, pp. 82–83.

[15] It is interesting to note that although Abercrombie stressed the need for housing to be given top priority he felt that most of the required rehousing necessitated by his plans would be completed on the basis of his own calculations by roughly 1957. After this time attention and resources could then presumably be shifted to other uses including highway construction. Patrick Abercrombie, *Greater London Plan 1944*, London: HMSO, 1945, p. 186.

the bottom up in a piecemeal fashion although conferring a number of local benefits was not, in itself, a sufficient condition for achieving the long-sought coherent, cohesive, convenient and compact pattern for London as a whole. The development of a fully articulated, triple-tiered road network, it was felt, would have the double merit of: (a) serving as a *prescriptive organizing device* for continuing the existing ordering principles on the one hand; while (b) at the same time acting as a *response to expressed demand* to reduce traffic congestion on the other.[16]

The extent of governmental commitment to the need for a strategic road network for London could be discerned in two separate ways during the 1950s and early 1960s. *Negatively*, although the top-tier road system was delayed in implementation and reduced in scope during this time *it was never formally abandoned by either the LCC or the Government.* Only one of Abercrombie's five proposed ring roads was in fact officially rejected by the Government—once again largely on the grounds of cost and the amount of disruption which it would cause.[17] In May 1950 the innermost, 11.1-mile-long "A" Ring which was designed to link the mainline railway stations in Central London was regretfully put aside by the Minister of Town and Country Planning after lengthy consideration; at a time when less than £1 million per year was actually being spent for the whole of the LCC's area on road improvements the cost of the "A" Ring was estimated to be at least £120 million.[18] At the then current rate of expenditure the construction of the "A" Ring would have required, in effect, the whole of the LCC's road budget for at least the next 120 years. It is significant that Abercrombie himself recanted a year before his death in 1957 and argued that, "after planning the 'A' Ring we came to the conclusion that it was completely impossible as an urban motorway largely on economic grounds". He went on to suggest, however, "I

---

[16] On these terms see David G. Williams, "The modal split", *Town Planning Review*, Vol. 42, No. 2, April 1971, p. 181.
[17] LCC, *Administrative County of London Development Plan 1951—Analysis*, London: LCC, 1951, p. 158.
[18] See, LCC, *London Statistics 1950–1959*, Vol. IV, New Series, London: LCC, 1961, table 198, p. 233; and compare with Edward Carter, *The Future of London*, Harmondsworth, Middlesex: Penguin Books, 1962, p. 155.

am still unrepentant and think the 'A' Ring should be abandoned, and the *'B' Ring... should take its place*".[19]

Another more positive indication of continuing governmental concern in this field was that despite the enormous expense involved belief in the need for high-speed, purpose-built roads within the city remained unwavering in many influential quarters. As the Deputy Chief Engineer of the LCC tellingly remarked to a conference on urban motorways organized by the British Road Federation in 1956, the fact that no large-scale motorways existed in London was due "not to hostility to the principle but to economic policy".[20] The 1960 Development Plan *Review* indicated even more explicitly that although lack of funds had slowed road planning during the 1950s,

> The possibility of urban motorways has been kept in mind. Indeed the most promising pattern for these would be the ring radial layout, modified in detail as necessary to meet traffic engineering and general planning needs.[21]

There was little professional disagreement on the need for and the value of urban motorways in engineering terms. At the local government level it was held that the real essence of the traffic problem in most cities was, according to the LCC's Deputy Chief Engineer, F. A. Rayfield, the familiar one of "lack of road space, and if this additional space is to be provided, better results will be obtained by motorways at less cost than in any other way".[22] At the Central Government level, W. H. Glanville, Director of Road Research at the Department of Scientific and Industrial Research, and J. F. A. Baker, Chief Engineer (Highways) at the Ministry of Transport, held that even a "very heavy expenditure on the

---

[19] Patrick Abercrombie, "Remarks", British Road Federation (Ed.), *Urban Motorways*, London: BRF, 1957, p. 31. Italics added.

[20] F. A. Rayfield, "Remarks at the British Road Federation Conference on urban motorways", BRF (Ed.), *Urban Motorways* (1956), p. 31.

[21] LCC, *Review* (1960), p. 66, and see also p. 69. Italics added. For another indication of the relationship between the road proposals in the World War advisory plans and the subsequent LCC Development Plans see the statement by senior LCC planner and architect Arthur Ling, who suggested that the Development Plans were "in effect the first stages of the execution" of the Abercrombie Plans. Peter Shepeard et al., "The New London", text of a BBC Radio broadcast which took place on the Third Programme, 28 March 1950, typescript, p. 8.

[22] Rayfield, "Remarks", BRF (Ed.), *Urban Motorways* (1956), p. 32.

improvement of existing roads and intersections can only to a very limited extent ease traffic flow".[23] According to Glanville and Baker, a comprehensive solution to the traffic problem required "new roads and, as will be seen, there is evidence to show that greatest benefits are likely to come from building such new roads as urban motorways.[24]

The Council indicated in their official 1960 Development Plan *Review* that many of these points had been accepted and that attention needed

> to be given to the planning and design of a *new road system*, possibly based on motorway principles.... The Council is fully aware of this need and has decided to start the necessary investigations so that further proposals may be submitted at subsequent Reviews of the Plan.[25]

To gather information for the proposed new road network an initial expenditure of £5000 was approved in December 1960 for preliminary work on a large-scale traffic survey to be jointly supervised by the LCC and the Ministry of Transport.

It is important to note that long before the survey was actually commissioned the following set of long-term road planning assumptions had been reconfirmed as public policy and could be summarized as follows:

(i) *That a significant increase in the supply of road space available for vehicular movement was essential to meet growing traffic demands and that the necessary increase should be created largely through the construction of new roads* although limited, related measures such as traffic management and parking controls would also be simultaneously employed.

(ii) That the new top-tier roads should form a multi-lane, high-

---

[23] W. H. Glanville and J. F. A. Baker, "Urban motorways in Great Britain?", in BRF (Ed.), *Urban Motorways* (1956), p. 31.

[24] Glanville and Baker, "Motorways", in BRF (Ed.), *Urban Motorways* (1956), p. 23.

[25] LCC, *Review* (1960), p. 69. Italics added. See also on this long-standing acceptance of the motorway solution, R. Nicholas, "The effect of the national road system on urban problems", in BRF (Ed.), *People and Cities*, London: BRF, 1964, pp. 235–236; and Simon Jenkins, "The politics of London motorways", the *Political Quarterly*, Vol. 44, No. 3, July–September 1973, p. 268.

speed, limited access, and grade-separated *system* to enable them to perform their basic purpose—the *physical canalization* of various types of vehicular movement and hence the segregation of differing kinds of activity patterns.

(iii) That at the strategic level these roads should assume a *ring-radial configuration based on the accepted compact, mono-centric concept of urban order.*

Once again the ring-radial pattern of motorways seemed to effectively fuse the growing importance of current traffic concerns and the traditional long-term planning objectives in a single design.

Technically the proposed road pattern appeared, at least in principle, to satisfy the primary requirement of a road system which the LCC felt to be the ability "to carry without undue delay and as safely as possible the volume of traffic which wishes to use it".[26] Administratively an interest in a solution based on a strategic road plan of this kind was clearly evident from a variety of sources at both the central and local government levels and the proposed Greater London Council seemed to afford an excellent opportunity to put this plan into practice.[27] As car ownership continued to increase it became evident, by the earlier 1960s, that a major interest in road building was developing and that the amount of funds required for construction to proceed might at last become available in the relatively near future.

Between 1955 and 1960 the LCC increased its road expenditure per annum by nine-fold. It was held by the authorities that this increase was "urgently needed to meet the growing traffic demand..."[28] and the actual amount spent on roads during this period rose from less than £0.5 to more than £4.5 million per year. The MOT had developed a "rolling programme" which allowed local authorities to plan at least 5 years in advance[29] and thus attempt to meet the growing traffic

[26] LCC, *Analysis* (1951), pp. 147–148, and for another indication of this basically supply-oriented approach see p. 160.

[27] For support in addition to the sources already cited, see Royal Commission on Local Government in Greater London, *Report*, London: HMSO, Cmnd. 1164, 1960, p. 117.

[28] GLC, *Movement in London*, London: GLC, 1969, p. 7.

[29] See J. A. G. Griffith, *Central Departments and Local Authorities*, London: George Allen & Unwin, 1966, p. 187.

demand. At last apparently the continuing commitment to a traffic strategy for London could begin the difficult transition from accepted policy to physical reality.[30]

REINFORCING—AND NARROWING—
THE MAIN ROAD COMPONENT

Given the accepted highway design for London one of the largest remaining obstacles in the development of the proposed new road system was a scarcity of detailed information regarding existing movement patterns and an inability, more importantly, to *predict* how these patterns would change in the future. Clearly a survey was needed which had predictive capabilities to guide the required organizational action.

As a means of bringing the required travel information up to date the LCC with the "whole-hearted support" of the Minister of Transport, Ernest Marples, began drawing up plans for a large-scale traffic survey in London in late 1960.[31] It was decided that because of the complexity of the project that it should be carried out by an Anglo-American group of independent consultants who had already gained experience in developing a research methodology for studying transport problems of this type in the U.S.[32] The principal firms selected to carry out the proposed "London Traffic Survey" (LTS) were Freeman, Fox (London), Engineering Service Corporation (Los Angeles), and Wilber Smith and Associates (New Haven). The consultants' brief called for "the collection, analysis and presentation

---

[30] See on the LCC's enduring interest in this sphere, John Craig, "The 1943 London Plan: a perspective", *Official Architecture and Planning*, Vol. 33, No. 12, December 1970, p. 1076 and the map on p. 1078.

[31] LCC, *Minutes 1960*, pp. 810–811. Such a survey had earlier been suggested by the Nugent Committee who were charged with studying road building in London on the assumption that more funds would increasingly become available. *Report of the Committee on London Roads*, Cmnd. 812, London: HMSO, 1961.

[32] There was a widespread technical interest in the American studies in Detroit and Chicago, for example, which had been mounted during the late 1950s. One official urged, "American methods must be studied and applied to English situations". Peter Wood, "Studying traffic in towns", *Journal of the Town Planning Institute*, Vol. 49, No. 8, September/October 1963, p. 271.

of basic information on current traffic movements *required for main road planning in Greater London*".[33]

Both major political parties were broadly in agreement on the need for a fresh traffic study as a foundation for the road construction programme which was expected to follow. Neither the survey nor the proposed need for construction were viewed as political issues at least partly because of their widely recognized *technical* merit. The Conservative Bow Group argued, for example, that new high-speed roads within urban areas were essential to the resolution of the traffic problem but that they needed to be sensitively sited and related to more general problems of movement. The Group advocated "a carefully planned system of fast urban roads giving facilities for the speedy flow of public transport and such private vehicles as are essential to the economy of the city...".[34] A Conservative study group under the chairmanship of R. A. B. Butler held that a "basic preliminary" to such a road building programme was "a full traffic survey".[35]

A Fabian Society group under Peter Hall argued in a similar way that urban motorways would play an essential part in the future reconstruction of existing cities but that

> Road improvement schemes have hitherto been carried out on an entirely unscientific basis, unrelated to any reliable estimate of future traffic flows. The Ministry is only now beginning to finance basic studies on the origin and destination of traffic, such as the London Traffic Survey, without which road planning must remain guesswork. But even the London Traffic Survey is restricted to road traffic....[36]

---

[33] Freeman, Fox et al., *London Traffic Survey*, Vol. 1, "Covering letter to the LCC", London: LCC, 1964, no page given. Italics added. See also for an indication of the extent of the main road emphasis, Robert J. Juster, "The London traffic survey", *Journal of the Town Planning Institute*, Vol. 49, No. 9, November 1963, p. 302.

[34] Timothy Knight et al., "Let our cities live", Conservative Political Centre Pamphlet No. 222, London: Conservative Political Centre, December 1960, p. 12. Compare with a similar study undertaken at about the same time in the U.S., Wilfred Owen, *A Total Strategy for Urban Areas*, Washington, D.C.: The Brookings Institute, 1959, pp. 147–148.

[35] "Change and Challenge", Conservative Political Centre Pamphlet No. 227, London: Conservative Political Centre, February 1962, pp. 16–17.

[36] Peter Hall et al., "The face of Britain", *Socialist Commentary*, September 1961, pp. xvi-xvii.

The Fabians then went on to stress the need to relate urban motorways to a "comprehensive communications plan".[37]

Both the Labour and Conservative parties thus accepted without major disagreement the need for quantification and the collection of empirical data as a necessary prerequisite for detailed siting of the proposed new road system. *A major reservation of both, however, was the fear that the survey might be too narrowly based.* It was felt that the proposed survey should be organized in such a way that the relationship: (a) between transportation and land use on one hand, and (b) among various public and private transport modes on the other, would be considered *comprehensively*. Given, however, this fear of a "tunnel vision" approach being prematurely adopted the survey itself was welcomed as a necessary first step in gaining knowledge about patterns of vehicular movement in the Capital.[38]

A number of observers also commented in a similar vein on the need to reintegrate road planning with the existing development plans for London which were almost entirely concerned with *land-use* matters. It was felt that the merger of these two components was particularly important in view of the stress which was laid on the Greater London Council acting as a new *strategic* planning authority.[39] Once again the problem was not a new one, and there had for some time been concern about the separation of highway and land-use planning.

Abercrombie expressed the concern in 1944 that there had not been enough co-ordination between road planning and other forms of planning. Roads were often left out of planning schemes, he argued, on the largely administrative grounds that they were subject to a different minister.[40] In the early 1960s Peter Self pointed out in a

---

[37] See also for an excellent restatement of many of the classical ordering principles for the city compact, Hall, "The Face" (1961), p. xviii. There was, however, one important divergence from these principles: a recognition of the need to make the city more polycentric in form through the creation and strengthening in major district centres. This point will be developed in more detail in Chapter 5.

[38] The term "tunnel vision" was suggested by the planning correspondent of *The Times*, Tony Aldous.

[39] See on this, for example, the "Report of the Planning and Communications Committee", 17 November 1964, *GLC Minutes 1964*, London: GLC, 1965, p. 147.

[40] Abercrombie, *GLP (1944)*, p. 66.

114 Strategic Planning in London

similar organizational criticism that "the Ministry of Transport's present methods completely prevent any local authority from planning highways as part of a general pattern of development".[41] He then went on to pointedly indicate that "Unless reformed these methods would cripple the work of a Greater London Council".[42] Buchanan also maintained, in *Traffic in Towns*, that

> very few of the statutory development plans really face up to the future problems of traffic and transport. Most of them seem to have been stultified by a feeling of hopelessness that funds would ever be available on anything like the scale required.... We think the plans need re-examining with a more optimistic view of the financial side, with the objectives and values clearly stated, and above all with a determined effort to get them onto a sound quantitative basis.[43]

It is worth studying how these suggestions were dealt with in practice in the attempt to reintegrate various movement and planning components.

In spite of these integration attempts the comprehensive and cohesive bundle of public policy principles initially put forward by Abercrombie inevitably became separated from each other as they were assigned different orders of priority and "allocated" to powerful operating departments with comparatively limited spatial and functional perspectives during the process of implementation.[44] This organizational subdividing or *factoring* of planning policy meant that housing, for example, was considered by one large LCC department while the roads which served them were the

---

[41] Peter Self, "Town planning in Greater London", Greater London Papers, No. 7, London: London School of Economics, 1962, p. 23; and see also, Planning Advisory Group, *The Future of Development Plans*, London: HMSO, 1965.

[42] Self, "Town planning" (1962), p. 23.

[43] Colin Buchanan et al., *Traffic in Towns*, London: HMSO, 1963, p. 192. In passing it is extremely interesting to note that in this brief statement on integration Buchanan touched upon, and made recommendations with regard to all three types of planning uncertainty identified by Friend and Jessop. Briefly these can be summarized and paraphrased as follows: (i) Uncertainty about Related Choices—"We need to take a wider view, a more co-ordinated approach..."; (ii) Uncertainty about the Environment—"We need more detailed surveys and more up-to-date information and (iii) Uncertainty about Policy—"We need clearer objectives, more policy statements...". J. F. Friend and W. N. Jessop, *Local Government and Strategic Choice*, London: Tavistock Publications, 1969, pp. 88–89.

[44] See for a comment on the spatial aspect Donald Foley, *Controlling London's Growth*, Berkeley: University of California Press, 1963, p. 118.

responsibility of the functionally quite separate Engineering Department.[45] One of the objectives of the original advisory plans was to knit together discreet functional activities as well as spatial entities around a common set of ideas but as various components of the cohesive policy began to disengage from one another during the implementation process the vitally important *relationship* among the ordering principles and the essentially contextual character—and value—of the plans themselves received less and less overall attention. Once again Abercrombie had earlier argued with regard to the holistical nature of planning that, "the touchstone of what constitutes a planning scheme is this matter of relationships, the accommodation of several units to make a complete but harmonious whole".[46] But as the long shelved, main-road component began to rapidly grow in importance the entire balance between the plans' major sub-components altered and the top-tier road network began to acquire the status of a strategically broad but functionally narrow end in itself.

In fact a narrowing of organizational concern was evident in two different yet essentially related spheres. In the first place as the cohesive planning components began to separate and as additional road funds became increasingly available the *strategic* character of the proposed road system was heavily emphasized by both the Ministry of Transport and the LCC–GLC highway planners. The development of new quantitative techniques and the clear but limited objectives which the traffic engineering professions sought to achieve gave their work an area-wide significance. This essentially "top-down" approach to planning, as the next chapter indicates, was to have important political as well as technical and organizational effects.

In addition one of the effects of the alteration of planning balance mentioned above was that at least partly for organizational and

---

[45] See on the internal organizational problems arising from planning, Peter Self, *Metropolitan Planning*, Greater London Paper No. 14, London: Weidenfeld & Nicolson, 1971, pp. 3–5.
[46] Patrick Abercrombie, *Town and Country Planning*, First Edition 1933, Third Edition revised by D. Rigby Childs, London: Oxford University Press, 1959, p. 11, Chap. I, p. 7.

methodological reasons land-use planning was not so much reintegrated with highway planning as it was increasingly dominated, and in many important ways eventually *redefined in terms of* mainroad planning. As one observer suggested regarding the restricted perspective adopted by the land-use/transportation surveys which were initiated in the early 1960s, "the role and treatment of land use in transportation studies was restricted to its influences on transport".[47] Both the provision of public transport services and the pattern of land use in London was largely taken as given in the original survey design and were of interest only to the extent that they impinged on private vehicular movement. Although the survey was based on the classical grounds that traffic was a function of land use the essentially *reciprocal* character of this relationship and the complex impact of various transportation modes on each other and on land use patterns generally was either very narrowly considered or neglected entirely.[48] The traffic survey for London played an important part in reinforcing the delayed main road component of the Capital's long-standing policy for creating a cohesive urban order but at the same time it should be noted that this reinforcement was purchased at the price of segregating that component by means of a systematic narrowing of organizational perspective.

Although the LTS was to knit together a number of separate organizations around a central information base the basic highway construction orientation of the survey meant that a number of contextual considerations such as: (a) community-level movement problems including the relation between the GLC and the London Boroughs, (b) the nature of the relationship between public and private transport, and (c) the way in which major land-use patterns had changed since the Abercrombie Plans had been adopted, were all beyond the scope of the proposed inquiry.[49] The importance of

[47] D. N. M. Starkie, "Transportation planning and public policy", *Progress in Planning*, Vol. 1, No. 4, Oxford: Pergamon Press, 1973, p. 317.

[48] For the original theoretical statement on this topic and a major influence on the early American traffic studies see Robert B. Mitchell and Chester Rapkin, *Urban Traffic: A Function of Land Use*, New York: Columbia University Press, 1954.

[49] In a similar way Council officers had for some time been concerned about the lack of strategic planning co-ordination but in spite of the establishment of a number of co-ordination councils the goal remained a distant one. See LCC, *Minutes 1957*, London: LCC, 1958, p. 654.

this initial narrowing of the definition of the problem is difficult to overemphasize.

THE LONDON TRAFFIC SURVEY AND ITS INITIAL ORGANIZATIONAL IMPACT

Several illustrations can be used to indicate some of the reasons for this narrowing of organizational concern and factoring of public policy. Firstly, the perceived urgency of the traffic problem meant that organizational attention was firmly fixed on vehicular congestion in spite of the periodic attempts to achieve a balance between the various transport modes. The belief that *the* major problem of movement was the traffic problem and this problem had a strongly inevitable component was widely accepted. As the Royal Commission on Local Government in London suggested,

> We have... approached our subject with the conviction that road traffic is an essential factor in the life of a great city; that it will grow with the growth of a city... and that it is a phenomenon not to be regretted but welcomed.... The Londoner is determined to be mobile and to lead the fuller, more varied and more concentrated life that mobility... makes possible.[50]

The Steering Committee of *Traffic in Towns* were rather more fatalistic about traffic: "We are not conscious of any exaggeration", they wrote, "in saying that we have been appalled by the magnitude of the problem and the speed with which it is advancing upon us."[51] Alan Altshuler has observed that planners often endeavour "in their recommendations to help the inevitable to occur in more orderly fashion, not to redirect the stream of change".[52] If a policy of co-operating with the inevitable were to be pursued with regard to the space which the automobile increase seemed to require the solution seemed to be as difficult to avoid as the problem itself; as the Steering Committee of the Buchanan Report stated flatly;

---

[50] Herbert Commission, *Report* (1960), p. 106. The Commission then went on to point out the importance of public transport, since, however, public transport considerations had been deliberately excluded from the Commission's terms of reference the amount of space given to this topic was limited.

[51] Report of the Steering Committee, *Traffic in Towns*, London: HMSO, 1963, para. 17.

[52] Alan Altshuler, *The City Planning Process*, Ithaca, New York: Cornell University Press, 1965, p. 102.

"Beyond any question, there will have to be a great deal of urban road-building in British cities."[53]

Another factor which played a part in narrowing the focus of the survey, apart from the sheer momentum of the traffic problem and a condition approaching institutionalized panic, were the organizational arrangements which grew out of the survey methodology itself. One observer has suggested that in terms of methodology, rather than results, transport studies were "arguably the most developed part of urban planning at the present time...".[54] More specifically, Herbert Gans has asserted that the large-scale traffic surveys undertaken in the U.S. differed from traditional planning in that: (1) they were well financed, (2) they accumulated a great deal of complicated data, (3) they were undertaken by interdisciplinary teams who were united by their interest in *economic efficiency* and who at the same time were concerned with a relatively small number of ends compared with traditional land use planners; and (4) finally, that they were *metropolitan* in area.[55] Since a good deal of the thinking underlying the traffic survey was drawn from American experience where the automobile was accepted largely without question as the principal mode of transport it may be worth while adding that most of these surveys were also heavily biased in favour of highway building.

The LTS broadly accorded with each of these points. For example, after a good deal of discussion between the Ministry of Transport, the LCC and the consultants it was decided that the survey would cover the whole of the built-up area bounded by the Green Belt thus giving it a metropolitan character. Although the LCC were initially reluctant to consider traffic flows outside their own 119-square-mile area they were persuaded by the consultants

---

[53] "Report", *Traffic* (1963), para. 19. See also on the perceived inexorable character of the automobile growth approaching near universal ownership and a criticism, Mayer Hillman *et al.*, *Personal Mobility*, London: Political and Economic Planning, 1973, p. 75.

[54] R. M. Kirwan, "Economics and methodology in urban transport planning", in J. B. Cullingworth and S. C. Orr (Eds.), *Regional and Urban Studies*, London: George Allen & Unwin, 1969, p. 188.

[55] Herbert Gans, "City planning in America", in *People and Plans*, Harmondsworth: Penguin Books, 1972, pp. 81–82.

that a much broader geographical consideration of the problem was required.[56] The justification of the extension of boundaries was based, as Abercrombie had argued some time before, on the strategic grounds that "...it is manifestly absurd to cease our scrutiny of the stream of motors the moment they cross the municipal boundary line".[57]

In June 1961 an expenditure of £600,000 was approved for the first stage of the project and data for the area-wide survey began to be collected. The amount of funds approved was approximately 3 times the original LCC estimate based on their smaller and more traditional origin and destination survey design. A good deal of the impetus for broadening the survey in spatial terms and a significant proportion of the total finance required came from the Ministry of Transport. Through their power over grants the MOT exercised considerable control over choice and order of priority of major road schemes and as more capital became available the survey was seen as a device for allowing priorities for the whole of the London area to be determined for main roads.[58]

In terms of the actual operation of the survey itself it was decided to divide London into 900 "traffic zones" to facilitate detailed study of the origin and destination of vehicles within the Capital. The first objective of the survey was to establish, through statistical analysis, current volumes between the traffic zones. It was decided that this would form Phase I of the project and the information required would be collected in a variety of ways including a 2 per cent sample of 50,000 households. In spite of the fact that a clear minority of people in London were car owners the survey was so arranged that

---

[56] For a detailed discussion of the establishment of the LTS and its internal impact on the LCC, see Michael Goldrick, "The administration of transportation in Greater London", unpublished Ph.D. Thesis, London School of Economics, 1967, chaps. 3 and 4.

[57] Abercrombie (1933), p. 130. Ironically one of the major criticisms of Abercrombie's road plan was that it did not make use of such a survey, see Michael Thomson *et al.*, *Motorways in London*, London: Gerald Duckworth & Co., 1969, p. 149.

[58] See on the order of priority, Ministry of Transport and Civil Aviation, "Memorandum of Evidence", Royal Commission on Local Government in Greater London, *Memoranda of Evidence from Government Departments*, London: HMSO, 1959, p. 165.

eight out of ten of the households interviewed had at least one automobile.[59] Material gathered in this way was also to be supplemented by road-side interviews, traffic counts, an inventory of existing public and private facilities and an analysis of journey times. Information from all of these sources were to be related to one another using a complex formula and a *synthesis* of travel requirements would be projected into the future and form the basis of Phase II of the study.

The LCC were initially dubious about the value of long-range forecasting. In addition to being biased in favour of conducting the survey only within their own area they were also in favour of using the survey to achieve relatively short-term objectives. As Goldrick indicated, "Whenever a conflict arose over short- or long-term objectives, participants were prone to opt for short-term goals".[60] Despite this early doubt, however, Phase II of the survey was allowed to proceed in 1964 since it was felt that a "close estimate" should be made of travel needs in 10 and 20 years time respectively.[61] One of the principle practical reasons for extending the time horizon was that a major highway project often required 8 years or more from conception to construction. It was essential, the Ministry of Transport contended, that sufficient lead-time should be built into the survey to allow forecasts of traffic demands to be made as far ahead as 1981.[62]

The interpretation and evaluation of the complex information generated by both phases of the survey was largely placed in the hands of the transport planners at the LCC and the MOT. Although British Rail and London Transport were each invited to take part in the formulation of a comprehensive transportation plan at the policy

---

[59] Originally it was proposed that *nine* out of ten of the households visited should be those with automobiles. See LCC, *London Statistics 1952–1961*, Vol. 5, New Series, London: LCC, 1963, p. 187.

[60] Goldrick, "Administration" (1967), p. 72.

[61] LCC, *London Statistics 1951–1960*, (1963), p. 187.

[62] Interestingly the LCC had earlier argued that a large-scale origin and destination survey was likely to be a "difficult and inconclusive business" partly because of the immense amount of data which it would generate. More importantly the Council maintained that such a survey was not really required since the movement of traffic was "fairly well known" to those involved in dealing with the problem. LCC, *Analysis* (1951), p. 145.

Unwrapping the Box 121

level as part of the consultant's methodology the contribution of both organizations, in common with almost all of the other agencies and local authorities involved, consisted of supplying information about their activities. Rather than taking an active part in shaping policy the public transport authorities played a rather more passive role by contributing to the survey's inventory base without really altering its fundamental road bias. As one observer noted, the LTS

> ...was a major innovation in planning methodology which placed a fund of technique and data at the disposal of transportation planners that others could not match. It was based on analytic methods that were unfamiliar and often unintelligible to most of those then involved in conventional town planning. The geographic scope of the Survey also gave the transportation planners detailed information about the entire Greater London area whereas the work of town planners had been confined to much more restricted areas. Furthermore, the traffic and road planners had a virtual monopoly of the LTS.[63]

Halfway through Phase II and soon after the creation of the GLC the Motorway Box was unveiled in the spring of 1965.

UNWRAPPING THE BOX

Shortly after the LTS was initiated one of the clients clearly indicated the use to which its expected findings would be put. As the LCC explained in 1963,

> When the survey is completed it will be possible to establish the nature and volume of the complex traffic flows on the main motorways and trunk routes leading into London, *to establish the need for... ring roads* and other new and improved roads within the survey area, and to enable their capacity and best location to be decided.[64]

In effect the survey was to provide the material which would allow an empirical case to be made for the familiar, predetermined solution to London's traffic problem: a ring and radial motorway system. In an important sense the Geddesian cycle of "survey,

---

[63] Goldrick, "Administration" (1967), p. 248. Michael Thomson also commented: "One must presume there were few people at County Hall who understood the LTS methodology...." Thomson, *Motorways* (1969), p. 176.
[64] LCC, *London Statistics 1952–1961*, Vol. 5 (1963), p. 187. Italics added. See also on the preconceived pattern, Gerald Foley, "London's motorways: an unwise investment", *Official Architecture and Planning*, Vol. 32, No. 12, December 1969, p. 1480.

analyze and plan" had been altered so that the survey could be used as an instrument to provide quantitative support for the long-standing plan.[65]

Paradoxically the ring road proposals were both predetermined and, in an important sense, premature. More than a year before the completion of the second phase of the study the recently elected Labour Council (elections were held in 1964) stated in 1965: "Phase II of the traffic survey is expected to show that the urban motorway 'box' and the links of the radial motorways converging on London will be a minimum requirement."[66] The Council argued that because of the urgency of traffic demands revealed by the LTS one of the GLC's essential tasks was to press ahead as quickly as possible and that "sufficient information" was available to not only outline the Motorway Box well before the survey's end but to describe it in some detail.

According to the initial description the Box was to be approximately 35 miles long and 8 lanes in width and would form a rough rectangle in inner London, 4 to 6 miles from the Central Area. Whenever possible it would be located along railways and other "seams in the urban fabric" to lessen its disruptive environmental impact.[67] In particularly sensitive places such as parks and historic areas it was suggested that the motorway would be carried in cuttings or tunnels beneath ground level. In terms of actual form the Box was to consist of four "legs": the East and the West Cross routes each roughly 6 miles in length, and the North and the South

---

[65] G. H. C. Cooper, a member of the group which produced *Traffic in Towns*, warned against precisely this type of approach at the time when phase I of the LTS was still in progress. "Too often...", he wrote, "we rely on traffic counts which have been arranged only to support road proposals that have already been conceived". G. H. C. Cooper, "Towns and traffic", *Journal of the Town Planning Institute*, Vol. 49, No. 5, May 1963, p. 138.

[66] "Joint Report of the Planning and Communications Committee and the Highways and Traffic Committee", *Minutes 1965*, Council meeting of 6 April 1965, London: GLC, 1966, p. 349.

[67] Historically several attempts at siting major roads along railways have been made. See, for example, Sir Charles Bressey and Sir Edwin Lutyens, *Highway Development Survey (Greater London)*, MOT Report, London: HMSO, 1937, p. 6; and for a later example, a British Road Federation report on urban motorways, "London Needs", London: BRF, 1960, p. 3.

Cross routes each roughly 10 miles in length. Parts of the East and the West Cross were already under construction before the Box was revealed and soon after its announcement the GLC began appointing independent consultants to investigate the most effective and painless ways in which the North and South Cross routes could be "inserted" in areas like Battersea, Greenwich, Hampstead and Hackney through "corridors of opportunity" designated by the GLC.[68]

Two very difficult problems remained, however. In spite of all the attempts to sensitively site the inner ring the GLC's housing committee chairman, Mrs. Evelyn Denington, indicated that 12,500 families largely living in "areas of unsatisfactory housing" would be displaced by the Box.[69] A significant proportion of the GLC's housing reserve would be required to rehouse those who were forced to move as a direct result of its own construction efforts. In addition a further major problem was the staggering expense of the project. Despite the fact that the majority of the cost of the Box was to be covered by grants from the MOT the enormous expense of the project meant that the GLC would still be required to bear a heavy burden. The estimated cost of the motorway was £450 million in total—at 1965 prices—or roughly £12 million per mile—making it one of the most expensive roads ever to be constructed.[70]

Although the Box was put forward by the GLC as a positive contribution to relieving London's chronic traffic congestion it is worth considering another less immediately apparent set of external forces which was also at work. Since the completion of the London–Birmingham section of the M1 in 1959, it was proposed that a number of the MOT's inter-urban motorways including the M1, the

---

[68] The corridors were to cover almost 3000 acres of inner area land which was reserved for their use. GLC, *Minutes 1965*, Question Reply, 6 April 1965, pp. 315–316. The initial consultants for the South Cross, Messrs. Husband and Co., were specifically directed to consider tunnelling along the route. For a later development of this approach along the same section, see Colin Buchanan & Partners, *Greenwich and Blackheath Study*, A Report to the GLC, London: GLC, April 1971, p. 52.

[69] GLC, *Minutes 1965*, Question Reply, 25 May 1965, p. 407.

[70] The MOT were to contribute 75 per cent of the capital cost of the Box.

M11, the M12, the A13, the A2, the M23, the M3 and the M4 would be slowly driven from all directions toward Central London.[71] In spite of the fact that these roads speeded traffic *between* towns *within* towns like London the new roads simply made existing congestion worse. The problem was not really that of *through traffic* since only a tiny proportion of traffic, as the LTS demonstrated, did not begin or end its journey within London. The real difficulty was that the new radials systematically funnelled high-speed, long-distance traffic from outside the GLC's boundaries ever closer to London's jammed Central Area.

The "nasty, nagging problem" of the radials, seemed to a pessimistic Buchanan writing in 1958 to have "no satisfactory answer".[72] The attempted solution developed by the LCC–GLC, with the continuing assistance of the MOT, however, turned on the idea of deflecting the radial-borne traffic as well as distributing its own internally generated traffic through the agency of the proposed inner ring. In spite of the expense and disruption which the Box would cause the justification for the motorway was based partly on *defensive* grounds since it was argued that the ring would act as a physical barrier to prevent the radials—and their highspeed traffic—from encroaching further.[73]

Clearly the radials helped to force the pace. When asked why the Box was being built so close to Central London along the north the retiring Chairman of the Roads Committee, Richard Edmonds, remarked ruefully that, "events overtook us".[74] The Council, he explained, were faced "with a situation in which six major motorways were heading into London without the means to accommodate

[71] See, for example, a proposal by the MOT to extend the M1 into inner London even before the main section had been completed. Ministry of Transport, *London–Yorkshire Motorway*, London: HMSO, 1959, p. 7; see also GLC, *Movement in London*, London: GLC, 1969, p. 12. In some cases the rate of progress was very slow indeed.
[72] Colin Buchanan, *Mixed Blessing*, London: Leonard Hill, 1958, p. 199.
[73] In 1958 the British Road Federation submitted a memorandum to the LCC which "stressed the urgent need for a limited access inner ring road from which urban motorway radials would run to connect with the inter-city motorways planned to link London to the rest of the country". BRF, *Annual Report 1958*, London: BRF, 1958, p. 8.
[74] *Hampstead and Highgate Express and News*, 15 April 1965, p. 1.

their traffic".[75] A Ministry of Transport official also indicated a similar concern in the early 1960s and neatly summarized the perceived problem. "The national motorway network development is now becoming fact", he wrote, "and fast motorway traffic is being dumped onto an archaic city street network."[76]

The newly created GLC were at pains to raise this problem with the Ministry of Transport and a worried delegation attended the Ministry on 18 November 1964, 5 months before the Box's official announcement:

> Among the matters raised with the Minister was the need for the integration of the national motorway system with the new and necessary network of urban motorways, *proper emphasis being given to the construction of ring roads to deflect traffic from the historic central areas of London*....[77]

Consequently the Box was so designed that all six of the national motorways entering inner London terminated along its boundary.

Initially at any rate defensive considerations of this kind played an important part in speeding—as well as justifying—the planning of the Motorway Box. If long-distance traffic could be physically *canalized* in inter-urban "conduits" there was no reason in principle apparently why the same type of thinking could not also be employed *within* urban areas to carry this type of traffic by means of purpose-built channels and thus lessen its pervasive environmental impact.[78] In protective terms this kind of often literally concrete planning meant that two complementary functions would be simultaneously performed by the inner ring from this point of view alone: (a) in the first place the Box was to act as a *barrier* to further radial

[75] Michael King, *Evening Standard*, 1 April 1965, p. 14.
[76] Wood, "Traffic" (1963), p. 265. The Chairman of the British Road Federation, Lord Derwent, drew the seemingly logical inference, when he remarked that the next phase of the national road construction programme should be "to extend motorways into and through built-up areas so that the benefits of rural motorways are not dissipated...". BRF, *Annual Report 1956*, London: BRF, p. 7.
[77] GLC, *Minutes 1965*, Council meeting of 4 December 1964, London: GLC, 1966, p. 201. Italics added. It is significant that more than 18 *months* before the unveiling of the Primary Road Network the ring proposals mentioned above were couched in a *plural* form.
[78] For the original ideas on traffic canalization see again H. Alker Tripp, *Road Traffic and its Control*, London: Edward, Arnold & Co., 1938; and H. Alker Tripp, *Town Planning and Road Traffic*, London: Edward Arnold & Co., 1942.

126 Strategic Planning in London

advance in physical terms; and (c) secondly, the Box was to also provide a complete circular *by-pass* for the Central Area. As the Council explained in their initial statement of policy on the Box:

> Although the work of the London Traffic survey is not yet complete, sufficient information is already available to give an indication of the scale and pattern of the future demand for travel. An urgent task facing the Council will be the development of a policy and a plan for meeting such demands. Such a policy may well entail a change of emphasis from the attention given in the last few years to radial routes to one of ring or diverting routes.[79]

Only by physical canalization, apparently, could traffic be satisfactorily controlled.

Even though the Box represented a major increase in London's road capacity the Council indicated that it was only a "minimum requirement" given the level of demand revealed by the LTS and that it was to form only a part of a much broader "London transportation plan" to be produced by the Council in 1967 or 1968 and included in the statutory *Greater London Development Plan* which the GLC were also charged with producing.[80] Despite the fact that the Box was from the point of view of the highway authorities only an initial measure it was nevertheless generally welcomed—particularly by the motoring organizations and the Press. The British Road Federation, for example, congratulated the GLC on their announcement and indicated how much urban motorway planning had been accelerated in the late 1950s and the early 1960s during the period when Ernest Marples was Minister of Transport. The BRF commented, "only six years ago we were told that motorways would have no place in London up to 1980".[81] The *Daily Mail* enthusiastically hailed what it called "the super-commuter motorway" and published a guide to its use.[82] Many motoring correspondents were convinced that London was on the verge of a new age.

---

[79] GLC, *Minutes 1965*, 6 April 1965, p. 347.
[80] See again, London Government Act, 1963, Section 25(3); and GLC, *Minutes* 1965, 6 April 1965, p. 353.
[81] "Super M-Way for London", *Daily Mirror*, 2 April 1965.
[82] Denis Holmes, "Guide for the super commuter", *Daily Mail*, 26 March 1965. On the relationship between new highways and commuting in the U.S. see Altshuler, *City Planning* (1965), p. 73.

THE FORM AND FUNCTION OF THE PRIMARY ROAD NETWORK

Although a certain amount of opposition to the Motorway Box was evident almost from its announcement the GLC continued to push vigorously ahead with consolidating its strategic road planning powers.[83] In July 1966, just over a year after the unveiling of the Box, two important events occurred. At a Council meeting held on 19 July, it was announced that the title of the London Traffic Survey, with the concurrence of the MOT which would continue to provide most of the funds, would be changed to the London Transport Study and an additional £418,000 would be spent on a third and final phase of the project.[84] The purpose of Phase III was to broaden the scope of the study and to consider a "number of alternative public-transport networks, road networks and land-use concepts..."[85] which would lead to a more "balanced" approach to movement planning. At the same Council meeting, however, it was announced that a vast "Primary Road Network" was to be constructed in London, consisting of three ring roads—including the Motorway Box—and twelve radials, all built to motorway standard.[86]

The Primary Road Network announcement was, like the earlier Motorway Box unveiling, premature. As the Council indicated,

> Much work remains to be done before stage III of the traffic study (the London transportation study) is completed, but, in the meantime, a start can be made on the study of those aspects of the problem which it is already clear call for attention.[87]

---

[83] See also on the GLC's fluid position in this field, Gerald Rhodes & S. K. Ruck, *The Government of Greater London*, London: George Allen & Unwin, p. 97.

[84] Apparently, Phase III of the LTS was only finally agreed on by the clients in 1966. The consultants, however, had put forward the idea that the survey should be broken down into three parts since its beginning in 1961. See Goldrick, "Administration" (1967), p. 91.

[85] Joint Report of the Planning and Communications Committee and the Highways and Traffic Committee, *GLC Minutes 1966*, Council meeting of 19 July 1966, London: GLC, 1967, p. 435.

[86] One of the reasons why public transport began to receive increasing attention was the simple fact that Phase II indicated that not even a far more extensive eight-lane motorway system than was actually proposed could accommodate all of the indicated demand for vehicular movement. GLC, *Greater London Development Plan—Statement*, London: GLC, 1969, p. 25, and Goldrick, "Administration" (1967), p. 227.

[87] "Joint Report", *GLC Minutes 1966*, 19 July 1966, p. 425.

Once again, however, the GLC also indicated that they were drawing heavily on *previous* planning. The Highway and Traffic Committee wrote in their 1966–1967 Report:

> the Committee's chief activity in the year has been the continued integration of the plans inherited from the Council's predecessors into the new forward planning—planning which covers the creation of a system of highways in London of a kind and on a scale not hitherto envisioned....[88]

A new system of highways was required because, it was argued, the existing road network was obsolete, and even a very heavy expenditure would not bring it up to the standard which could be achieved by constructing purpose-built motorways.

The head of the Highways and Transportation Department, Peter Stott, an engineer with a good deal of highway planning experience stated, for example, "Tinkering with the existing roads would be ineffective and uneconomic for our present system already differs markedly in character and orientation from current needs".[89] The concept of *economy* and *efficiency* which were almost axiomatic highway engineering objectives thus played an important part in the original justification of the Primary Road Network. Curiously, however, in view of the traditional engineering concern with cost, no attempt was made in the initial report putting forward the new road proposals in 1966 to indicate even roughly their estimated expense.[90] When the Primary Road Network was accepted "in principle" by the Council in July of 1966 critics argued that the GLC had, in effect, signed a blank cheque.

On 21 November 1967, when the LTS was still a year from completion, the Primary Road Network was more fully articulated by the newly elected Conservative Council which had taken office in April.[91] Although political control of the GLC had changed hands

[88] GLC Highways and Traffic Committee, '1966–67', typescript, pp. 2–3.

[89] Peter Stott, "Structure and management", *Traffic Engineering and Control*, Vol. 9, No. 1, May 1967, p. 36. The same quote can also be found, in verbatim form, in the Council's initial report on the primary system, see *GLC Minutes 1966*, Council meeting of 19 July 1966, p. 426; and see also for a similar line of reasoning, GLC, *Greater London Development Plan—Report of Studies*, London: GLC, 1969, p. 197.

[90] On the lack of costing see Stephen Plowden, *Towns Against Traffic*, London: Andre Deutsch, 1972, p. 113. For an indication of the power of the engineer with regard to planning proposals see Ken Hutchings, "Urban transport: public or private?", *Fabian Research Series* 261, London: Fabian Society, June 1967, p. 12.

[91] See, on the timing of the proposal, Thomson, *Motorways* (1969), p. 107.

Unwrapping the Box 129

the motorway proposals continued to enjoy a substantial measure of bipartisan support. If anything, the Tory party was more committed to the new highway proposals than the Labour party had been as their attempts to speed the pace of construction when in opposition demonstrated.[92] The new network, the Conservatives indicated, was to consist of three separate rings: the Motorway Box, an improved North Circular and a new South Circular, and substantial parts of Abercrombie's "D" ring which ran along the inner edge of the Green Belt plus the extended national radials. (For an indication of the outline of the Primary Road Network see Fig. 4.1.[93]) At the same time a fourth ring—the proposed Outer Orbital—which lay wholly outside the GLC's boundaries was also under active consideration by the MOT.

As the Primary Road Network was more fully described it became clear that the GLC had a powerful, and largely silent, partner also operating *within* its boundaries. Although most of the new highway announcement were made by the Council, the *Ministry of Transport continued to be directly involved in main road planning and construction in the Capital.* To give an indication of the extent of the Ministry's involvement it was decided that the GLC would only be completely responsible for the Motorway Box, for the new South Circular, and for the inner radials. The MOT, however, would be the highway authority for the improved North Circular, for the entire "D" ring and for all of the outer radials.[94] Simply in terms of mileage most of the highway responsibility for the ringway system rested not on the GLC but with long heavily involved MOT.

---

[92] See on this the motion put forward by the Leader of the Opposition, Sir Desmond Plummer, *GLC Minutes 1965*, Council Meeting of 30 November 1965, London: GLC, 1966, p. 818; or a letter to the *Daily Telegraph* dated 18 July 1966 by the Conservative leader, making much the same point: the need to speed road building.

[93] "Joint Report of the Planning and Communications Committee and the Highways and Traffic Committee", *GLC Minutes 1967*, Council meeting of 21 November 1967, London: GLC, 1968, p. 694.

[94] On the relationship between the GLC and the MOT see GLC, "Phasing the primary road network", GLDP Background Paper, B. 485, July 1971, p. 1; and Highways and Traffic Committee, GLC, "The work of the highways and traffic Committee 1966–67", GLC, typescript, p. 12. In fact the Ministry was also actively at work even on some parts of the network which could be assumed to be the responsibility of the GLC. See, for example, on the new South Circular, GLC, "Ringway 2", London: GLC, 1969, pp. 14–15, for an outline of a "delta" being built by the MOT.

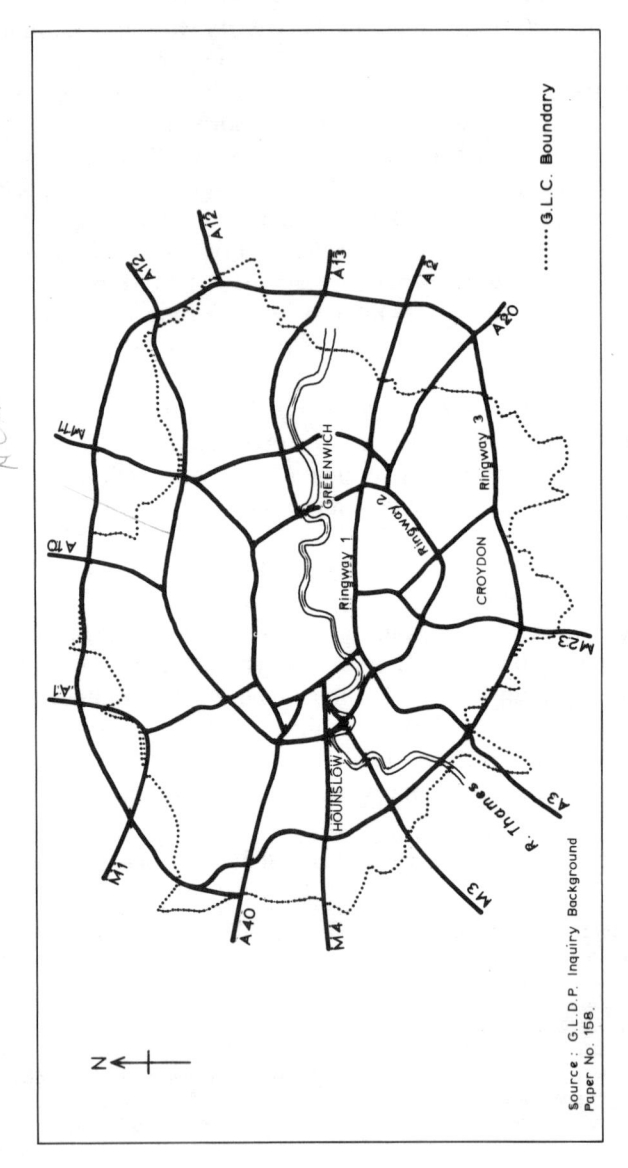

FIG. 4.1. Primary road network.

Unwrapping the Box 131

The circular motorways within the Greater London area jointly proposed by the GLC and the MOT, which were later renamed Ringways One (formerly the Motorway Box), Two (formerly the North and South Circulars) and Three (formerly the "D" Ring), were to run at distances of 4, 7 and 12 miles from the Capital's Central Area. The purpose of the Primary Road Network, the Council declared, was not merely to facilitate traffic movement but to establish a basically circular geometric pattern for London since the LTS's findings indicated a far more extensive pattern for orbital movement than the "motorway box could serve".[95] The newly established circumferential routes would help lessen the strain on both the outdated inherited street pattern and on the newly extended national radial network. It was argued by the Council that

> The major shortcomings of the present system are that its pattern is mainly radial, which limits diversity of movement; the existing network is seriously incomplete; and most roads have to carry all kinds of traffic, whether for long journeys, short journeys, local access, or general distribution.[96]

Two points were involved: the new roads would not only have substantial intrinsic value but they would also serve as part of the top level of the proposed triple-tiered *system* for streaming traffic within the Capital.

"Beneath" the purpose-built Primary Road Network which was to be approximately 400 miles in length two other road tiers were also defined. A second tier largely consisting of major existing roads almost 1000 miles in length and the lowest level which was to be made up of the thirty-two London Boroughs' (plus the City of London) 7000-mile local road system were also outlined. Thus three levels—primary, secondary and local—were to be united in a single system. Because of its strategic orientation and its close operating relationship with the MOT the Council was particularly concerned with the top two tiers of the proposed road system.[97]

[95] GLC, *Minutes 1966*, 19 July 1966, p. 426; and see also GLC, *Minutes 1967*, 21 November 1967, p. 694.
[96] GLC, *Greater London Development Plan—Statement*, London: GLC, 1969, p. 22.
[97] GLC, *GLDP—Statement* (1969), p. 177. On the complex relationship between the various authorities involved see Colin Buchanan and Partners, *North East London*, A Report to the Greater London Council, London: GLC, June 1970, p. 96; and Chapter 2, p. 50.

Initially the Council indicated that the proposed Primary Road Network and a good deal of the improvements required to up-grade the Secondary Road Network, including major interchanges, would be completed by the early 1980s. Top priority was to be given to the construction of the innermost ring which was, once again, the only ringway for which the GLC had sole responsibility, and it was expected that it would be completed by 1977. Although several other major planning and road projects were under consideration by the GLC, the Chairman of the Highways and Traffic Committee, Robert Vigars, stated unequivocally, "The motorways must come first: it is a case of getting our priorities right".[98] Because of the overriding importance of dealing with the traffic problem at the strategic level other projects, such as road improvements and the redevelopment of the rapidly growing major shopping centres within Greater London, "would have to fall by the wayside", Mr. Vigars added.[99]

Because of the urgency of the traffic problem one of the essential goals of the GLC and the MOT was the largely instrumental one of increasing the efficiency of the road system and the proposed *hierarchy* of road types was expressly designed to serve this end. With regard to the Secondary Road Network, for example, it was argued,

> The overriding considerations must be to maintain high operational efficiency. Because of limited resources, expenditure on secondary roads must be carefully planned *so as to promote the efficiency of the whole road system rather than merely to secure local advantage.*[100]

In spite of this rather mechanistic, basically supply-oriented approach to alleviating the problem of traffic congestion it became clear that even given the most optimistic estimates on future highway grants by the MOT construction of the full Primary system would impose an extremely heavy strain on the Council's financial resources and borrowing ability.

One means of attempted short-term economizing initially considered by the GLC consisted of building certain parts of the

---

[98] Muriel Bowen, "Motorways have GLC priority", *The Sunday Times*, 29 October 1967, p. 3.
[99] Bowen, "Motorways" (1967), p. 3.
[100] *GLC Minutes 1967*, 21 November 1967, p. 697. Italics added.

motorways to a width of only four lanes. During a later second stage of construction as more money became available these roads would be subsequently widened to either six or eight lanes, depending on demand.[101] In the long term, however, this method of construction meant that the cost of the ringways would be higher than if they were built in a single stage. After consideration the idea of staged construction was eventually dropped by the GLC in 1970 because of the difficulty of widening those parts of the network which were carried below ground level and because of the additional expense involved.[102]

Another device for dealing with costs which *was* regretfully accepted by the Council in view of limited funds and mounting expenses was to spread the road system's construction over a longer period of time. The completion date of the system was steadily pushed forward in time and it was finally announced that in spite of the often repeated urgency of the traffic problem substantial parts of the network would not be completed until the 1990s and beyond.[103] This prescheduling also signalled a change in the order of priority of construction. Ringway One—the motorway which had been accorded the highest priority since the project was originally announced in 1965—was quietly placed much lower in the construction programme and was not scheduled to be completed until almost the turn of the century. Ringway Two, which was relatively cheaper and less controversial, was simultaneously discreetly brought forward, "thus giving London its first complete orbital road".[104]

In spite of proposed changes in the width of the motorways and with regard to their order of priority the GLC and the MOT never deviated from the proposed ring and radial *pattern* itself. When the Council submitted its delayed Greater London Development Plan (GLDP) in 1969 the familiar road proposals formed a central

[101] GLC, *Movement in London*, London: GLC, 1969, p. 13.
[102] See GLC, *Minutes 1970*, Council meeting 27 January 1970, p. 43; and GLC, "GLC to revise spending programme", GLC Press Release No. 29, 21 January 1970, pp. 1–3.
[103] See GLC, *Minutes 1970*, 27 January 1970, p. 43; and GLC, "Primary roads review—order of priority", GLC Press Release No. 363, 15 July 1970, pp. 1–3.
[104] "Joint Report of the Strategic Planning Committee and the Environmental Planning Committee", GLC, *Minutes 1970*, p. 23.

134 Strategic Planning in London

component of its planning strategy.[105] Once again, curiously in view of the stress which was placed on economic considerations, no attempt at *overall* costing was made in any of the major planning documents produced for public study when the plan was submitted for formal approval in 1969.[106] Even more curiously given the importance of the project no attempt was made in any of these documents to indicate: (a) the total amount of land required for the road system, or (b) the number of houses which would be directly affected as a result of its construction.

Not until 4 years after the initial acceptance of the Primary Road Network by the Council was an attempt to assess the overall *impact* of the proposals made public. The Council's estimate suggested that the *combined* costs of the GLC and the MOT for constructing the Primary system would be roughly £1400 million and an additional £550 million would have to be spent on upgrading the Secondary Road Network—thus making a total cost of roughly £2000 million.[107] In addition it was estimated that the Primary network alone was to also take 6200 acres of urban land and directly result in the destruction of at least 20,000 homes.[108] Although less than 1 per cent of London's population would be directly involved the road plans would still mean that something of the order of 100,000 people

---

[105] On the GLC's delay in submitting the GLDP see Donald G. Hagman, "The Greater London Development Plan Inquiry", *Journal of the American Institute of Planners*, Vol. 37, No. 5, September 1971, p. 290.

[106] See, for example, GLC, *GLDP—Statement* (1969), Ch. 5; GLC, *Tomorrow's London: A Background to the Greater London Development Plan* (1969), Ch. 7; and GLC, *GLDP—Report of Studies* (1969), p. 200 and p. 314. The *Report of Studies* probably came the closest to making an estimate but the figures supplied were only of a partial character and did not include the full costs of *completing* the Primary and Secondary networks.

[107] See on the various GLC attempts to estimate the impact of the highway programme, GLC, *Minutes 1967*, 21 November 1967, pp. 697–698; GLC, "Revise", P/R No. 29, 12 January 1970; and GLC, *Minutes 1970*, p. 43. The estimates in the text are taken from: GLC, "Proposed", GLDP Background Paper B. 158 (August 1970), p. 5; and GLC, "Secondary" (November 1969), on the grounds that, in very rough terms, half as much would be spent on the Secondary system as on the Primary Road Network.

[108] GLC, "Proposed", GLDP Background Paper B. 158 (August 1970), p. 5. As an example of the GLC's vagueness it was estimated in another document, *Tomorrow's London*, that the housing figure was to be somewhere between 20,000 and 30,000 homes, see p. 69 of that publication.

would require rehousing as a result of the proposed road system's construction over a period of 30 years or more. For a summary of the impact of the Primary Road Network see Table 4.1.

TABLE 4.1. LONDON'S PRIMARY ROAD NETWORK IMPACT: A SUMMARY OF THE GLC–MOT PROPOSALS

Authority	Project	Costs (£m.)	Length (miles)	Area required (acres)	Dwellings affected
GLC	Ringway One	480	25.1	1048	7585
	Ringway Two (South)	305	25.1	1007	5705
	Inner radials	118	11.0	305	1825
	GLC Total	903	61.2	2360	15,115
MOT	Ringway Two (North)	114	—	220	1780
	Ringway Three	206	—	2800	450+
	Outer radials	173	—	790+	2235
	MOT Total	493	—	3810+	4465+
Combined GLC–MOT total	Completed project	1396	—	6170+	19,580+

SOURCE: GLC "Proposed Primary Road Network", GLDP Inquiry Background Paper B. 158, August 1970, p. 5.

In terms of *form* the huge road plan proposed by the GLC and the MOT was strikingly similar, at first glance, to Abercrombie's geometric ring and radial design put forward during World War Two in the *County of London Plan (1943)*. Apart from the innermost "A" Ring which was dropped, significantly, for reasons of cost in 1951, each of the remaining four rings directly corresponded with the Abercrombie proposals.[109] Ringway One (formerly the Motorway Box) bore a close resemblance to the much earlier path proposed for the "B" Ring, Ringway Two clearly resembled the "C" Ring and Ringway Three was largely based on the "D" Ring. Outside of the Greater London area the planned Outer Orbital Route was evidently

[109] On the "A" Ring see p. 107.

patterned on Abercrombie's outermost "E" Ring. Oddly however in spite of occasional references to the "D" Ring in Council Minutes very little in the way of explicit acknowledgement was made to Abercrombie's influence regarding the Primary Road Network as a whole.[110] Not until several years after the unveiling of the Motorway Box in 1965 did the GLC publicly acknowledge that the basic road pattern from which they worked was already more than 20 years old.

In 1969 when the Greater London Development Plan was formally submitted the Council stated:

> The studies are the first overall examination of the planning of London since the Abercrombie Plan twenty-five years ago. It is not surprising that they question whether the assumptions are still influencing present policies are valid....[111]

Paradoxically, in the same document the Council revealed that during the intervening quarter of a century one fundamental assumption—the most desirable shape for the main road network—had evidently remained unchanged. In concept, the GLC quietly admitted in 1969, the proposed motorway proposals were "... similar to the rings proposed by Abercrombie and Forshaw in the County of London Plan of 1943, with the omission of the innermost ring".[112] In addition to the evident similarity between the *form* of the road pattern put forward by Abercrombie and later reaffirmed in the GLC-MOT proposals a high degree of policy continuity could also, apparently, be discerned with regard to the *functions* which the road system was designed to perform.

Close to the heart of the case for the proposed new system of roads for London was the traditional assumption that only by means

---

[110] On the "D" Ring see *GLC Minutes 1967*, 21 November 1967, p. 694. In more detailed studies the "C" Ring was also mentioned, once again, however, without reference to either Abercrombie or the *County of London Plan (1943)*, see *GLC Minutes 1967*, 21 November 1967, pp. 696–697.

[111] GLC, *GLDP—Report of Studies*, p. 1. It is difficult to tell from this quote whether the *County of London Plan (1943)* or the *Greater London Plan 1944* is the "Abercrombie Plan" referred to above, both plans, as Chapter 3 indicated, heavily influenced government policy in London.

[112] GLC, *GLDP—Report of Studies* (1969), p. 9. On the similarity of form see two studies written by GLC planners in 1970, C. M. Buchanan, *London Road Plans 1900–1970*, Research Report No. 11, London: GLC, December 1970, p. 3; and John Craig, "The 1943 London Plan: a perspective", *Official Architecture and Planning*, Vol. 33, No. 12, December 1970, p. 1076.

of supply-oriented, *physical canalization* would it be possible to divide traffic into appropriate flows based on journey length, speed and purpose. It was also held by the highway authorities that this structural correction, and supplementation, of the existing road network would simultaneously confer substantial local area planning benefits and city-wide movement advantages. This concrete approach to creating vehicular segregation—which might conveniently be termed the *hard planning* approach—was at least as old as the proposed main-road pattern for the Capital and was well known to Unwin and Tripp as well as to Abercrombie himself.[113] With the rediscovery and elaboration of these ideas in 1963 by Buchanan an added boost was given to the importance of using large-scale road-construction measures to divide traffic, in a rather mechanistic way, into its desired streams.[114]

The *basic* differentiation was, once again, to be made between *through* and *local* traffic by means of a combination of tactical area "push" and strategic motorway "pull". From this simple combination of precinct, or environmental area, *restriction* and arterial, or primary distributor, *attraction* (using Abercrombie and Buchanan's phraseology respectively), a number of benefits were to flow. Specifically, Abercrombie suggested in 1944 that the proposed road system would: (a) divide roads into a triple-tiered hierarchy of arterial, sub-arterial and local levels; (b) canalize traffic into through and local flows; (c) relate London's road programme to the national highway system; and (d) provide the opportunity to adopt "the precinct principle of planning to render residential and other built-up areas free from through traffic".[115] This set of ideas was also apparently closely followed by the GLC and the MOT in their highway planning for London.

In the *GLDP—Statement*, for example, it was indicated by the

[113] On Unwin and Tripp's analysis of the problem see Raymond Unwin, "Memorandum", *Second Report of the Greater London Regional Planning Committee*, London: Knapp, Drewitt & Sons, 1933, p. 62; and H. Alker Tripp, *Town Planning and Road Traffic*, London: Edward Arnold, 1942, p. 58.

[114] Depending on the degree of canalization sought, it might be added, the logical conclusion of the hard planning approach would be the partial or complete recasting of cities which Buchanan called "traffic architecture". See Buchanan, *Traffic* (1963), p. 46 and p. 222.

[115] Patrick Abercrombie, *Greater London Plan 1944*, London: HMSO, 1945, p. 70. See also on this topic, Abercrombie–Forshaw, *CLP (1943)*, p. 49.

Council that the case for the new road system rested on its ability to: (a) create a hierarchy of primary, secondary and local roads; (b) relieve "the existing main roads of longer-distance traffic, thereby enabling them to function as secondary roads more effectively"; (c) make "orbital journeys easier, so avoiding journeys across Central London"; and (d) provide "good access from all parts of London to the national and regional motorway system".[116] Colin Buchanan and Partners, acting as consultants to the GLC, reaffirmed each of these points in 1970 and then went on to add another by indicating that the new road proposals would also "Provide opportunities which do not exist today for improving the environment by the withdrawal of traffic from residential and shopping area [sic]."[117]

Evidently the strategic highway authorities' intention was, in a manner very reminiscent of Abercrombie and Buchanan's earlier suggestions, to improve the way in which the city *worked* and thereby to improve its overall *efficiency* and *environment* in structural terms. This type of *hard planning* had two separate components. To summarize this type of thinking once again at the upper level the new ringways would act, as a result of their basic *geometry*, to canalize traffic "horizontally" by serving:

(1) as a *barrier* to further radial advance;
(2) as a *by-pass* to prevent traffic from crossing the central area;
(3) as a *boundary* divide which would distribute traffic circumferentially along the periphery of inner and outer London;
(4) *as a pressure valve* which would collect and remove traffic generated within major activity centres such as Central and inner London.[118]

---

[116] GLC, *GLDP—Statement* (1969), p. 23. See also GLC, *GLDP—Report of Studies* (1969), pp. 99–101.

[117] Colin Buchanan and Partners, *North East London*, A report to the Greater London Council, June 1970, p. 77. In general the local roads received very brief treatment in the Greater London Development Plan (1969). In the only sentence in the Plan which referred specifically to this vital component, the Council advised the London Boroughs that they should "ensure that local roads are adequate for local traffic and that they are suitably integrated with the overall road system". See *GLDP—Statement* (1969), p. 24.

[118] Compare this with Abercrombie's initial horizontal canalization proposals on p. 77.

Unwrapping the Box 139

This (p)horizontal aspect of the GLC–MOT proposals was to be complemented by a physical attempt to canalize traffic "vertically" as well.

The *hierarchical* nature of the proposed road system would, it was held, also canalize traffic in a "vertical" manner by moving traffic "upward" or "downward" from one tier in the hierarchy to another. By means of the attraction of the high-speed motorways long-distance traffic would be induced to move upward to the Primary Road Network level, thus freeing both the secondary and local roads from the type of vehicular movement.[119] *After* the building of the strategic road network, the Council argued, it would be possible, rather as an afterthought, to decide the use to which the local roads would be put by local option. Matters might be so arranged, the GLC suggested, that these roads could

> fill up with local traffic, or if people want in a particular area to restrict traffic by banning the entry of vehicles, they can do so in the knowledge that it will be generally possible to find other means—*even walking*—of making a comparatively short journey. Any such local restriction of traffic would not interfere with people making longer journeys or threaten to disrupt the commercial life of London.[120]

In terms of *intent*, apart from initial construction difficulties, the creation of the Primary Road Network would seem to confer a number of wholly advantageous structural benefits on the way in which London worked, allowing it to maintain its commercial and industrial efficiency and at the same time help to lessen the disadvantageous effects of through traffic.

The result of the combination of "horizontal" and "vertical" canalization which the new road proposals prescribed meant that a high degree of physical control could be exercised over the flow of traffic. The hard planning approach adopted by the GLC and the MOT was apparently simply a continuation of Abercrombie and

---

[119] Compare, once again, with p. 115. It is worth recalling that Buchanan had suggested that in city centres traffic might be literally segregated vertically by building on several "decks". On this, see also H. Alker Tripp, *Town Planning and Road Traffic*, London: Edward Arnold, 1942, p. 27; and Peter Hall, *London 2000*, London: Faber & Faber, 2nd ed., 1969, pp. 208–209. Because of the expense of this type of approach it has only occasionally been attempted.

[120] GLC, "Ringway", London: GLC, 1969, p. 6. Italics added.

140 Strategic Planning in London

Buchanan's ideas regarding the part which *geometrical* and *hierarchical* road factors should play in creating a desirable urban form. Evidently the authorities had, using the work of two of the most noted planners of the century, created a strategy of traffic control for an entire city-region.

In fact on closer examination a number of significant differences in emphasis and even of intent can be found between the GLC–MOT proposals on one hand, and the earlier Abercrombie–Buchanan prescriptions on the other, with regard to the form—and even more importantly, with regard to the functions which the proposed road system was designed to perform.

Although it was true that *only a metropolitan* authority like the GLC—with the considerable direct assistance and advice of the MOT—had the resources and ability to transform the Abercrombie–Buchanan road proposals into practice on the scale of a city as vast as London, it was also true that this strategic approach generated a number of unintended problems.[121] Because of its basic strategic orientation and close working relationship with the Ministry the GLC tended to approach its highway planning role in very much a "top down" manner.[122] It is important to remember that the GLC was a *strategic* rather than a *comprehensive* planning authority and a number of its road proposals depended for effect not only on the co-operation of the Ministry of Transport but also, at the local level, on the Council's relationship with the powerful London Boroughs. As the GLC began to find to its cost its relationship with the Boroughs was often a good deal less than wholly satisfactory and the Boroughs' support was essential for bringing the road *system* in its entirety into being.

Nor was this difficulty in relations confined to the Boroughs. One of the first lessons learned during the controversy which grew out of the road proposals was that even very broad "policy plans", such as the GLDP (1969), have quite specifically perceived *local* effects on

---

[121] On the GLC's concern in this regard, see Greater London Group, *The Lessons of the London Government Reforms*, evidence submitted to the Royal Commission on Local Government, London: HMSO, 1969, p. 2.

[122] See also on a comment of the GLC's approach, Peter Self, *Metropolitan Planning*, Greater London No. 14, London: Weidenfeld & Nicolson, 1971, p. 32.

individuals, organizations and on other authorities within the planned areas, and that these effects are often seen as having a threatening character. As Tripp presciently remarked in 1942, regarding the importance of planning detail: "When replanning a town, the task of projecting and surveying lines for a new and ambitious system of main roads will be found to be as child's play as compared with the detailed application of the scheme."[123] The various ways in which this lesson was brought home to the Council and the manner in which the movement planning process in London was gradually broadened technically, organizationally and politically will form the basis of the next chapter.

---

[123] H. Alker Tripp, *Town Planning and Road Traffic*, London: Edward Arnold, 1942, p. 34.

CHAPTER 5

Widening the Movement Planning Process: The Fall of the Primary Road Network

> The notion that the motor car is a sacred object, to which all the functions of a community must give way, is a superstitious and irrational one; and the fact that many people believe it doesn't make it any the less so. By giving the motor car priority over any other form of transportation, highway planners are robbing us of something more important than public transport: the possibility of choice.—Lewis Mumford, "Letters to the Editor", *Journal of the American Institute of Planners*, Vol. XXVII, No. 1, February 1961, p. 76.

> The instincts and the hunches of Abercrombie's time are giving way to the objective study of social motivations and the increasingly elaborate methods of quantiative analysis and the reduction in almost every field covered by planning. Some of this is heavy stuff...there can come a point when you have to take yourself in hand and ask yourself what the whole exercise is in aid of.—Colin Buchanan, *The State of Britain*, London: Faber & Faber, 1972, p. 33.

REDEFINING THE PROBLEM

Although nominally pursuing the prescriptions put forward by Abercrombie and Buchanan for controlling London's traffic, the GLC–MOT proposals were in many important ways actual reversals of the two men's earlier ideas. The complete "hard planning" approach for physically canalizing traffic, and more broadly, for creating the type of urban order which both men originally advocated was gradually but fundamentally altered over time to accord with the strategic problem perception of the top-tier authority. During this process several aspects of the original

Widening the Movement Planning Process 143

Abercrombie–Buchanan approach were almost completely inverted. Although the *shell* of the Abercrombie road plan continued to persist it became increasingly divorced from both the city's changing structure and from the original intent of its designers.

The combined GLC–MOT approach to road planning meant that although the traditional road *pattern* remained intact many of the *purposes* which it was designed to perform were radically altered. At least partly as a result of this organizational alteration a growing gap began to appear between those two components of movement planning which Abercrombie and Buchanan had sought most to beneficially combine: strategic highway proposals on the one hand and community level planning considerations on the other. Rather than binding London together, the Primary Road Network proposals revealed a major lack of co-ordination between the strategic and local planning levels and acted almost as a wedge driven between them.

In a similar way in 1938 when the Bressey proposals for major road improvements in London were being considered a commentator remarked: "The present danger is not so much that road development will not be planned as that they will be planned 'compartmentally' without proper relation to other planning requirements..."[1] The "compartmentalization" reflected in the GLC–MOT's rather narrow and top-heavy approach to road planning and the way in which the Abercrombie–Buchanan strategy was inverted can perhaps be best illustrated by briefly considering, once again, the two central components of the traditional hard planning approach—*geometry* and *hierarchy*.

In terms of geometric pattern it is instructive to note the extent to which London's actual structure had altered over time while the physical form of the strategic road network had remained broadly

---

[1] National Survey, "Report of the National Survey and National Planning Committee of the Institute", *Journal of the Town Planning Institute*, Vol. XXIV, No. 7, May 1938, p. 241. As a means of illustrating how the original proposals contained in the Abercrombie Plans had narrowed and become separated from "other planning requirements" it is worth pointing out the "B" Ring (later redesignated Ringway One) was initially intended to form the spine of "an almost continuous inner green belt". *County of London Plan* (1943), p. 58. No trace of the inner green belt idea remained in the GLC's strategic road proposals, however.

unaltered since World War Two. One of the most fundamental changes which had occurred in post-war London was a rapid growth in major suburban shopping centres outside of the central area. In the *Greater London Development Plan (1969)*, six "major strategic centres" were identified: Ealing, Wood Green, and Ilford north of the Thames, and Kingston, Lewisham, and Croydon south of the river. The increase in the size of these centres and the *GLDP's* recommendations that their growth be continued meant that a new *polycentric* form for London was being proposed as official policy, and the long-held, monocentric concept of urban order for the city was quietly but effectively abandoned.[2] In addition to serving as shopping and major office sites the new strategic centres, the GLC indicated, would also serve as "particularly good centres for providing arts, culture, entertainment" and other facilities required for large gatherings, and the London Boroughs effected were directed by the GLC to "secure the standard of development which their importance will justify".[3] Thus although the monocentric concept of urban order which served as the strategic basis for Abercrombie's road pattern had ceased to exist the shape of the road plan *based on that concept* continued to persist long after London's basic structure had altered and its alteration had been accepted as a matter of planning policy.[4]

Each of the major strategic centres which had been slowly growing for some time generated substantial amounts of traffic but no clear relationship in geometrical terms existed between the designated centres and the proposed Primary Road Network. One critic, John Blake, argued that the town centre developments and the strategic road proposals set forth in the *GLDP* were basically incompatible.[5] He contended,

---

[2] See, GLC, *GLDP Statement (1969)*, p. 44. For a parallel development in the U.S. see John Friedmann and John Miller, "The urban field", *Journal of the American Institute of Planners*, Vol. XXXI, No. 4, November 1965, p. 313.

[3] GLC, *GLDP Statement* (1969), p. 44.

[4] See, on the "profound conservatism" of the strategic road proposals, Maurice Ash, *A Guide to the Structure of London*, Bath: Adams & Dart, 1972, p. 71.

[5] John Blake, "Shopping and suburban development", in Judy Hillman (Ed.), *Planning for London*, Harmondsworth, Middlesex: Penguin Books, 1971, p. 83.

Widening the Movement Planning Process 145

The end result of the GLC's present policy is indisputable. Over the next 15 years or more, it should become progressively easier to make long-distance journeys *between* centres as the motorway construction programme proceeds, but progressively more difficult to move within town centres....[6]

The mismatch between the planning and highway components of the GLC–MOT strategy was made even worse by the fact that each of the major centres lay astride existing major roads which were to form essential components of the Secondary Road Network.[7] As development of the designated centres and the Primary Road Network proceeded congestion in and around the centres might well actually increase as additional local traffic was thrown on to the existing secondary roads.[8] Thus although the GLC was both the strategic highway authority and the strategic planning authority its roles were combined in such a way that disadvantageous traffic effects at the community level could be created at several key points *as a direct result* of its own road building activities in the Capital.

In terms of the road pattern's basic geometry it is perhaps also worth considering, in view of London's changing form, the grounds on which the traditional ring and radial road pattern continued to be defended. Colin Buchanan and Partners, acting as consultants to the GLC, based their case for the Primary system on a paradoxical combination of inertia and historical inevitability. In *North East London*, a document produced by the Buchanan partnership in 1970, they contended, for example,

> A point needs to be made regarding the *pattern* of the primary network. It is perfectly true to say that the essential pattern was settled long before the London Traffic Survey was started. In fact the pattern is quite plainly a fairly direct derivative of the proposals advanced in the County of London Plan and the Greater London Plan of 1943 and 1944 respectively. We do not think this procedure of "plan before survey" necessarily invalidates the pattern of the primary network. The fact seems to be that Abercrombie, although unable to

---

[6] John Blake, "London's proposed motorways: some unanswered questions", *Building*, 11 September 1970, p. 95.
[7] See also on this topic Ash, *A Guide* (1972), p. 72; and Colin Buchanan and Partners, *North-east London*, London: GLC, 1970, p. 84.
[8] According to the GLC only 10 per cent of the secondary road budget was to be spent on improving traffic congestion within the strategic centres—80 per cent was to be spent on the secondary system as a whole and the remaining 10 per cent was to be spent on improvements in the Central Area. GLC, Press Release, "Secondary roads—new GLC plan", 11 December 1960, p. 1.

quantify and predict in the manner which is possible with the help of today's analytical tools, had a very good instinct as to the pattern of road required.... History plays a part in these matters, and cannot be ignored. It is difficult to change the lines of proposed roads when they have been "on the map" for a period of years and have become accepted.... Indeed it might be thought that an extraordinary feature of London planning is the way in which the concept of a ring and radial road system has survived for many years even though practically nothing has been built. We ourselves have certainly seen no reason to challenge the basic pattern at this late stage.[9]

Apart from raising the problem of the actual substantive contribution of the London Traffic Survey to main road planning one possible reason for challenging the traditional road pattern "at this late stage" was simply that it no longer fitted its context.

Treating an historical geometric road pattern as if it possessed a high level of *intrinsic* value and could thus be easily and safely isolated from its urban surrounding had been criticized by students of planning on more than one previous occasion. One of the major criticisms of the "slavish adoption" of predetermined road patterns came, curiously enough, from the working party which had produced *Traffic in Towns*, under the chairmanship of Colin Buchanan. In 1963, 7 years before the publication of the *North-East London* document, the Buchanan Report had argued,

> In some cases it appears that ring roads have been intuitively adopted in the first instance as part of the plan and at a later date "origin-and-destination" surveys have been taken to demonstrate that they would carry enough traffic to justify their construction. The results of such surveys are nearly always favourable to the ring road, for the simple reason that practically any new road cut through a densely developed area will, as a drain cut across a sodden field fills with water, attract enough vehicles to justify its existence in terms of flow. But if a wider view is taken the actual contribution to relieving the centre is extremely uncertain. It is not being inferred here that a ring road is in no circumstances likely to form part of an urban network. The objection that is taken is against the slavish adoption of the ring as a standardized pattern.[10]

The dangers of treating a proposed road system as a kind of "unmoved mover", which while changing its surroundings remained itself unchanged was the source of some concern to other observers as well.

Two transport economists, M. E. Beesley and J. F. Kain,

---

[9] Colin Buchanan and Partners, *N.E. London* (1970), p. 82.
[10] Buchanan, *Traffic in Towns* (1963), pp. 42–43, and see also p. 37.

suggested that the Buchanan approach had almost entirely ignored the tendency for modern western cities to decentralize.[11] Even more disturbingly it was entirely possible that construction of the proposed road system would actually accelerate changing patterns of land use and produce almost the opposite of the coherent, convenient and compact city which its designers had originally hoped to achieve. Once again rather than holding an increasingly mobile city together the construction of the Primary Road Network might well *increase* the already growing tendency for the city to decentralize both population and employment. "The moral of all this", one observer succinctly noted, "is not that the GLC's planning and transport policies are necessarily wrong but that considered together they cannot both be right."[12]

In addition to the problem of relating pattern to purpose in *geometrical* terms a parallel and in some ways even more fundamental difficulty remained: the problem of constructing an effective road *hierarchy* after a basic shift of emphasis had taken place in terms of organizational approach. Both Abercrombie and Buchanan had initially laid a good deal of stress on the importance of protecting the *local* environment from the deleterious effects of through traffic by means of the hierarchical nature of the road system. Abercrombie suggested, for example, that a number of measures including the actual closure of some local roads should be employed to allow traffic-controlled precincts to be created. After creating precincts in Central London the *County of London Plan* (1943) proposed "to extend the precinct system of planning to social entities of all kinds" throughout the London area.[13]

In an analogous way Buchanan originally suggested that "environmental areas" should be established as the *first* step in controlling

---

[11] M. E. Beesley and J. F. Kain, "Urban form, car ownership and public transport: an appraisal of traffic in towns", *Urban Studies*, Vol. 1, No. 2, November 1964, p. 194.

[12] Blake, "Shopping" (1971), p. 84. On the complex interrelationship between changes in transport and land use and the difficulty in modelling the reciprocal effects see Doreen B. Massey and Martyn Cordey-Hayes, "The use of models in structure planning", *Town Planning Review*, Vol. 42, No. 1, January 1971, p. 38.

[13] *CLP* (1943), p. 51. See also on the overriding importance of *neighbourhood* concerns, J. H. Forshaw, "Town planning and health", The Chadwick Public Lecture, delivered 11 November 1943, Westminster: P. S. King & Staples, p. 7.

148 Strategic Planning in London

traffic. Once delineated these "urban rooms" would spread throughout the city. As indicated earlier, Buchanan wrote, regarding his basic approach:

> Attention is first turned to the environment, to delineating the areas within which life is led and activities conducted. Gradually, for the whole town, working *outwards* from a large number of points, the cellular structure takes shape, and as it does so, by a complementary process, the pattern of the network declares itself. This, we submit, is the right order, and thus are vehicles and the arrangements for their movement kept in the right place—the place of service, no more, to the buildings and the activities therein.[14]

The establishment of the environmental areas (or precincts) would thus serve as an *essential prerequisite* for controlling traffic and would also form the basis for planning the intermediate and top tiers of the new road system.

In practice, however, this logical sequence was reversed in terms of order of priority and the pattern of the Primary Road Network was declared well before any concerted attempt was made to consider the environmental requirements of the proposed local areas.[15] The Greater London Council, because of its strategic orientation, was much more concerned with the traffic "pulling" power of the Primary Road Network and much less able to actually protect the local environment through the "squeezing out" of extraneous traffic. The two basic components of the complete Abercrombie–Buchanan policy for controlling traffic—local area "push" and strategic highway "pull"—were thus increasingly separated from one another and the local component was relegated to a distant second place in terms of importance. Because of the heavy emphasis placed on the Primary Road Network by the top-tier authorities and the relatively small amount of effort actually put into setting standards for, and physically limiting traffic within, local areas the GLC and the MOT were in effect only following half a policy—even worse in many ways, given the traditional bottom-up

---

[14] Buchanan *et al.*, *Traffic in Towns* (1963), p. 52. See Chapter 3, p. 93. See also on traffic segregation Peter Wood, "Studying traffic in towns", *Journal of the Town Planning Institute*, Vol. 49, No. 8, Sept./Oct. 1963, p. 265.

[15] For an example of this type of approach see GLC, *Westway: An Environmental and Traffic Appraisal*, GLDP, Inquiry Background Paper B. 494, London: GLC, July 1971.

approach for establishing a traffic hierarchy, they were pursuing the wrong half.[16]

The splitting of the traffic "push–pull" canalization policy and the lack of development of parallel environmental and movement strategies clearly worried Colin Buchanan and Partners. The organization of the planning system in London, they noted, meant that highway schemes were being pushed well ahead of wider planning concerns.[17] In *The Conurbations*, a report prepared for the British Road Federation, the Buchanan partnership wrote:

> ...even if new primary highways networks are built, a major environmental problem will remain in the areas lying between networks.... This problem has not yet been fully understood; more work is needed to develop techniques for assessing environmental capacities... and for seeing, in the transportation planning process, a real integration in the design for road accessibility and good environments. In all the conurbations the effort and manpower now being expended on planning for good environments (with regard to the impact of traffic) is comparatively small. At the present rate of progress in this field, motorway boxes may be completed before the more ubiquitous environmental problems are grappled with.[18]

The organizational arrangement for planning in London which had been established by law and practice did not, however, lend itself to dealing with the problem as a whole. The direction of events, as observers noted, very much tended to favour the strategic, top-down approach—often apparently with only the sketchiest knowledge of, or even concern with, local affairs.

As Peter Self noted regarding the road proposals put forward in the *Greater London Development Plan*: "The measures needed to improve the mobility of Londoners were spelled out in detail, but measures needed to protect the urban environment against traffic

---

[16] For an illustration of two of the few attempts to actually create environmental areas in London and the attendant difficulties see Mayer Hillman and Irwin Henderson, "Towards a better kind of environmental area", *New Society*, Vol. 25, No. 562, 12 July 1973, p. 75.

[17] On this point see Buchanan, *N.-E. London* (1970), p. 97. See also the suggested legislation put forward by the GLC to reduce the deleterious effect of the new roads and the increased costs involved, GLC, *Environmental Effects of the Construction of Primary Roads—Illustrative Examples*, GLDP Inquiry Background Paper B. 383, London, GLC, October 1970, p. 3.

[18] Colin Buchanan and Partners, *The Conurbations*, London: The British Road Federation, 1971, p. 100.

nuisance were indicated only broadly and left mainly to further action" by the local authorities involved.[19] The GLC also rather sadly conceded that under the terms of the London Government Act, 1963, there was a "split in London between roads, traffic planning and local planning", and went on in a fine piece of understatement to concede

> achieving close relations with local planning activity has its particular difficulties. Close co-ordination... is vital at planning, design and implementation stages for a proper local environmental assimilation. This is not easy to secure....[20]

Because of the continuing lack of co-ordination between the governmental tiers in Greater London the GLC's powerful but narrow road proposals were put forward without any direct means of controlling their local impact.[21]

The fragile and carefully constructed bottom-up model of hierarchical traffic canalization had been almost completely overturned. The Buchanan Partnership indicated that as events progressed

> ...the GLC will have virtually all the transportation and highway responsibilities together with the strategic planning responsibilities, whilst the boroughs will have important local planning functions but practically no responsibilities for traffic and transport except in respect of local roads. The Minister of Transport will stand in the background as a provider of grant aid, but very much in the foreground in respect of the trunk roads for which he is the highway authority. We are not sure that this will prove to be a workable arrangement.[22]

In spite of the doubts and reservations about the administrative arrangements for implementing planning in London the Buchanan Partnership, acting in their role as consultants to both the Greater London Council and the British Road Federation, gave considerable support to their clients' interest in constructing a large-scale com-

---

[19] Peter Self, *Metropolitan Planning*, London: Weidenfeld & Nicolson, 1971, p. 31.

[20] GLC, Subject Evidence—Stage 1, *Transport*, GLDP Inquiry Proof, E12/1, London: GLC, November 1970, p. 194.

[21] See on this topic at a more general level, David G. Williams, "The modal split", *Town Planning Review*, Vol. 42, No. 2, April 1971, pp. 194 f., and see also The Greater London Group of the LSE, *The Lessons of the London Government Reforms*, Evidence submitted to the royal commission on local government in England, London: HMSO, 1968, p. 34.

[22] Buchanan, *N.-E. London* (1970), p. 97. See also on the splitting of powers, Carl Tusker, "A motorway in London: learning from Western Avenue Extension", *The Surveyor*, 24 July 1970, p. 33.

plex of urban motorways in the Capital. This support for the overriding importance of the Primary Road Network in terms of order of priority meant that precincts, or environmental areas, as set forth in the *County of London Plan* and *Traffic in Towns* respectively, were treated less as the *essential prerequisite* for determining the pattern of the proposed triple-tiered road hierarchy for London and more as belated embellishments for a *fait accompli.*

WIDENING THE MOVEMENT PLANNING PROCESS

As the case for construction was more closely examined a number of other disturbing features regarding the road proposals also began to become evident. For example, in many ways the case for the new road hierarchy rested on three basic assumptions. In the first place it was assumed that constructing the new purpose-built system would be the most economical way to use the scarce public funds available for increasing mobility.[23] Secondly, it was held that the additional road capacity would increase efficiency and facilitate the movement of that traffic which was essential "to the future prosperity and functioning of London".[24] Finally it was argued that the proposed hierarchy of roads would protect the environment by separating through traffic from local traffic.[25] The triple *intent* of the GLC–MOT proposals was thus that the new road system would be *economical, efficient* and *environmentally beneficial.*

A growing number of observers suggested, however, that the actual *impact* of the joint proposals would be very different from the objectives put forward by the public authorities involved. The whole of the highway policy turned, apparently, on the rather mechanistic belief that a substantial expansion in the road space available would allow an increasing degree of physical canalization between different types of traffic to take place—including the

---

[23] GLC, *Greater London Development Plan—Statement*, London: GLC, 1969, p. 24; and see also GLC, *Greater London Development Plan—Report of Studies*, London: GLC, 1969, p. 199.

[24] GLC, *GLDP—Statement* (1969), p. 22; and see GLC, *GLDP—Report* (1969), p. 163.

[25] GLC, *GLDP—Statement* (1969), p. 23; and GLC, *GLDP—Report* (1969), p. 201.

152 Strategic Planning in London

separation of through and local traffic and essential and optional traffic. This hard planning, top-down approach to traffic control meant, as noted earlier, that although the GLC lacked local planning powers it nevertheless continued to press ahead with its plans for making the city work more efficiently largely through the traffic attraction potential afforded by the Primary Road Network.[26] Increasing stress was thus laid by the top-tier authorities on aiding the city's ability to function as a complex, higher-order machine for producing and distributing goods and services in the hope that by so doing community life would also be simultaneously improved through the removal of extraneous local traffic.[27]

In one of its publications the Council pointed out that

> Goods need to be delivered to and from the docks, to factories, warehouses and shops.... Increased prosperity has produced an increased demand for all types of goods and services but unless these goods can be moved freely to and from their destinations London's commercial prosperity will wane, and with it the living standards of its citizens. The convenient movement of goods is essential to London's economic well-being.[28]

Large-scale road construction seemed once again to be the inescapable answer to achieving these objectives.

Even the most ardent of the road-proposals defenders admitted, however, that new construction was only a *partial* answer to London's movement problems. According to the GLC's own studies in many areas, particularly in inner London, the potential traffic

---

[26] See, for example, GLC, "Transport in London: a balanced policy", London: GLC, March 1970, p. 11.

[27] It would perhaps at this point be worth while recalling Abercrombie's initial division of London into three parts: Community London, Monumental London and Mechanistic London. The mechanistic component had clearly become the dominant factor while the community component had been largely redefined to accord with the assumed movement insulation afforded by the road system element of Mechanistic London. In a very similar way Monumental London could be seen as having been redefined and was now largely limited to the new motorways themselves. See Patrick Abercrombie and J. Forshaw, *County of London Plan* (1943), London: Macmillan and Co., 1944, p. 13. See also Buchanan's structural criticism of the out-of-date road system, Buchanan (1963), p. 191; and Chapter 3, p. 96.

[28] GLC, Transport (1970), p. 1. For a similar view see the comment made by Richard Marsh, the then Labour Minister of Transport, during the opening of part of Ringway One's East Cross Route, MOT Press Release, No. 226, "Transport Minister opens Blackwall Tunnell approach road", 25 April 1969, p. 1.

Widening the Movement Planning Process   153

flows which would be generated *after* the construction of the Primary Network would be "greater than the design capacity of a dual four-lane highway".[29] In effect this meant that traffic congestion could not be solved simply by increasing the supply of road space *without building motorways which were dual five lanes or more in width* and thus further worsening the already heavy "take" of housing and land in the inner city. For both practical and political reasons the policy which one of the GLC's critics attacked "as the indiscriminant provision of road space" simply could not be indefinitely pursued.[30] The problem facing the top-tier authorities became less that of how to provide new high-speed roads and more of how to devise an integrated transportation policy for the Capital. The real point therefore became at what point and by what means the balance between private and public transport was to be struck. It proved to be an extremely difficult decision to make.

Both Abercrombie and Buchanan had previously argued in favour of creating "movement systems" in large urban areas which would draw on and co-ordinate all of the relevant transport modes available.[31] An even earlier observer, Rees Jeffreys, had also commented before World War One: "No solution of the traffic problem will be found until the questions of tramway, railway and road communications are considered together by one authority."[32] In spite of periodic attempts no such authority existed in London 60 years later at the time of the announcement of the Primary Road Network. At this time the GLC was primarily a strategic *highway* agency rather than a comprehensive transport authority and responsibility for public transport in the metropolitan region was divided between

---

[29] GLC, *GLDP—Report* (1969), p. 199; and see also the statement by Peter Stott, the GLC's principle highway engineer, "Structure and management", *Traffic Engineering and Control*, Vol. 9, No. 1, May 1967, p. 38.

[30] J. Michael Thomson (*et al.*), *Motorways in London*, London: Gerald Duckworth, 1969, p. 142. In addition see for a supporting opinion, South-East England Young Liberal Federation, "The motorway box briefing", Undated, typescript, p. 4.

[31] See Abercrombie and Forshaw (1944), p. 14 and pp. 69–70; and Colin Buchanan, "Transport and the community", an inaugural lecture delivered at the Imperial College, University of London, 18 February 1964, p. 177.

[32] Quoted by C. M. Buchanan, *London Road Plans 1900–1970*, Research Report No. 11, London: GLC, December 1970, p. 8.

two publicly owned but largely independent organizations—London Transport and British Rail.[33]

The GLC and the MOT were agreed on the need to create a single movement "mechanism" for the Capital. The idea took some time to take shape, however. In the U.S. it had been suggested that

> ...we expect mass transit operations to act like private enterprises and highway agencies like bureaus. We are not technologically prepared to serve well the classical city writ large; we are not administratively prepared to integrate regional transportation activities.[34]

In a sense both of these contentions were challenged in London. Soon after the creation of the new governmental system for Greater London in 1965 the MOT was reorganized and the former London Highway Division was replaced by the much broader London Policy Division.[35] In 1967 when the full Primary system was announced the GLC indicated its

> ...ultimate object must be to assemble all the diverse elements of transportation policy—whether they stem from the provision of new highways—into a single mechanism, where their interaction one with another can be observed and adjusted.[36]

With the active support of the MOT the problem of co-ordinating interauthority relations in the movement sphere became a major source of governmental concern.

After a good deal of discussion and negotiation between the GLC and the MOT a White Paper, *Transport in London*, was published in 1968.[37] The Council with very little party political dissension took the

---

[33] A loose Transport Co-ordinating Council for London had been created in 1966 which included all of the relevant movement authorities but it was advisory rather than an executive body.

[34] Lowdon Wingo, "Urban space in a policy perspective: an introduction", in Lowdon Wingo (Ed.), *Cities and Space*, Baltimore, Md.: The John Hopkins Press, 1963, pp. 16–17.

[35] Michael Goldrick, "The administration of transportation in Greater London", unpublished Ph.D., London School of Economics, 1967, pp. 238–239.

[36] GLC, "London's roads—a programme for action", London: GLC, 1967, p. 6. Significantly this pamphlet was withdrawn later and replaced by "Transport in London: a balanced policy".

[37] MOT, *Transport in London*, Cmnd. 3686, London: HMSO, 1968. This document followed the publication of an earlier White Paper, which suggested the need to establish broad transport authorities in the major conurbations, MOT, *Transport Policy*, Cmnd. 3057, London: HMSO, 1966.

position that it was prepared to play a leading part in the establishment of a conurbation transport authority provided that satisfactory administrative and financial arrangements could be made. The broad recommendations put forward in the White Paper suggested that: (a) transport planning in the Capital should be integrated; (b) London Transport should be placed under the control of the GLC, although detailed day-to-day matters would be the responsibility of a London Transport Executive; (c) attempts should be made to more closely co-ordinate British Rail and GLC financial policy; and (d) finally, the GLC's control over highways would be extended to cover all principal roads in London, including ultimately the MOT's trunk routes. These recommendations were made law with the passage of the Transport (London) Act, 1969; under the terms of the Act, London Transport was placed under the control of the GLC in January 1970 and the transport authority's accumulated debt was written off by the Government. Partly as a result of this legislation and partly as a result of the merger of the planning and transportation departments the opportunity at last existed for the GLC with its broadened transport powers to create an integrated movement system for the Capital.[38] Unfortunately this opportunity was only partly grasped. The continuing power of the original Primary Road Network proposals was such that the acquisition of formal powers of control over public transport made no significant impact—apart from rather vague proposals for motorway buses—on either the purpose or pattern of the new road system. Rather than actually being *integrated* with highway planning for Greater London, London Transport activities, because of the extent to which the motorways were taken for granted by the Council, were simply *superimposed* upon the existing plans. Although what transpired initially was an addition, rather than an integration of functions, the planning process in London was thus formally widened, at last, to include public as well as private modes of transport. Because these two

---

[38] For organizational arrangements in general see Michael F. Collins and Timothy M. Pharoah, *Transport Organization in a Great City*, London: London School of Economics and George Allen & Unwin, 1974. See also Gerald Rhodes and S. K. Ruck, *The Government of Greater London*, London: George Allen & Unwin, 1970, p. 114.

modes had developed over time in a parallel and largely separate fashion, they were in fact *contiguous* rather than complementary in character.[39]

The steady increase in the recognition of the importance of public transport to a certain extent redressed its earlier omission from the 1963 London Government Act and from the early phases of the LTS.[40] The belated recognition of the kind of benefits which public transport was capable of providing was coupled with mounting political concern regarding the cost and destruction which would be caused by the highway programme. These two factors operating in conjunction eventually had a significant impact on the seemingly immutable ring and radial road proposals. Paradoxically the attempt to broaden the movement planning process in technical and organizational terms played an important part in politically calling into question, and ultimately of undermining, the case for the Primary Road Network.

THE GROWTH OF OPPOSITION

The highway proposals contained in the *Greater London Development* Plan (1969) not only symbolized a long-held concept of urban order; they also revealed a complex balance of power among a number of differing and occasionally competing organizations within the metropolitan area. This balance was, however, like the actual structure of the city itself, dynamic rather than static. As the implications of the road proposals became evident at the local level a number of public and private organizations in Greater London began to take a much closer look at the arguments upon which the ringway proposals were based.

As a result of this analysis a continuing and on more than one occasion an extremely sharp controversy surrounding the highway plans developed of an intensely political kind. Although this debate was concerned, in Easton's phrase with the "shaping and sharing of

---

[39] It should be added that this was not by any means peculiar to London. See Wilfred Owen, *The Accessible City*, Washington, D.C.: The Brookings Institute, 1972, p. 44.

[40] On the need to widen the 1963 Act see Stott (1967), p. 38.

power", it was not *party* political until a relatively late stage in the development of the proposal. Both the Labour party, which had initially proposed the Motorway Box, and the Conservative party, which had long pressed for increased road building, were broadly in agreement on the need for and the shape of the new road system. Not until 1969 did the Labour party begin to quietly dissociate itself from its own proposals. As late as April 1970 when the GLC elections were held *The Times* remarked that it was "impossible to vote against the ringways by voting either Conservative or Labour, because although both parties appear to be back-pedaling, Labour much the harder, neither has openly repudiated them".[41] Because of this bi-partisan accord the real question for several years even with the raising interest in public transport was not *whether* the ring and radial pattern would form the key component of the Council's planning strategy but *when* the roads would be constructed. Other concerned groups did not, however, share as readily in the two partys' belief that the advantages of the new highways would outweigh their disadvantages. In a sense the emerging polycentric shape of the Capital was also mirrored in the proliferation of active interest groups throughout the metropolitan area.

Banfield has suggested that the policy produced by one urban organization in the attempt to maintain (or enhance) its position often results in other organizations feeling threatened by the change proposed. As a result these organizations react defensively and a political controversy results.[42] As it became increasingly apparent that the GLC–MOT road plans were concerned not merely with the more efficient distribution of traffic but more broadly with the distribution of real resources the question of which areas and groups benefited and which lost during the process of construction assumed a high level of importance. Although it was undeniably true that a good deal of survey and quantification work had gone into the GLDP, it was also true that the fundamental assumptions upon which this work had been based could be evaluated politically as well as factually since the document was concerned with the

[41] Michael Bailey, "Both parties stand clear of ringway eruptions", *The Times*, 17 March 1970.
[42] Edward Banfield, *Political Influence*, Glencoe, Ill.: The Free Press, 1961, p. 263. See also Altshuler (1965b), p. 409.

ordering of priorities among competing concepts of what constituted the public good. As Long cogently observed, "The question is not whether planning will reflect politics but whose politics it will reflect".[43] In controversies of this type, governmental units, as another observer noted, often act as "contestants, rather than as neutral referees, in the struggle for political power".[44] Among those organizations which were most concerned by the plan's implications were several of the London Boroughs and a large number of neighbourhood and amenity groups within the city.[45]

The often unclear relationship between the GLC and the Boroughs was particularly strained with regard to the road proposals. In 1965 the suggestion of the London Boroughs' Association that a joint working party be established to study highway matters was rejected by the GLC. In spite of repeated urgings, the GLC maintained that it preferred to deal with the Boroughs concerned on an individual basis.[46] Many of the Boroughs resented what they believed to be the GLC's uncompromising attitude with regard to its highway planning. On several occasions the Boroughs were notified of decisions which had been made and which would affect their areas through public announcements.

As an example of Borough opposition the London Borough of Lambeth in a report prepared for the Highway and Works Committee argued that the GLC's motorway proposals were "premature". The report stated:

> The alignment of the motorway box and associated radial routes does not appear to have been based on the provision of an integrated transportation policy, including a modern public transport system.... It appears to be an ad hoc solution developed from past proposals which were based on traffic data which must now be out of date.[47]

---

[43] Norton E. Long, "Planning and politics in urban development", *Journal of the American Institute of Planners*, Vol. XXV, No. 4, November 1959, p. 168.

[44] Bertram Gross, quoted by Frank Smallwood, *Greater London*, Indianapolis, Ind.: Bobs–Merrill, 1965, p. 97.

[45] On the political implications of the plan see David Donnison (*et al.*), "Observations on the Greater London Development Plan", Background Paper, GLDP Inquiry, B603, November 1970, p. 11.

[46] See GLC, *Minutes 1965*, London: GLC, p. 336; and see also Greater London Group (1968), p. 31.

[47] Planning Correspondent, "Motorway for London premature", the *Guardian*, 12 January 1966.

A number of other Boroughs including Camden, Lewisham and Tower Hamlets which felt similarly threatened also publicly indicated concern with the GLC's policy.

The Boroughs were not, of course, the only organizations to initially voice concern and ultimately to challenge the motorway programme. Abercrombie had noted in 1943 that "From time to time the local inhabitants have expressed their spontaneous opposition to road proposals...".[48] After the announcement of the Motorway Box a number of "local inhabitants" began to form local protest organizations to oppose the GLC–MOT plans. By the time of the publication of the GLDP 5 years later over 100 groups scattered throughout the metropolitan area had emerged. Although these organizations were largely concerned with specific parts of the Capital a number were also linked with two umbrella organizations with a city-wide perspective: The London Motorway Action Group (LMAG) and the London Amenity and Transport Association (LATA). These groups—particularly the LMAG chaired by Douglas Jay, M.P.—played an important part in what became the battle of the ringways.

The individual protest groups involved varied widely in size and composition. Houseboat owners living off Cheyne Walk formed the Chelsea Boat Owners' Association and complained that the West Cross Route of Ringway One would threaten their continued existence on the Thames. Groups formed in Hampstead and Greenwich expressed concern about the danger caused to the architectural character of their areas by the construction of the new roads. At a strategic level a "Homes Before Roads" group ran canditates in a number of areas during the 1970 GLC elections and managed to gain 100,000 votes. The LMAG contended simply that it was "fighting to save London from Destruction by Motorways".[49] Letters were written to the press, M.P.s of both parties joined the opposition, and local protest meetings were held throughout the Capital. One organization, the Hampstead Motorway Action Group, went as far as announcing that it was going to form a limited company and sue

---

[48] Abercrombie (1944), p. 21.
[49] LMAG, "Local appeal letter launching the Motorway Fighting Fund", 8 May 1970.

160 Strategic Planning in London

the GLC over the legality of the whole scheme. David Wilcox wryly noted that "ringway-bashing" had become a favourite public sport.[50]

ANALYSING THE PLAN—THE GLDP INQUIRY

The road proposals had remarkably few supporters. The ring and radial plans were condemned by most of the press, several leading academic commentators, the Town and Country Planning Association and the Royal Institute of British Architects. Very few outside observers indeed could comment, as the British Road Federation did, that the GDLP was "magnificent".[51] As opposition continued to grow unabated some type of public examination of the plan was clearly called for. In December 1969 it was announced by the Government that a far-ranging inquiry would be held to "probe and evaluate, fully and searchingly, the policies embodied in the plan, the objections made to them and possible alternative strategies".[52] Although it was not the only forum for debate during the period 1970 to 1972 the GLDP Inquiry became one of the central focal points for assessing the multitude of conflicting messages generated in the Capital by the road proposals.

Almost 30,000 objections were received to the plan. About 75 per cent of these objections related to the motorways.[53] Although it was initially held by a government minister that it would be "neither right nor proper to set up some kind of Roskill-type commission to examine the Development Plan proposals of a large and competently staffed authority..." it was finally agreed by the Government, at least partly because of the strength of the opposition that a high-level panel headed by an independent judicial chairman would

[50] David Wilcox, "The Greater London Development Plan", in Judy Hillman (Ed.), *Planning for London*, Harmondsworth: Penguin Books 1971, p. 18.
[51] "The GLDP inquiry: Stage 1 Transport", *Official Architecture and Planning*, Vol. 34, No. 6, June 1971, p. 471.
[52] Statement by Anthony Crosland, then Secretary of State for Local Government, quoted in Department of the Environment, *Greater London Development Plan—Report of the Panel of Inquiry* (the Layfield Report), Vol. 1, London: HMSO, 1973, p. 13.
[53] See on the road objections the statement of concern issued by the Inquiry Panel, Ministry of Housing and Local Government, Press Release, 1 October 1970; see also J. Michael Thomson, "Transport: the motorway proposals", in Hillman (1971), p. 86.

Widening the Movement Planning Process 161

be appointed.[54] The chairman eventually selected to preside over the Inquiry was Frank Layfield, a barrister with considerable planning experience.

By the time the Inquiry actually began its session in July 1970 the debate between the GLC and its critics had become very acrimonious indeed. It was asserted, for example, that the Council had been deliberately suppressing information. Michael Thomson, a transport economist at the London School of Economics, and Terence Bendixson, the Planning Correspondent for the *Guardian*, charged that the third volume of the London Transportation Study (formerly the London Traffic Survey) was being withheld from public examination.[55] When the third volume of the LTS was finally released these critics argued that a good deal of the most important information had been left out of the public document. Those who opposed the road proposals also suggested, even more fundamentally, that the major LTS parameters which formed the basis for the study's projections were all incorrect. Population and employment in the Capital were both falling rather than increasing as the LTS had suggested and automobile usage was not increasing at anything like the rate which was initially predicted.[56] The LTS information had been collected for the year 1962 and by the time that the GLDP Inquiry began it was almost 10 years out of date.[57]

If it was true as one observer suggested that in London "great decisions are made with little understanding of the consequences for those interests which are not plainly visible to the decision-makers"

---

[54] Letter from Kenneth Robinson, Minister of Planning and Land, to Douglas Jay, M.P., unpublished, 15 July 1969; in addition see Letter from Douglas Jay to Kenneth Robinson, regarding the form of the inquiry, unpublished, 27 June 1969.

[55] See, for example, Terence Bendixson, "Box Mania", the *Guardian*, 24 January 1969.

[56] See Blake (1968), p. 35. For the original projection see GLC, *Movement in London*, London: GLC, 1969, p. 8. In addition see Thomson (1969), p. 25.

[57] A new study—The Greater London Transportation Survey—was, however, carried out during the course of the Inquiry at an additional cost of £400,000. The two traffic studies cost a total of £1,400,000. House of Commons, *Second Report from the Expenditures Committee, Urban Transport Planning, Session 1972–73*, Vol. II, *Minutes of Evidence*, London: HMSO, 14 December 1972, p. 125; and see K. A. J. Crawford, "The 1971 Greater London Transportation Survey", *Quarterly Bulletin of the Intelligence Unit*, No. 16, September 1971, pp. 15–16.

then it was also true that during the course of the Inquiry decision-makers were made aware of a very broad spectrum of divergent opinion.[58] The Inquiry was "almost certainly the largest statutory inquiry ever held in this country".[59] Among the formal objectors were twelve London Boroughs and the City of London and thousands of individuals, business firms, and neighbourhood action groups. Tens of thousands of pages of evidence were produced during the course of the proceedings which lasted from 7 July 1970 to 9 May 1972. There were 326 actual appearances during the 237 days when the panel was in session, and panel members visited all of the areas of London for which specific objection had been registered.

Briefly four general strands of opposition emerged during the 22 months which the Inquiry panel sat. All of these arguments were in direct opposition to the GLC's contentions regarding the benefits which the Primary Road Network would confer. In terms of impact rather than intent it was held that:

1. The proposed ring and radial road network would be *uneconomic*. One of the most powerful of the objections to the primary and secondary proposals was simply the real amount of public money at stake. It was contended that it was "the most costly peacetime public investment project ever proposed by a British authority—as large as if not larger than the British share of the Concorde, Channel Tunnel and Third Airport put together...".[60] Whether this would be the best use of scarce public resources available was open to serious question.

One commentator observed that the price of Ringway One would be £20 million per mile and in certain areas where tunnelling was employed it would have been even higher. To bring the road system into being every family in London, many of whom lacked access to an automobile and lived in inadequate housing, would have to contribute the equivalent of £800.[61] Once again the precise cost of

[58] Banfield (1961), p. 339.
[59] *Layfield Report*, Vol. I (1973), p. 3.
[60] Douglas Jay, "Preface" to, Michael Thomson (*et al.*), *Transport Strategy in London*, GLDP Inquiry, Proof E12/20, London: LMAG and LATA, 1971, p. 3.
[61] See Simon Jenkins, "The politics of London motorways", the *Political Quarterly*, Vol. 44, No. 3, July–September 1973, p. 262.

the road proposals was difficult to determine for two reasons: (a) continuing inflation, and (b) increased compensation. Between 1967 and 1970 the GLC estimated that the cost of the Primary Road Network had increased by more than 50 per cent from £650,000,000 to £1,400,000,000. If the secondary system also increased by a similar amount the total cost by official reckoning would have been of the order of £2,100,000,000.[62] A Borough Chief Planning Officer suggested to a critic, however, that the true cost of Ringway One alone would be £3000 million.[63]

One of the reasons for suggesting that the MOT (which was subsequently merged with a new Department of the Environment in 1970) and the GLC had underestimated the costs involved was the assertion that the motorways had been very narrowly conceived in physical terms. Although the GLC had for some time been campaigning for increased compensation to benefit those whose homes were not actually demolished but who would nevertheless suffer from increased noise, vibration and dirt as direct result of construction it was suggested that these costs had been left out of its own accounting. If these "second-order" effects were taken into account it was argued that the total costs of the project could well double, and the benefits might be substantially less than the GLC's elaborate cost–benefit study had originally suggested.[64] The attempt which grew out of the concern with "land-scrapping" motorways to widen the movement planning process *spatially* by protecting buildings and paying increased compensation—as well as by widening movement planning *functionally* by more closely integrating public transport—meant either higher costs or less road mileage or both.[65] More attention began to be devoted to thinking about developing movement corridors rather than merely buying the land required for the road structure itself.

[62] Thomson (1971), p. 197.
[63] W. R. C. Halpin, "Letter to the Editor", the *Daily Telegraph*, 18 July 1966.
[64] On this see John Blake, "London's proposed motorways: some unanswered questions", *Buildings*, 11 September 1970, p. 94; and Thomson (1969), p. 147.
[65] On various suggestions for reducing the impact of new roads see the White Paper, "Development and Compensation—Putting People First", Cmnd. 5124, London: HMSO, October 1972; and see also Department of the Environment, *New Roads in Towns*, London: HMSO, July 1972.

2. The proposed ring and radial road network would be *inefficient*. Quite apart from problems of expense it was also argued by the highway plan's critics that the new road system simply would not work. One of the principal justifications for building the new top-tier highways was that they would allow through traffic and local traffic and essential and optional traffic to be separated from one another. A number of difficulties arose in this sphere, however.

In the first place it was argued that it might not be possible to differentiate between these various traffic types in practice. One influential writer had earlier remarked; "...it has yet to be shown that traffic is really 'canalizable' to the extent necessary to provide effective insulation..." to local areas; the growth of automobile ownership and usage meant that the "legitimate traffic" of people living within these tactical areas alone would be sufficient to destroy their peace and quiet.[66] Physical planning could only effectively prevent traffic from entering these areas by completely recasting the city.

In addition it was held that the fastest growing type of traffic in London was optional rather than essential traffic. The journey to work was steadily declining as a percentage of overall traffic while shopping, leisure and recreational trips were all growing rapidly. In one of its publications the GLC contended that it was because of these *social* trips that the new roads were required.[67] Critics held, however, that the problem of the journey to work should receive top priority, "Yet the whole approach of the LTS and the GLC systematically diverts attention from this to other less important problems".[68] Apart from the question of priorities an even more basic problem began to become evident: the construction of the Primary Road Network might not actually reduce road congestion but could well stimulate an increase in optional, social travel.

According to GLC sources by the mid-1980s even with the new motorways in place and parking controls operating demand during

[66] C. D. Buchanan, *Mixed Blessing*, London: Leonard Hill Ltd., 1958, p. 158.

[67] See on this GLC, "New Roads in West and North Central London", GLC pamphlet, June 1967, unpaginated.

[68] See Thomson, (1971), pp. 163–164. See also on the difficulties of distinguishing between essential and optional traffic, D. J. Reynolds, *Economics, Town Planning and Traffic*, London: Institute of Economics Affairs, 1966, p. 79.

peak hours would exceed the capacity of the Secondary Road system in Central London by 50 per cent.[69] In another Council publication it was asserted that a local environmental study for 1981 had

> already shown that for the area selected the projected motorway and secondary routes will divert a substantial proportion of traffic from the local streets. *However, it also indicates that much of this could be replaced by locally generated traffic* which is expected to increase as car ownership rises.[70]

Although the GLC contended that new road construction would help to meet the growth in demand several critics argued that the ringways would help to increase inessential traffic, some of which would inevitably be local in character. The position was therefore a good deal less than completely clear.[71]

3. The proposed ring and radial system would be *environmentally disadvantageous*. Even if the problems of cost and congestion could be satisfactorily resolved it was still contended that the environmental damage which would be caused by the construction would be unacceptable. The attempt to canalize traffic physically meant the destruction of tens of thousands of homes.[72] Many argued, however, that London's biggest environmental problem was that of substandard or inadequate housing rather than movement. According to official estimates well over one million people lived in "Housing Problem Areas" in the Capital.[73] The construction of the motorways would mean that waiting time for new housing for people other than those actually displaced by the new roads would certainly not diminish.

In addition research work such as Buchanan's study of North-east London, indicated that noise problems could mean doubling the number of houses which the GLC had initially proposed to buy.[74] It

[69] GLC, "A secondary roads policy", Consultative Text, London: GLC, November 1969, p. 3.
[70] GLC, *Movement* (1969), p. 14. Italics added.
[71] On this topic see LMAG, "Ringway 2", typescript, November 1969, p. 4. See also Ken Hutchings, "Urban transport: public or private", *Fabian Research Series* 261, London: Fabian Society, June 1967, p. 13; and Owen (1972), p. 114.
[72] See LMAG, "Appeal Letter", May 1970.
[73] GLC, *GLDP—Report* (1969), p. 28.
[74] Colin Buchanan and Partners, *North-east London*, London: GLC, 1970. See also GLC, *Urban Design Bulletin*, London: GLC, 1970, for proposals for dealing with noise problems.

was also argued that interchange problems and the impact of the Secondary Road Network had received insufficient attention. In many ways, it was held, the secondary roads would be as environmentally harmful as the motorways themselves because of the number of people who lived nearby and who would be subjected to increased traffic levels.[75]

4. The proposed ring and radial system would be *inequitable*. Closely linked with the problem of environmental effects was the perceived fairness of the proposals. In effect it was contended that inner area dwellers who had the most to lose because of construction would also have the least to gain while the converse was true of those who lived in middle-class, car-owning, outer London. The "two Londons effect" meant that inner areas of the city which were traditionally Labour party supporting, were being reconstructed according to some observers to benefit Conservative-held outer areas.[76]

The one section of inner urban motorway which *had* been constructed—Westway—was uniformly held to be a particularly bad example of attempting to build a new urban road "on the cheap". The $2\frac{1}{2}$ mile section which had been completed ran, in some cases, only a few yards from multi-storey flats. All of the parties involved were agreed on the need to broaden planning to avoid a repetition of this project.[77] There was also a more general concern with treating those who lost land or property more equitably.

In total it was thus argued by a host of disparate individuals and groups that the effect of the Primary Road Network would be uneconomic, inefficient, environmentally disadvantageous, and inequitable.

---

[75] See on environmental effects, Cornelius Murphy, "New deal for motorway victims", *Official Architecture and Planning*, Vol. 35, No. 2, February 1972, p. 83; and Wilcox (1971a), p. 31.

[76] On this see Terence Bendixson, "Transport: the two cities", Hillman (Ed.) (1971), pp. 99–112.

[77] On Westway see GLC, *Westway: An Environmental and Traffic Appraisal*, GLDP Inquiry, Background Paper, B494, July 1971.

THE FALL OF THE PRIMARY ROAD NETWORK

Although the GLC vigorously contested the objections put forward by its critics it became increasingly clear during the course of the GLDP Inquiry that the Council had begun to lose the initiative. There was certainly no clear and unambiguous evidence that the majority of Londoners shared in the belief of many of the objectors that the effect of the Ringways on the Capital would be disastrous. By the same token, however, there was reason to believe that basic doubts had been raised in the minds of a number of people regarding the real value of the road proposals on political, economic and technical grounds. Of particular concern to many was the relative priority accorded to the road proposals in relation to other public projects such as housing for example.

Early in 1970 the British Road Federation conducted a poll of 2000 Londoners which revealed that 80 per cent favoured the building of more new roads in the Capital. Later in the same year, however, Willmott and Young found that when a similar sample were asked to *rank* a list of proposals for allocating public funds building new urban motorways finished at the bottom of the list of ten proposals. While 66 per cent of the sample felt that the most important way to use funds would be to give increased aid to old people, only 8 per cent felt that roads should be placed at the top of the list.[78] In effect this conflicting evidence meant that the Council had not really conclusively proven its case at a time when the burden of proof fell very much on the initiating authority. It could be argued that the finding which emerged during the Inquiry was the Scottish verdict—Not Proven—with particular regard to the *scale* of the motorway proposals and the extent to which they were *integrated* with broader planning and movement concerns.

Many of the GLC's most vehement critics accepted the need for some road-building. At the Inquiry it was argued, for example, by the London Motorway Action Group and the London Amenity and

---

[78] See British Road Federation, Press Release, "London Ringways: 80 per cent support the GLC plan", 16 March 1970; and *New Society*, Press Release, "Urban motorways not popular with Londoners", 9 December 1970.

Transport Association that certain motorways—Ringways One and Two and those inner radials proposed within Ringway Three—should be scrapped and that Ringway Three should be constructed as an outer by-pass for the metropolitan area. By pursuing this reduced plan it was estimated by LMAG and LATA that 90 per cent of the housing scheduled for destruction under the original GLC–MOT plan would be saved and costs could be reduced by an estimated £1500 million.[79] Several other groups and individuals suggested that the amount of road building proposed—particularly in inner London—should be drastically reduced and the remaining roads which were constructed should be built to a high environmental standard.

Throughout the Inquiry, however, the GLC doggedly clung to the original road pattern which it had put forward in 1966.[80] One of the factors which apparently strengthened the GLC's resolve to continue with the full Primary Road Network was the quiet but firm support which the Council continued to receive from the Ministry of Transport. The London Borough of Kensington and Chelsea indicated in a report produced during the Inquiry that the GLC had received a letter from the Minister of Transport dated 13 May 1968, which contained the following assurances:

> The desirable form of the primary road system has been examined by the Ministry and the Council within the Joint Highways Planning Organization of the Transport Co-ordinating Council for London. This examination has led to the conclusion that there is a need for a system of primary roads designed to improve orbital movement in London and relieve suburban roads and the central area as a whole... *The Minister accepts the need for such a system.*[81]

The roads were also a matter of *planning* concern for the Central

---

[79] Jay (1971), p. 11. For an example of opposition to Ringway 3 by one of the outer London Boroughs see London Borough of Ealing, "'D' Ring Road—Ealing Council Protest to Ministry of Transport", 6 November 1969. Note the persistence of Abercrombie's terms.

[80] See, for example, the *Greater London Development Plan Statement Revisions*, which was prepared after the Inquiry had been in session for some time. Although the document emphasized greater traffic restraint and placed more emphasis on public transport the plans for the Primary Road Network remained unaltered. GLC, *GLDP—Statement Revisions*, London: GLC, February 1972, p. 39.

[81] London Borough of Kensington and Chelsea, "Planning Committee Report", 22 April 1971, unpaginated. Italics added.

Government and it was evident that complete co-ordination had not been achieved between the Ministry of Transport and the Ministry of Housing and Local Government which dealt with planning matters. One of the ministers involved, the Minister of Planning and Land, wrote to a correspondent just over a year after the Ministry of Transport had given their assurances: "As you know the Government are in no way committed to the Greater London Council's road proposals...."[82] Partly as a means of increasing co-ordination in this type of matter and partly as a result of political pressure several administrative modifications were adopted at both Central and local governmental level.

Two major organizational changes occurred which attempted to further widen the movement planning process by formally combining planning and transportation concerns. In the first place the planning and transportation departments at the GLC were merged in 1969 to form a single Department of Planning and Transportation. Secondly, at the Central Government level the Ministry of Transport, the Ministry of Housing and Local Government and the Ministry of Public Building and Works were brought together to form a new "super-Ministry"—the Department of the Environment (DOE) in 1970.[83] By and large, however, these changes came too late to have much real effect. Within the GLC the impact of these co-ordinating devices on the GLDP was described as "disappointingly small".[84] The inflexible highway proposals continued to dominate planning considerations in spite of these formal organizational changes and the concern expressed by Peter Self regarding the need to mesh the vertical integration of the road system with a horizontal integration of planning needs continued to present a major source of difficulties.[85]

These difficulties were clearly in evidence as the GLDP Inquiry progressed. After listening to testimony for almost 2 years from July

[82] Robinson (1969), p. 2.
[83] The Department of the Environment replaced the co-ordinating role held briefly by Anthony Crosland, Secretary of State for Local Government and Regional Planning.
[84] Self (1971), p. 31.
[85] Peter Self, *Bureaucracy or Management*, An Inaugural Lecture, London: G. Bell & sons, 1965, p. 25. See also Greater London Group (1968), p. 34.

170 Strategic Planning in London

1970 to May 1972 the Panel of Inquiry agreed with critics that the GLC had been over-ambitious in its road planning and that problems of vertical and horizontal integration had not, in fact, been properly related to each other. Although the Layfield Panel acknowledged that the Council's transport policy had developed during the 3 years since the GLDP was produced in 1969 the Panel contended that the Council's proposals were still far from satisfactory. As the Panel witheringly remarked

> That the primary road programme is intended to relieve secondary and local roads to a specified extent, that the relief will bring about relative environmental improvement, that contributory management schemes will be carried out, that environmental areas will be delineated, that the adverse consequences of road construction will be minimized and counteracted, are all stated in the Plan as expressions of faith. But, except for the important conditions precedent to action in regard to extended and improved land acquisition and compensation powers, these expressions of faith are not stated in the Plan in a sufficiently clear and practical form to give any confidence that they can or will be carried into effect...[86]

The Panel asserted that the GLDP suffered from over-ambition; from inconsistency of treatment of substance; from a failure to relate information to policies; from a failure to relate policies to aims; and from a failure to present aims in meaningful terms.[87]

It was suggested in the Panel's report that a modified transport policy needed to be put forward which would adopt a more comprehensive approach to London's problems. One of the principal aims expressed by the Panel was to stress the interdependence of the various elements which collectively constituted a movement strategy for London. As the Layfield Report suggested,

> Any effective transport strategy should contain policies for handling a number of essential and interdependent elements. These elements include public transport, highway networks, restraint and management, environmental improvement and both short and long term changes in the nature and location of the generators and attractors of traffic.[88]

As a result of the attempt to harmonize these factors the Panel became convinced during its process of evaluation that three orbital roads (plus the Outer Orbital which was to be constructed by the

[86] Layfield, Vol. I (1973), p. 278.
[87] Layfield, Vol. I (1973), pp. 24–27.
[88] Layfield, Vol. I (1973), p. 281.

Widening the Movement Planning Process 171

DOE outside the GLC's boundaries) would be far in excess of what would be required for essential vehicular movement in the Capital.

As the GLC had noted earlier, research studies alone could not determine what a correct level of road investment should be. The maintenance of the highway plan, the Council contended when the GLDP was published, was as dependent on local feedback as on strategic studies.[89] The feedback which the Council received from both community groups and the Panel of Inquiry indicated that the road plan would have to be significantly reduced in size. The Panel and protestors such as LATA and LMAG were also agreed on the need to: (a) give top priority to public transport; (b) introduce additional traffic restraint measures; (c) reconsider the roads which were collectively designated as the Secondary Road Network; and (d) scrap at least one of the orbital roads proposed within the GLC's boundaries. The Panel and the protestors differed sharply over which roads *would* be constructed, however. While the community groups in general favoured the building of Ringway Three through outer London the Inquiry Panel, although broadly in agreement, placed primary stress on building in addition, a dual three-lane Inner London Motorway with new radials brought in and terminated along its length.

In effect this meant that the Layfield Panel was recommending the construction of the ring—Ringway One, formerly the Motorway Box, formerly Abercrombie's "B" Ring—which had consistently aroused the greatest controversy.[90] The decision to proceed with the inner area road building was made on the oft-repeated technical grounds that Ringway One would: (a) relieve traffic in Central and Inner London, (b) link the inter- and intraurban motorway systems; (c) and help to assist in the redevelopment in areas of poor housing. By the conclusion of the Inquiry in mid-1972, however, the retreat from the full ringway plan had begun in earnest in *political* as well as in technical terms.

Partly because of the stimulation caused by the Inquiry itself the

---

[89] GLC, *Movement* (1969), p. 14. On "scientific" highway planning see Altshuler (1965), p. 79.

[90] See Layfield (1973), p. 445. Critics were furious, see, for example, LATA and LMAG, "Layfield and the Ringways, typescript, March 1973.

172 Strategic Planning in London

Ringways had at last become a party political issue. The Layfield Panel remarked that part of the problem with the GLDP was that

> ...the GLC, when faced with a variety of solutions to a problem, chose one on political grounds and then presented it as inevitable. We think it right that political considerations should form part of the planning process and that, when an authority decides on a plan, it should do it in accordance with political principles. What we do not accept, however, is that the choice should be presented as inevitable.[91]

At the same time that the Panel was collecting evidence several members of the Labour party—the party which had initially put forward the motorway proposals—became increasingly concerned with the city-wide implications of the road plans. The Deputy Leader of the Labour opposition on the GLC, Evelyn Denington, wrote in 1970, for example, that Londoners had already begun to reject the only firm part of the GLDP—the Primary Road Network proposals.[92] As it became evident that the full ring and radial network for the Capital was not necessarily inevitable and that there were several different ways in which London might approach its movement problems opposition in both the community and the Labour party mounted. By June 1972 the situation had drastically altered and the Leader of the Labour opposition, Sir Reg Goodwin, stated:

> Labour pledges itself to abandon the disastrous plans to build two motorways which threaten the environment of Central London.... We call on the GLC not to enter into any contracts which would authorize the commencement of work on any further motorway construction...before the GLC Elections in April next year so that Londoners as a whole can give their verdict on this urban madness.[93]

Labour argued that if elected it would scrap Ringways One and Two even if they were accepted by the Department of the Environment.[94]

In September 1972, after the completion of the Inquiry, matters had reached a point that the Conservative party which controlled the

---

[91] Layfield (1973), p. 26.
[92] Evelyn Denington, "London under pressure", *Town and Country Planning*, Vol. 38, No. 2, February 1970, p. 101.
[93] Quoted in *A Socialist Strategy for London—Labour Party Manifesto*, London: the Castle Press, 1973, p. 10. Italics added.
[94] See also on this subject Jenkins (1973), p. 267.

Widening the Movement Planning Process 173

GLC began a strategic withdrawal from the road proposals which they had so long defended. Although not as dramatic as Labour's retreat from the Ringways it was nevertheless clear that the Tories had also decided to significantly reduce the scale of road building in the Capital. The Conservative compromise was broadly that the most controversial and destructive components of the Ringway plans should be dropped and the remaining elements joined together to form a single inner ring. The North Cross route of Ringway One and the proposed new South Circular were both to be indefinitely postponed. The new ring was to be formed instead by linking the northern half of Ringway Two (the improved North Circular) with the southern half of Ringway One (the East, West and South Cross routes). It was held by a Conservative party spokesman that this would mean that a complete motorway ring could be finished, "within 12 years instead of perhaps 30 years".[95]

All of these changes underlined the fact that the motorway pattern was not as immutable as it had initially appeared. As the Layfield Panel, the most active opposition groups, the Labour party and the Conservative party, all demonstrated a number of alternative road plans could be conceived of and related to other movement elements to form a differing "bundle" of interrelated policies.[96] More fundamentally the multiplicity of local groups at work in the Capital indicated once again that major planning problems are never simply technical in character but that they always involve political considerations and that these considerations are sharpest when the local community is specifically threatened by public action.[97]

The road plans also revealed that in even the very largest of cities that there are *levels of rationality* and that the local community with

---

[95] Quoted by David Wilcox, "GLC Tories shelve half of those highly-controversial road plans", *Evening Standard*, 5 September 1972. For an earlier hint about the movement away from Ringway One by the Tories, see GLC Press Release, "New London road a step nearer", No. 371, 20 August 1971.

[96] See on a criticism of the GLDP for failing to put forward realistic alternatives, Thomson (*et al.*) (1969), pp. 4–5; and Peter Hall, "The future of London", in Hillman (Ed.) (1971), p. 149.

[97] See Altshuler (1965), pp. 4–5; and see also Sean Damer and Cliff Hague, "Public participation in planning a review", *Town Planning Review*, vol. 42, No. 3, July 1971, p. 227.

its own logic still remained "an important agency of social control".[98] The decision-making process surrounding the Primary Road Network proposals indicated, as Webber has remarked, that

> ...public decisions are becoming more varied, the publics themselves are becoming more diversified, the numbers of decision centres are increasing, the networks of influence among publics and decisions are becoming more intricately woven....[99]

Although one supporter of the GLC proposals was prepared to acknowledge that there were a number of communities of interest in London he advised planners not simply to take cognizance of "...the noisiest of them all, the conservationist, the anti-motor car brigade...".[100] This advice proved to be politically unacceptable, however.

In February 1973 two significant events occurred. After a discussion by the Cabinet it was decided that the Layfield proposal to build an inner London motorway based on the alignment of Ringway One and Abercrombie's "B" Ring would be accepted in principle. At the same time, however, events were moving in a very different direction in London. During the GLC elections Labour continued to assert its opposition to an inner ring and emphasize instead improving the quality of public transport and restraining automobile demand. The road proposals proved to be one of the major issues of the campaign and at last served as one of the ways in which the major political parties could be distinguished from one another in terms of their approach to urban movement and planning.[101]

In April 1973 after several years in opposition Labour regained control of the Greater London Council. Although it is notoriously difficult to explain the real *meaning* of local elections it is also true that the impact of the election was felt almost immediately.[102] The

[98] Martin Meyerson and Edward C. Banfield, *Politics, Planning and the Public Interest*, Glencoe, Ill: The Free Press, 1955, p. 297.

[99] Melvin M. Webber, "The roles of intelligence systems in urban systems planning", *Journal of the American Institute of Planners*, Vol. XXXI, No. 4, November 1965, p. 291.

[100] David Eversley, "What is London's future," *New Society*, Vol. 22, No. 522, 5 October 1972, p. 19.

[101] On this see *A Socialist Strategy* (1973), pp. 9–12.

[102] See, on the difficulty of interpreting the relationship between the vote and policy issues, Charles E. Lindblom, *The Policy Making Process*, Englewood Cliffs, N. J.: Prentice-Hall, Inc., 1968, p. 46.

new leader of the GLC, Sir Reg Goodwin, proved to be as good as his word. As his first official act he directed the Planning and Transportation Department to officially abandon the planning and construction of the two innermost motorway rings and the associated inner radials. The safeguarded land for the motorways which had been held by the Council—in some cases for years—was freed of restrictions and released for other purposes. Exactly 30 years after the publication of Abercrombie's *County of London Plan* (1943) and 10 years after the publication of Buchanan's *Traffic in Towns* (1963) the concept of urban order which both documents supported and in a sense which the Primary Road Network symbolized was effectively abandoned.

It would now perhaps be worth while to stop and attempt to devise an analytical model which might help to reduce the complexity of events and aid in the understanding of the way in which policy has been made and modified in the Capital during what became, in effect, a new Thirty Years War (1943–1973) over strategic planning and movement in the Capital.

CHAPTER 6

Ordering Change and Changing Orders: an Analysis of the Planning Process in Greater London

> ...it should be recognised that were the planning process not involved in politics, it would be irrelevant. It was no means of achieving its goals outside the political arena. Francine Rabinovitz, *City Politics and Planning*, New York: Atherton Press, 1969, p. 155.
>
> The historian tracing the development of London will highlight certain major policy statements such as the 1944 Abercrombie Plan or the current Greater London Development Plan. In practice, the city is undergoing a continual metamorphosis because of pressures which are outside...the jurisdiction of the planners.... However brilliant the plan initially, priorities change and modifications are required.—K. A. J. Crawford, "The 1971 Greater London Transportation Survey", *Quarterly Bulletin of the Intelligence Unit*, GLC, September 1971, No. 16, p. 15.

CHANGING ORDERS IN THE CAPITAL

Urban planning is concerned with controlling various aspects of the city's development. More properly it is a continuing public experiment which seeks to beneficially link purposeful action with changing circumstances. Since plans both reflect and reform their environment it is instructive to consider the way in which the relative emphasis accorded to each of these components had altered during the past 30 years.

Three different aspects of the planning process in Greater London will be examined in this chapter. First the *control measures* which are employed in translating intent into effect will be considered. Secondly, it will be argued that it is possible to identify *three interlocking policy modes* which have played a significant role in

Ordering Change and Changing Orders 177

shaping the post-war planning process in London. Finally some *lessons* will be drawn from the experience of the Primary Road Network and related to the suggestion raised in the first chapter that planning is an iterative process.

Two general points can perhaps be made initially with regard to the post-war planning process in the Capital. In the first place planning forms an important part of an on-going learning process which is concerned with identifying the nature and limits of public control powers in a long-established city such as London. In many ways this process has been an exercise in humility, and there has been a significant shift in the *type* of control measures which are being employed. Secondly, the strategic road system proposals for London can be viewed both as an attempt to create a large-scale physical artefact and as an illustration of the way in which the fundamental concept of urban order, in policy terms has altered since World War Two. The road proposals are thus of interest both substantively and symbolically and it would perhaps be useful to establish an analytical framework and examine the way in which planning policy for London has changed over the past 30 years. It would then be possible to go on to consider what has been learned during the period 1943 to 1973.

Returning to the first aspect of the planning process, planning has recently exhibited more humility because hard-won experience has demonstrated how limited the planners' concrete powers of control can be. This limitation is particularly evident when town planning has been interpreted as being *physical* planning and physical measures of control have been proposed to correct perceived problems. The efficacy of traditional or "hard" planning has been called into question in two different ways. Firstly, because of the pressure exerted by financial, environmental and order of priority constraints. Secondly, because of the way in which the initially perceived problem is redefined as attempts are made to resolve it.[1]

According to the initial diagnosis of the traffic problem, for example, the Primary Road Network was the essential condition for controlling London's traffic. Partly because of the constraints

---
[1] See on successive problem redefinition, Chapter 1, p. 18.

mentioned above and partly because of the way in which the problem has subsequently been reinterpreted a significant shift in emphasis in terms of planning tactics has recently taken place. Although the hard planning, physical construction, approach has by no means been abandoned it has been significantly reduced in scale and prominence. The more recent alternative approach to traffic congestion suggests that the problem is that there are *too many* private automobiles in use particularly in congested commercial centres, rather than that there is not enough road space available as traditional planning suggested. Instead of emphasizing construction, a more subtle "soft" planning approach has been adopted which is concerned, very briefly, with promoting public transport by means of operating subsidies, by increasing parking control measures, and ultimately by restraining private traffic in particularly congested areas by supplementary licensing or road pricing.[2]

Although it would be incorrect to assert that a coherent set of soft planning measures in the movement field have been worked out, a number of ideas based on this type of approach, such as bus lanes, are currently in operation and a number of others, such as the banning of private automobiles from Central London, are receiving careful consideration.[3] Most of these controls turn on economic and legal *restriction* rather than on *construction.*

Soft planning can be contrasted with the hard planning approach which was, for so long, held by a number of motoring organizations including the British Road Federation. Several years ago the BRF in a classical example of the physical construction point of view argued that the road policy which should be pursued by the relevant public authorities was

> ...the improvement of roads rather than the restriction of motorists. Its essence is segregation of traffic. Modernize all trunk roads.... Build in addition a number of special motor-roads on the analogy of railway tracks, for through traffic

[2] For an example of early thinking regarding traffic restraint see Alasdair C. Sutherland, "Land use and local traffic in the Central Area", *Planning Outlook*, Vol. IV, No. 4, 1958, p. 49. On road pricing see Ministry of Transport, *Road Pricing: the Economic and Technical Possibilities*, London: HMSO, 1964.

[3] See for a number of soft planning suggestions, House of Commons, Second Report from the Expenditure Committee, *Urban Transport Planning*, Vol. I, London: HMSO, December 1972, pp. xii–xv.

only.... Eliminate the ordinary cross-road, substitute fly-over bridges, subways, and feeder roads entering on the clover leaf principle, so that no entering traffic need cross the main stream.[4]

As the previous chapter demonstrated, however, the political tide has now turned and is running strongly against this type of full-scale, architectonic approach. In spite of a good deal of effort and the expenditure of several million pounds on strategic road planning in the Capital during the 1960s, as late as 1972 London still had only 5.9 miles of urban motorways in actual use.[5]

Part of the reason for this lack of construction and one of the reasons why traffic restriction is currently receiving more attention than large-scale road building is nicely illustrated by Thomson's description of a regularly recurring "pattern of progress". According to Thomson, this pattern consists of

(a) growing complaints about traffic congestion; (b) production of an ambitious plan; (c) modification of the plan to meet objections on grounds of cost and amenity; (d) implementation of the modified plan, subject to delays and further modifications due to financial constraints and new priorities arising from developments unforeseen at the planning stage.[6]

One of the things which clearly emerged from the controversy surrounding the Primary Road Network was that the GLC had over-estimated its own powers of control with regard to the London Boroughs and the public and had under-estimated the strength of non-party political opposition which both sectors were able to marshal. This increasing fragmentation of power and politicization of the planning process, however, meant that the GLC was placed in an untenable position regarding its ability to actually achieve its concrete objectives, given powerful and largely independent second-tier authorities and a substantial body of grass-roots opinion

[4] British Road Federation, "Times change, why not the roads?", London: BRF, 1938, unpaginated. See for a more recent condemnation of traffic restraint, W. H. Glanville and J. F. A. Baker, "Urban motorways in Great Britain", in British Road Federation (Ed.), *Urban Motorways*, London: BRF, 1956, p. 23; and P. F. Stott, "Structure and management", *Traffic Engineering and Control*, Vol. 9, No. 1, May 1967, p. 36.
[5] See Cornelius Murphy, "New deal for motorway victims", *Official Architecture and Planning*, Vol. 35, No. 2, February 1972, p. 81.
[6] J. Michael Thomson, *Motorways in London*, London: Gerald Duckworth, 1969, p. 98.

actively opposed to the perceived impact of the road proposals.[7]

The shift in emphasis from hard to soft planning which has increasingly occurred in Greater London can thus partly be explained on organizational and political (but not *necessarily party political*) grounds. The shift has not been easily achieved or universally welcomed. In many ways soft planning is the product of a lengthy war of attrition. After the 1973 GLC elections the defeated leader of the Conservative party, Sir Desmond Plummer, long one of the staunchest supporters of the Primary Road Network, sadly remarked, "We seem to have lost our will to achieve anything positive in London any more".[8] It is possible to contend, however, that although less direct in impact than hard planning, soft planning measures which are currently being developed could potentially possess a number of advantages. They could, for example, prove to be: (i) relatively less expensive than construction; (ii) less destructive to existing property and amenities; and (iii) less difficult to alter in the light of changing political priorities and community needs.

Another explanation of the retreat from creating a full-scale ring and radial system and taking a softer approach to controlling movement is simply that soft planning makes a virtue of a necessity.[9] Recasting London on the scale of building the complete strategic road system would be extremely costly and, as events have shown, politically unacceptable. Even more fundamentally, however, as examination of the Primary Road Network proposals proceeded it became evident that not only was this attempt to architectonically order movement in the Capital suspect on a number of purely practical grounds but that the underlying concept of urban form initially set out by Abercrombie and Buchanan needed to be carefully reconsidered to determine its continued overall relevance to Greater London in the 1970s.

This alteration in the type of control mechanisms employed by the GLC reflected not merely that the planners' direct, physical powers

[7] On the GLC's impossible position see David Eversley, "What is London's future?", *New Society*, Vol. 22, No. 522, 5 October 1972, p. 18.

[8] Quoted by Simon Jenkins, "The politics of London motorways", the *Political Quarterly*, Vol. 44, No. 3, July–September 1973, p. 270.

[9] The relationship between soft and hard planning in this sphere will be considered at the conclusion of this chapter.

of control were limited with regard to roads but that the coherent, convenient and compact city which planning had long attempted to create was probably unattainable purely in structural terms. Both the *type* of urban order sought and the *kind* of control measures available to achieve it have thus both been called into question during the past three decades.

Returning to the second point, the strategic road proposals are of interest both substantively and symbolically because of the way in which they illustrate how planning policy in the Capital has altered.[10] The motorway proposals were an attempt to beneficially order change based on a relatively well-worked-out concept of what form the Capital should assume. More generally it could be argued that, although one of the central purposes of planning is to order change *in Greater London at any rate the planning process has been compelled by circumstances to be as concerned with continuously incorporating changing concepts of order as it is with simply ordering change.* As Chapter 1 attempted to indicate the underlying concept of urban order is neither monolithic nor static.

One important aspect of the planning process—the traditional Master Plan—has often appeared to be both, however. As Herbert Gans has remarked, "The planners' certainty about how people ought to live resulted in a nearly static plan, a Platonic vision of the city as an orderly and unfinished work of art".[11] The plan as a "cartoon of utopia"[12] was less than wholly satisfactory, as the Greater London strategic road planning experience illustrates, because: (a) the form of utopia alters over time as objectives change; and (b) as noted earlier the actual ability of the planners to physically construct utopia—even if the vision had remained substantially unaltered—was severely circumscribed by a number of practical considerations.

---

[10] The remainder of this chapter is based on an expanded version of a previously published paper, D. A. Hart, "Ordering change and changing orders: an analysis of urban policy development", *Policy and Politics*, Vol. 2, No. 1, September 1973.

[11] Herbert Gans, "Regional and urban planning", David L. Shills (Ed.), *International Encyclopedia of the Social Sciences*, Vol. XII, New York: The Macmillan Co., and the Free Press, 1968, p. 130.

[12] Lowdon Wingo, "Urban space in a policy perspective", Lowdon Wingo (Ed.), *Cities and Space*, Baltimore: The John Hopkins Press, 1963, p. 4.

In spite of the fact that planning must fuse *both* the initiation of, and the response to, urban change traditional plans, composed of a cluster of implicit values, a set of underlying assumptions and a complex of intuitive beliefs, all woven together to provide guidance as to how and why public intervention should be undertaken has all too often exhibited a rigidity bordering on crystallization.[13] But as the city, and in some ways more importantly, expectations regarding the desirability of objectives, have changed over time, values have altered, associated assumptions have been questioned and their supporting beliefs challenged. It is thus useful to view planning as a continuous means of understanding and reinterpreting the confusion and complexity of London rather than solely as a blueprint for reform.[14] It is now possible to return to the question raised in Chapter 1 and to consider not merely *whether* planning is a process but in what *sense* it is a process and how the process has altered since World War Two in the attempt to comprehend and influence constant change.

It will be suggested in this analysis that it is possible to identify at least three different general ways of ordering Greater London and that each of these approaches has played an important part in guiding the process of planning in the Capital. An attempt will be made to briefly examine each of these interlocking policy "modes" in terms of their internal construction and to consider the way in which they interrelate to form the spatial, functional and temporal basis of the planning strand of the policy-making process.

COHESIVE POLICY: EXPLANATION AND ANALYSIS

The first policy mode to be examined, the Cohesive, has traditionally been employed in orthodox planning circles as the accepted answer to the question: how is planning policy produced? Typically

[13] The remark made by Peter Hall that "The terrible responsibility of the planner is that...he creates monuments that survive", could apply to certain types of plan with as much force as it does to large-scale physical artefacts. Peter Hall, "Transportation", in Peter Self (Ed.), *London Under Stress*, Welwyn Garden City: The Broadwater Press, for the Town and Country Planning Association, 1970, p. 59.

[14] See on blueprint planning Andreas Faludi, *Planning Theory*, Oxford: Pergamon Press, 1973.

the explanation in a condensed form runs roughly as follows: policy is *formulated* on the basis of intelligible and explicable objectives on the part of the planners which are formally cohesive, administratively integrated and nominally at least, rationally determined. This type of centralized rationality at the urban level is both one of the characteristic features of the planning process and one of its principle legitimations.[15] As a fairly common example of this kind of thinking it is maintained that "The planner's task is to allocate resources rationally, to achieve his aims according to a proper scheme of priorities".[16] More specifically, policy-making as a product of rational analysis[17] operates in the following manner in its most developed form: (i) a clearly recognized problem exists; (ii) the objectives of the policy-makers are known and it is possible to roughly determine whether they are being achieved; (iii) an "envelope" defining the action space available is both known and well defined with regard to possible alternatives; (iv) there is also an outcome envelope containing the consequences of available options; and (v) the policy-makers have a preference function with regard to the outcome envelope which allows them to select and rank alternatives in terms of order of priority.[18]

In fact on closer examination imagination and intuition often play a larger role than rational analysis as it is described above. Rather than systematically considering alternatives many plans are based on a single concept, or in Sir Geoffrey Vicker's phrase, "appreciation", of the city. Applied imagination therefore is an extremely important, if often little mentioned, method underlying plan making and policy formulation. Certainly it could be held that something of

---

[15] This type of logical goal pursuit is often contrasted with random change and public choice is therefore emphasized. Friend and Jessop, for example, have *defined* planning as "the process of strategic choice". J. K. Friend and W. N. Jessop, *Local Government and Strategic Choice*, London: Tavistock Publications, 1969, p. 97.

[16] GLC, *Tomorrow's London*, London: GLC, 1969, p. 42.

[17] See on this mode of explanation generally, with particular reference to foreign policy, Graham T. Allison, *Essence of Decision*, Boston: Little, Brown & Co., 1971, pp. 29–35.

[18] On this see David E. Boyce, Chris McDonald, and Andre Farhi, "An interim report on procedures for continuing metropolitan planning", Phildadelphia: typescript, University of Pennsylvania, 1972, p. 7.

the kind can be found in Abercrombie's thinking regarding the form the capital should assume.

As a means of conceptually illustrating this method of approach in London it is possible, as Chapter 3 indicated, to conceive of the city almost as a physical, living organism—or organic complex—occupying a clearly definable amount of geographical space.[19] This type of implicit intuitive order apparently played a major part in guiding the way in which problems were framed and resolution attempts drawn up. According to this model, for example, after a global survey of the city and its problems it then became possible to plan, as the *County of London Plan (1943)* and the *Greater London Plan 1944* did, for the resolution or reduction of those difficulties which had prevented the city from developing in an orderly manner and achieving a full and balanced maturity. The planners' task then became, working within the initially determined *spatial constraint* bounding the urban area, of *designing* a set of measures which would allow the city to continue its almost teleological development by correcting those obstacles in its path—usually of a physical nature—through physical means. As a result of detailed understanding of the city as a whole a number of literally concrete proposals were made as part of a continuing construction programme to allow it to reach a condition approaching a stable state.[20]

One particular aspect of this hard planning approach, the strategic road network proposed by Abercrombie and later reinforced by Buchanan was designed to play a fundamental role in helping to create the type of cohesive and contained city mentioned above. This suggested "circulation system" for the City Organic[21] meant, it was hoped, not only that mobility would be facilitated but that various areas could be physically delineated and the local environment simultaneously insulated. The synergistic effect of the triple-tiered road hierarchy on the city as a whole was thus to be,

[19] On this topic generally see Gilbert Herbert, "The organic analogy in town planning", *Journal of the American Institute of Planners*, Vol. XXIX, No. 3, August 1963, pp. 198–209.

[20] On the concept of a stable state see Donald A. Schon, *Beyond the Stable State*, London: Temple Smith, 1971.

[21] See for a view on this topic by one of Abercrombie's contemporaries, C. B. Purdom, *How Should We Rebuild London?*, London: J. M. Dent & Sons, 1945, p. 168.

according to the original Abercrombie–Buchanan approach, far more than equal to the sum of its individual parts.[22] Furthermore, *only through the agency of the road proposals, it was contended, could this classical order for London be achieved.*

The various planning components were therefore—like the city itself—carefully related to one another to form a complementary set of planning ideas that were inter-locking and mutually reinforcing. The holistical concern with relating various parts to the whole evidenced in this particular approach was further strengthened by two factors. In the first place it was assumed that the planning process rested on a broad-based *political consensus* regarding ultimate objectives. Both of the major parties, it was suggested, were agreed on the need for planning—although admittedly often for quite different reasons—and their active, long-term support had allowed many large-scale projects, such as the Green Belt, to be implemented. Political consensus of this type meant that the nature of what constitutes the public interest[23] was widely accepted and the planner was freed to play a strictly technical role in achieving the agreed upon goals growing out of this acceptance.[24]

Secondly, the planner as a technician was aided in his task by a high level of administrative co-ordination which gave *coherence* to the process of implementing the plan. The major problem after the formulation of the plan, it was felt, was of ensuring that it was properly executed and a powerful legal control system was created under the terms of the Town and Country Planning Act of 1947[25] so that deviations and alterations to the approved plan were either limited in scope or were only raised at uniform intervals when the plan was officially reviewed. As a proposal for change, however, the plan was essentially complete in itself from the moment of its

[22] On this approach see, once again, Chapter 3, pp. 99–101.

[23] See on the relationship between planning and the public interest, Martin Meyerson and E. C. Banfield, *Politics, Planning and the Public Interest*, Glencoe, Ill.: The Free Press, 1955, pp. 322–329.

[24] See also for a complementary analysis of the work of the LCC, with particular reference to the partnership between senior elected members and professional planners, Stephen J. Elkin, *Politics and Land Use Planning*, London: Cambridge University Press, 1974, p. 122–128.

[25] See the comments of Colin Buchanan, *The State of Britain*, London: Faber & Faber, 1972, p. 23.

186 Strategic Planning in London

acceptance. The original Abercrombie Plans for London, once again, provide excellent examples of how this general approach to a cohesive urban order could be formulated and attractively presented.

It is possible to identify a number of explanatory levels within the Cohesive Mode based on the previous summary and the related examples. Broadly these levels are concerned with three related sets of factors: the technical, the organizational and the political. Briefly this particular mode is illustrated in Table 6.1. As this figure indicates, this particular policy mode displays some degree of internal consistency and in many ways is intellectually appealing but the picture which it conveys regarding the nature of the policy-making *process* is a false one. As an explanation of how the planning process actually works the Cohesive Mode is at best incomplete and worst positively misleading—not least of all for the planners involved—regarding the way in which considered intent is translated into actual effect.

TABLE 6.1. THE COHESIVE POLICY MODE

Explanatory level	Cohesive policy characteristics
Planning process stage	Formulation
Method of operation	Applied imagination
Underlying concept of the city	Organic
Prescriptive requirement	Design
Component relationship	Complementary
Primary initial constraint stress	Spatial
Political climate	Consensus
Administrative co-ordination	Coherent
Goal relationships	Integrated
Proposal finality	Complete
Example	Abercrombie plans

FACTORED POLICY: EXPLANATION AND ANALYSIS

Policy cannot be easily separated from the administrative agency which created it and which is designed to give it effect. As John Friedmann has suggested, "the kind of implementing mechanism adopted will itself influence the character of the plan and the way in which it is formulated".[26] As Chapter 2 demonstrated this statement could apply with particular force to the way in which the Greater London Council was initially structured to deal with traffic problems, for example. Policy from this perspective is less the result of applied imagination and more the product of *organizational output*.[27] Using the same set of explanatory levels employed in examining the Cohesive Mode it is possible to construct a completely different policy profile—the Factored Mode—as a means of explaining the nature and operation of the policy-making process. According to this view of urban order and the means of achieving it something more is involved in policy making than merely carefully selecting among alternative means to achieve a given end. Policy, it can be argued from this perspective, must be considered within a broader and more realistic context and that context has a substantial bureaucratic component. The Factored Mode very briefly holds that the central point of the planning process is the *articulation* of policy at two different levels. In the first place the policy decided upon is simply made known to a wider audience outside of the originating agency. The formulation by informed and imaginative technicians working, initially at any rate, within the bounds of political consensus is made manifest through an indication of intent to public organizations and through press releases and local meetings to inform community groups and the public generally. In short, the plan goes public.[28] At a more subtle level, however, articulation in this context has quite a different meaning.

Policy is also articulated in organizational terms in a more important but less visible sense in that: (i) the organization undertaking planning is not a monolith but a constellation of departments and agencies; (ii) a problem is broken down in some manner and "allocated" to two or more departments or agencies on the basis of technical capabilities and spheres of influence; (iii) problem compo-

---

[26] John Friedmann, "A conceptual model for the analysis of planning behaviour", *Administrative Science Quarterly*, Vol. 12, No. 2, September 1967, p. 240.
[27] On this idea applied to the study of international relations see Allison (1970), pp. 78–96.
[28] On this see Committee on Public Participation in Planning, *People and Planning* (Skeffington Report), London: HMSO, 1969.

nents then assume a sub-optimal character in the sense that they are redefined by the various administrative units dealing with them as "the problem" on the basis of their own criteria for determining acceptable performance, their own professional perspectives and their own operating procedures, etc.; (iv) problem components broken down in this manner are seen by the operating departments and agencies involved as having primacy over other planning goals and their particular resolution is often equated with solving the problem in its entirety. This disaggregation of the problem means that the planning process may have rational elements but it is not wholly or even mainly rational, at least according to the rigorous, almost deductive view of urban order exemplified by the Cohesive Mode.

As Chapter 4 indicated factored policy often rests on a quite different underlying organizing concept with regard to the nature of the city. From this perspective there is less concern with the urban area in its entirety and more with those specific goods and services provided by the public authorities within its boundaries. The primary initial constraint is therefore *functional* rather than spatial and the local authority is often broken down into departments according to the specific service which they provide including transportation and housing, for example. Transportation matters in London are particularly difficult since it could be argued that the proposed Abercrombie–Buchanan triple-tiered road hierarchy was roughly paralleled by a triple-tiered organizational hierarchy consisting of the MOT, the GLC, and the London Boroughs. Interdepartmental and interauthority relations thus become matters of central concern. The "compartmentalization" of concerns evident in this description was also reflected in a rather more instrumental and more mechanistic view of the city itself.

As a conceptual illustrative device, the City Mechanistic, unlike the previous City Organic, could be conceived of as being wholly man-made and therefore wholly artificial.[29] It has no inbuilt purpose or pattern for "natural growth" and if substantial components of the

---

[29] On artificiality see Herbert A. Simon, *The Sciences of the Artificial*, Cambridge, Mass.: The MIT Press, 1969, pp. 4–5.

mechanism are performing inefficiently—such as the road system, for example—it is essential that they should be either modified or replaced to accord with changing purposes.[30] As the original Abercrombie–Buchanan proposals were developed by the MOT and the GLC during the 1960s the Primary Road Network was vigorously pushed ahead by these organizations and it became increasingly divorced from its context. The GLC–MOT road pattern bore a superficial resemblance to the Abercrombie–Buchanan strategy for movement but it almost completely lacked any real means of safeguarding the local environment which both planners had felt to be a fundamental matter of concern.

At a more general level the Factored Mode suggests that the city is neither mysterious nor sacrosanct—it is merely an extremely complex instrument for satisfying wants. Instrumental topics such as reducing traffic congestion, for example, are identified and pursued in a strategically broad but functionally narrow manner. Once isolated one of the planners' chief considerations becomes how best to provide for these identified objectives by *predicting* on the basis of expensive, long-term, large-scale surveys such as the London Traffic Survey, and its successor, the London Transportation Study, how traffic ownership and usage will grow. Given these predictions the highway planners task then becomes often—subject to resources constraints—how to meet the projected demand.

The various operating components of the planning process are once again like the functional subdivisions of the city itself, *contiguous* rather than complementary. Some measure of co-ordination at the administrative level is usually secured between public and private transport, for example, but the large and powerful operating departments or agencies involved often act in an almost semiautonomous fashion. As implementation proceeds the Master Planning concept and the importance of part-whole, strategic-local relationships are increasingly—perhaps inevitably—relegated to the background as one particular topic, such as road building, is energetically pursued almost as if it had acquired the status of

---

[30] On a condemnation of the inherited street system in this vein see GLC, *GLDP—Statement*, London: GLC, 1969, pp. 22–23; and GLC, *GLDP—Report of Studies*, London: GLC, 1969, p. 143.

becoming an end in itself.[31] In this type of fragmented situation although the administrative units may not be in open competition for the limited funds available there are important and evident differences of opinion regarding the timing and order of priority of projects.

As these differences became more pronounced although there may be nominal political agreement regarding the long-term objectives of planning, shorter term measures can become political issues. If these issues are sufficiently persistent or important they may develop over time into party political disputes with regard to either the substantive value of a proposed project or its phasing and relationships with other planning projects. Consensus may thus give way to a political climate in which the balance of power *alternates* between the major parties and the question of who benefits from particular proposals slowly gains in significance.[32]

According to this Mode the solutions which are put forward in response to present and project difficulties and which are accepted by one or both of the political parties are *continuously extruded* in quantitative and technical terms. Suggestions become increasingly specific and resource expenditure considerations more detailed as they progress from the planning authority to the various operating agencies involved. Ultimately, it is hoped, the proposals will be put into effect—backed by a high degree of organizational commitment.[33] It is the administrative proposals rather than the city in its entirety which develops according to this view. Once again a good example of this type of approach is the GLC–MOT backed Primary Road Network as set out in the *Greater London Development Plan (1969)*. The policy-making process from this perspective consists of steadily refining concepts and techniques and applying them in the

---

[31] See Gerald Rhodes, "Highways, traffic and transport", in Gerald Rhodes (Ed.), *The New Government of London: The First Five Year*, London: Weidenfeld & Nicolson, 1972, pp. 293–294.

[32] See on the question of who benefits in organizational terms, Peter M. Blau and W. Richard Scott, *Formal Organizations*, London: Routledge & Kegan Paul, 1963, pp. 42–44.

[33] On commitment see P. H. Levin, "On decisions and decision making", *Public Administration*, Spring 1972, pp. 19–44.

attempt to increase the efficiency of the physical city in operating terms.

The Factored Mode, as Table 6.2 indicates in broad outline, reveals a very different view of both London and the planning process in the capital than that sketched earlier with regard to the Cohesive Mode. The Factored approach, as Chapter 4 demonstrated, stresses a fundamental concern with the way in which London works, and how its "performance" may be improved in structural terms. It also reveals the crucial importance of the relationship between organizations as the initial cohesive plan inevitably fragments over time. The participation of *public organizations* in the planning process therefore becomes a matter of some concern as attempts are made to implement policy proposals.[34] The matter does not end here, however, and it is possible to identify a third general policy mode which serves as a further means of explaining the way in which the city is ordered.

TABLE 6.2. THE FACTORED POLICY MODE

Explanatory level	Factored policy characteristics
Planning process stage	Articulation
Method of operation	Organizational output
Underlying concept of the city	Mechanistic
Prescriptive requirement	Prediction
Component relationship	Contiguous
Primary initial constraint stress	Functional
Political climate	Alternating
Administrative co-ordination	Semi-autonomous
Goal relationships	Segmented
Proposal finality	Continuous extrusion
Example	Development plans

---

[34] On some of the problems of inter-agency agreement regarding a major planning project see J. K. Friend, J. M. Power and C. J. L. Yewlitt, *Public Planning: The Inter-Corporate Dimension*, London: Tavistock Publications, 1974, pp. 83–104. See also for an example in Greater London, Michael F. Collins and Timothy Pharoah, *Transport Organization in a Great City*, London: George Allen & Unwin, 1974, pp. 563–567.

DIFFUSED POLICY: EXPLANATION AND ANALYSIS

The final view of the way in which planning policy is made in London—the Diffused Mode—rejects both of the previous concepts of urban order on the grounds that they are partial in character and that they do not take sufficient cognizance of political considerations in the widest sense of the term. The diffused policy approach indicates that decision-making is far less centralized in operation than even the Factored Mode would suggest. Policy, from this stance, is shaped by *political outcome*[35] rather than simply being the result of applied imagination or the consequence of organizational output.

Two central propositions are contained in this Mode as Chapter 5 attempted to indicate. First it is clear that planning is a matter of opinion as well as a matter of fact and opinions are rarely wholly in accord or remain unchanged over time. *Evaluation* of a given policy therefore becomes at least as important as the prediction of future activity patterns even given the most imaginative of designs or the most far-sighted of surveys. Feedback, as the extended controversy which emerged during the Greater London Development Plan Inquiry indicated, becomes as significant as initial formulation and policy must, of necessity, undergo a substantial amount of *modification* as conflict and compromise occur.

This school of thought holds that policy has a sequential and incremental character because of the limited amount of control which traditional "top-down" planning in either spatial or functional terms is actually capable of providing. As Lindblom suggests, a policy maker "who appreciates a next chance, exploits feedback and keeps his eye on ills to be remedied will come to take it for granted that policy making is typically serial, or sequential".[36] Further, this need not be a disadvantage since an order imposed from above, without regard to community concerns—even if it could be achieved through hard planning measures—would be tantamount to stagnation for the city.[37]

[35] See again Allison (1971), pp. 162–180.
[36] Charles Lindblom, *The Policy Making Process*, Englewood Cliffs, New Jersey: Prentice Hall, Inc., 1968, p. 25.
[37] On an early criticism of architectonic planning of this type see J. M. Richards, "London plans", *The Geographical Magazine*, May 1943, pp. 1–13.

Once again the planning process for this Mode is a reflection of a particular view of the nature of the city. As a means of conceptually illustrating this particular view it could hold that Greater London is a sophisticated, higher-order machine concerned with the exchange and processing of information. "Any metropolis", Karl Deutsch has written, "can be thought of as a huge engine of communication, a device to enlarge the range and reduce the cost of individual and social choices."[38] The flows of information and goods thus become the focal point of planning concerns. Competing sub-centres may arise both in terms of building complexes, such as the major strategic centres, and of organizations, such as the London Amenity and Transportation Association, bargaining for power to determine how local areas are to be effected by decisions made by the strategic authorities. The City Organic and the City Mechanistic are thus supplanted by a new model order: the City Cybernetic.[39]

This particular type of policy-making process implies at least some degree of conflict among various organized groups with the planning authority itself acting as a leading contestant. This explicit conflict is based essentially on a *problem-oriented* approach but the nature of the problem is redefined, as Chapter 1 suggested, as various groups and organizations become involved in the process. As Macmurray has suggested, "The process of bringing people together in, say, a local association... is as important as the information they supply; indeed it may change the very social situation which it was set up to discuss."[40] "Political facts" are marshalled to support the resulting opposing points of view.[41] Although it is true that public conflict can lead to the production of more information to buttress positions and can cause the issues and values involved to be

[38] Karl Deutsch, "On social communication and the metropolis", in Larry S. Bourne (Ed.), *Internal Structure of the City*, London: Oxford University Press, 1971, p. 222. For an attempt to increase this type of choice in an emerging New City see Lord Llewelyn-Davies, "Changing goals in design: the Milton Keynes example", *New Towns: The British Experience*, Essays introduced by Peter Self, London: Charles Knight & Co., 1972, p. 105.
[39] See, for example, Richard L. Meier, *A Communications Theory of Urban Growth*, Cambridge, Mass: The MIT Press, 1962.
[40] Trevor Macmurray, "How not to have participation", *Town and Country Planning*, Vol. 39, No. 5, May 1971, p. 264.
[41] John Dewey, *The Public and Its Problems*, Denver, Colo.: Henry Holt & Co., 1927, p. 6.

clarified this clarification is purchased at the expense of slowing the whole of the policy-making process. Attention becomes concentrated on those planning proposals which are particularly contentious and which cannot be contained within the bounds of traditional party political methods of dealing with disputes. Active interest groups emerge at the local, and occasionally, as in the case of LATA and LMAG, at the city-wide level concerned with blocking proposed local government activities or with changing actual policy. The struggle may thus assume an *adversarial* character in political terms[42] and administrative co-ordination becomes as a result more piecemeal and fragmented.

It is important to stress that although opposition to the Primary Road Network was initially based on local political concerns the community groups involved also developed *technical* arguments for challenging the GLC–MOT proposals.[43] Basically these groups held that there was, as Chapter 5 indicated, a fundamental mismatch between: (a) the Abercrombie–Buchanan concept of urban order; (b) the GLC–MOT narrow, hard planning approach for achieving it; and (c) the emerging polycentric city. The cumulative effect of this controversy was that it became increasingly difficult in political or organizational terms to execute any large-scale physical plan for an established city such as London. Previous policy is often therefore continued and is departed from in a marginal way by using softer measures of control.

In a paradoxical way the Diffused Mode is particularly concerned with *temporal* matters. In the first place there is an interest in using the motorways, for example, to reduce travel time. At the same time, however, because planning had become increasingly politicized and pluralistic, lengthy inquiries are required to consider proposals of this type, however, to hear objections and to incorporate modifications.[44] The planning process has thus developed a pronounced and time-consuming iterative character. It is therefore

---

[42] Paul Davidoff, "Advocacy and pluralism in planning", in Andreas Faludi (Ed.), *A Reader in Planning Theory*, Oxford: Pergamon Press, 1973, pp. 277–296.

[43] See, for example, Michael Thomson, "Transportation strategy in London", GLDP Inquiry Proof E12/20, London, typescript, January 1971.

[44] This can be contrasted with planning under the LCC. See, for example, Elkin's study of World's End in Chelsea, Elkin (1974), pp. 27–52.

essential, as Medhurst has suggested, to "think not so much of a plan being an orthographic document, that is a fixed and finite drawing on paper, but more as a continuously operated flexible process in a machine which computes a continuous flow of data".[45]

An example of many aspects of this particular policy mode can be found in the Greater London Development Plan Inquiry in which various components of the Plan—particularly the roles to be played by public and private transport—could be seen as almost competitive in character. Once again using this example and the preceding summary it is possible to illustrate the Diffused Policy Mode by means of the same set of explanatory levels employed earlier with regard to the Cohesive and Factored Modes. Table 6.3 gives a brief outline of the diffused Mode.

TABLE 6.3. THE DIFFUSED POLICY MODE

Explanatory level	Diffused policy characteristics
Planning process stage	Modification
Method of operation	Political outcome
Underlying concept of the city	Cybernetic
Prescriptive requirement	Evaluation
Component relationship	Competitive
Primary initial constraint stress	Temporal
Political climate	Adversarial
Administrative co-ordination	Sequential
Goal relationships	Problem oriented
Proposal finality	Iterative
Example	GLDP inquiry

POLICY MODE INTERACTION

Each of the three previous approaches to the problem of establishing and maintaining an urban order presented in a condensed form on the previous few pages is, of course, simplified. In addition, they are rarely found in the unalloyed forms presented

---

[45] Franklin Medhurst, "The planning context", in Douglas Jones (Ed.), *Communications and Energy in Changing Urban Environments*, London: Butterworths, 1970, p. 27.

here: most plans and the planning process itself are in fact a combination of these approaches. Perhaps it would be useful to view the explanatory levels not as completely compartmentalized by the three modes but as a set of dimensions or continua. Because of this overlapping character it is entirely possible for any given plan, at various points in the planning process, to exhibit characteristics of all three policy modes; the real question is one of relative emphasis.

Another point should be made. These policy modes grow directly out of the analysis of the post-war planning process in Greater London. They are limited in terms of their applicability to a particular set of conditions and they should not be construed as a complete or universal explanation of the way in which urban planning policy is made and modified. Nevertheless, for the purpose of the present study the three modes serve as useful analytical tools and given the qualifications outlined above it may now be possible to draw some conclusions based upon them and the examples presented earlier in the text.

First the plan as a land-use map for the city with its "connotation of irrevocability, infallibility, and inviolateness",[46] simply cannot be sustained. In a sense plans, as suggested earlier, float on the surface of a pool of values, beliefs and assumptions. When all of these factors are closely related to one another it is possible to attempt to employ the Cohesive Mode. When divergence from the original norm begins to occur, however, there is some danger that the plan will be reified by its defenders and treated as if it had a value in and of itself.[47] It has, of course, nothing of the kind. The more sweeping and visionary a plan is, the more dependent it becomes on its political and administrative environment for continuing support. If this support is not forthcoming the plan becomes increasingly irrelevant. As a critic has asserted, planning to create a large-scale physical structure often calls "for a measure of goal consensus, for a quality of prediction, a hierarchy of command and a degree of

[46] Norman Deckman, "The planner as a bureaucrat", *Journal of the American Institute of Planners*, November 1964, p. 327.

[47] On reification see David Silverman, *The Theory of Organizations*, London: Heinemann, 1970, p. 150.

control that do not exist in the normal context of public affairs."[48]

The rejection of this type of traditional Master Planning does not—as some commentators seem to suggest—mean that the *concept* of public planning must be abandoned. It does, however, serve to indicate that extremely detailed, end-state planning for the city as a whole cannot be made to work except under a very specialized and rarely realized set of circumstances. The alternative to the problem of achieving the high level of rationality required by the Cohesive Mode need not, on the other hand, be the extreme form of Diffused Policy perhaps best exemplified by Lindblom's "disjointed incrementalism".[49] Organizations and individuals, as Webber has pointed out, *do* plan and large-scale changes *do* occur.[50] The point is once again that policy cannot be satisfactorily explained as if it were only the result of applied imagination, or the consequence of organizational output, or the product of political outcome. It is an interweaving of all three of these elements because no single agency—however imaginative and well informed—has the power to put its proposals into effect without having them altered—and in some cases completely transformed—by the complex interaction of ideas, of organizations and of political interests which continuously occurs within the Capital. In a very broad and only partially physical way, plans are a function of their environment and they retain their value and predictive power only to the extent that an effective relationship between the two levels is achieved and maintained.

The second point, following from the first, is that because these modes continuingly interact, as Table 6.4 illustrates, they form a policy chain or spiral and it is this type of movement which shapes the planning process. It could be contended that none of these modes *in isolation* provide a satisfactory explanation of what has occurred in terms of strategic road planning in Greater London during the past 30 years. If a *process approach* combining all three

---

[48] Melvin Webber, "The role of intelligence systems in urban systems planning", *The Journal of the American Institute of Planners*, November 1965, p. 291. See also on this Francine F. Rabinovitz, *City Politics and Planning*, New York: Atherton Press, 1969, p. 78.

[49] See, for example, Charles E. Lindblom, *The Intelligence of Democracy*, New York: The Free Press, 1965.

[50] See also for a criticism of disjointed incrementalism, Chapter 1, pp. 21–22.

198 Strategic Planning in London

modes is adopted, however, it allows a more realistic and more comprehensive description of the way in which urban policy is made to be put forward than would be possible either: (a) by merely examining each mode in turn; or (b) by treating the modes collectively as if they were a simple historical progression.

TABLE 6.4. A COMPARISON OF POLICY MODES

Explanatory level	Policy mode characteristics		
	Cohesive	Factored	Diffused
Planning process stage	Formulation	Articulation	Modification
Method of operation	Applied imagination	Organizational output	Political outcome
Underlying concept of the City	Organic	Mechanistic	Cybernetic
Prescriptive requirement	Design	Prediction	Evaluation
Component relationship	Complementary	Contiguous	Competitive
Primary initial constraint stress	Spatial	Functional	Temporal
Political climate	Consensus	Alternating	Adversarial
Administrative co-ordination	Coherent	Semi-autonomous	Sequential
Goal relationships	Integrated	Segmented	Problem-oriented
Proposal finality	Complete	Continuous extrusion	Iterative
Example	Abercrombie plans	Development plans	GLDP inquiry

Once again it is important to mention that the *relative stress* placed on a particular explanatory component plays an important part in this process at any particular point in time. An organization, for example, evaluates progress as well as predicts future courses of events. The real point is the stage in the policy spiral when this occurs and its relative importance in relation to other factors.

The present study has been an attempt to gain an understanding of the way in which a major policy issue close to the heart of the planning process in Greater London—urban movement—has been shaped by combined technical, organizational and political considerations. Through combining these considerations at both the descriptive and explanatory levels it is hoped that it has been possible to move at least a limited way toward a broader and more comprehensive understanding of the policy making process.

A concern with comprehensiveness is a matter of continuing interest in planning circles and it has a legitimate and impressive pedigree stretching back to the founders of the town planning movement. Many modern writers have stressed the need to view the city as a set of interrelated parts forming a complex system.[51] The importance of the relationship among urban elements which this approach stresses, coupled with a growing concern regarding the temporal dimension of planning, has served to indicate that there are at least two different types of comprehensiveness. The more traditional of the two is that of "plan comprehensiveness"[52] in which sub-components of the city are abstracted and related to one another with the assistance of operational research and quantitative modelling techniques. Planners are regularly exhorted to take a wider view and the creation of the Planning and Transportation Department at the GLC and the Department of the Environment at the Central Government level are both organizational manifestations of this type of thinking.[53]

It could be contended, however, on the basis of the experience of the Primary Road Network, that at least as much attention should be devoted to a consideration of "process comprehensiveness"[54] since planning must be concerned with continuing impact as well as with

---

[51] See, for example, J. Brian McLoughlin, *Urban and Regional Planning: A Systems Approach*, London: Faber & Faber, 1969; and George Chadwick, *A Systems View of Planning*, Oxford: Pergamon Press, 1971. It is perhaps worth noting in passing that there are different kinds of system just as there are different types of plan and it would be possible to conceive of the city as an organic, or a mechanistic, or a cybernetic system.

[52] On this see Alan Altshuler, "The goals of comprehensive planning", in Faludi (Ed.) (1973), pp. 193–209; and John Friedmann, "A response to Altshuler", in Faludi (Ed.) (1973), pp. 211–215.

[53] As noted earlier, however, these reforms came too late to have any real effect on the strategic road proposals.

[54] See Roger Montgomery, "Improving the design process in urban renewal", *Journal of the American Institute of Planners*, Vol. XXXI, No. 1, February 1965, p. 7.

initial intent.[55] It is evident, therefore, that because planning is "fed through" itself, the concept of urban order and the means of achieving it can be neither rigid nor final. As Alonso has suggested, "...there is always a future beyond the stage projected".[56] New orders, as the policy modes presented in this study indicated, are constantly emerging and one of planning's major tasks is to graft one upon another in the light of continuously changing demands and means of control. Even the most complete and elaborately documented of plans is the origin rather than the object of this process. In many ways it is the process itself rather than the plan which is the real product of planning.

SOME LESSONS OF STRATEGIC PLANNING

It is now evident that the kind of coherent, convenient and compact city long advocated by Abercrombie and Buchanan cannot be achieved solely through restructuring the city through physical hard planning. While some of the traditional ordering principles which both men supported continue to survive, such as horizontal containment of both the Central Area and the metropolitan region as a whole by means of legislation and restriction, many others which are directly related to new, large-scale construction, such as complete hierarchical traffic canalization, are no longer considered to be politically or economically realistic. In the first major policy document produced after the 1973 GLC elections, *London: The Future and You*, it was made clear that major new road construction would be largely abandoned for the present at least.[57] In particular the attempt to use hard planning measures to re-create Abercrombie's geometry in the Capital by means of a ring and radial road pattern have been effectively defeated. In terms of both geometry and

---

[55] See also on the question of comprehensiveness Peter Self, "Is comprehensive planning possible and rational?" *Policy and Politics*, Vol. 2, No. 3, March 1974, pp. 193–203; with particular reference to those circumstances in which comprehensive planning might be easier to achieve.
[56] William Alonso, "Cities, planners and urban renewal", in James Q. Wilson (Ed.), *Urban Renewal*, Cambridge, Mass.: MIT Press, 1966, p. 439.
[57] GLC, *London: The Future and You*, London: GLC, 1973. On the need to restrict and direct new growth in terms of employment and offices see paras. 15 and 16.

hierarchy 1973 has marked a major change in the relationship between strategic road planning on the one hand and the concept of urban order on the other.

In fact strategic road planning is a symbol of at least three different factors:

(i) A concept of urban order.
(ii) An indication of organizational control capabilities.
(iii) A reflection of political priorities.

On the basis of experience it could now be argued that the 1940s unitary concept of urban order which initially underlay the Primary Road Network was, by the 1970s, no longer really relevant; that the organizational capability of the GLC to actually control planning policy, particularly at the local level, had been over-estimated; and that the high political priority accorded to the full motorway programme, given the limited real resources available for replanning the Capital was, as the Layfield Panel noted, over-ambitious. The physical pattern for Greater London which the Primary Road Network symbolized, as this study has attempted to demonstrate, has been shattered by events. What is it possible to learn about the planning process as a result of this experience?

One factor which clearly emerges from this study is the lack of *contingency planning* which took place. Although there was some attempt to briefly test alternative road patterns, for example, during the closing phase of the LTS they were not systematically explored and related to wider planning concerns. In some ways the production of once and for all "one-off" alternatives has now begun to replace the traditional one-off Master Plan.[58] Rather than creating single and simple alternatives at the beginning of plan-making process perhaps it would be possible to think in terms of producing and up-dating various options based on parallel policy "bundles" consisting of related proposals. These bundles and packages would be continuously maintained over time so that the balance between *future anticipation* and *experiential adaptation*, mentioned in Chapter 1, could be altered as circumstances changed, technically, organizationally and politically.

[58] See, on the latter, once again Beckman (1964), p. 327.

While it would be unrealistic to expect that the GLC could have anticipated all of the alterations which have occurred in urban transport policy since the announcement of the Motorway Box (Ringway One) in 1965, at least some of the rigidities in the planning process might have been reduced by a more lengthy consideration of the options available.[59] By using continuous planning consciously based on continuing options at least some of the problems inherent in what could be called the military staff college approach might be avoided. Wingo has observed that policy makers dealing with planning matters have been on occasion "Like generals brilliantly prepared to fight the preceding war... trying to solve the problem that was".[60] Analysis of the recent trends, stated objectives and the intended and unforeseen impact of policy would all play a part in the preparation and preservation of alternative paths for the organization to pursue as political and economic factors alter over the course of time.

Clearly the rapid collection, analysis and presentation of information will assume a high degree of importance in strategic planning. Feedback of a continuous and systematic kind is beginning to be viewed not as a regrettable interruption of the planning process but as a central and integral component.[61] It has been suggested machinery be established to monitor and regularly report on the state of London's economy and it is possible that this approach will be broadened to include other topics as well.[62]

In addition to the need for making more use of *continuing* contingency planning and more active monitoring another related lesson which can be drawn from this experience is the need to

---

[59] It is in fact difficult to explain precisely why the GLDP did not more systematically consider alternatives. At least part of the explanation must be in terms of the historical orientations described in Chapter 3 which pointed quite clearly to a single model of the city.

[60] Lowdon Wingo, "Urban space in a policy perspective", in Lowdon Wingo (Ed.), *Cities and Space*, Baltimore, Md.: John Hopkins Press, 1963, p. 4.

[61] For a development of this idea see F. Wedgwood-Oppenheim, D. A. Hart and B. W. Cobley, "An exploratory study in strategic monitoring: establishing a regional performance evaluation and policy review unit for the north west", Department of the Environment Report, Birmingham: typescript, 1974. (Forthcoming, *Progress in Planning*, Vol. 5, Part 1, Oxford: Pergamon Press.)

[62] On the establishment of this machinery see GLC, *London: The Future and You—Population and Employment*, London: GLC, 1973, unpaginated.

carefully relate both hard and soft planning measures to one another to create a *plastic type of control system*.[63] One potential example of this type of thinking is the Transportation Policy and Programme (TPP) which allows all of the various movement modes to be considered together in a single document and regularly reviewed.

This type of approach would mean that various soft planning projects such as traffic restraint and parking controls could be carefully related to emerging hard planning projects such as possible future urban motorways to achieve the greatest benefit from both kinds of planning. Although there has been a movement away from the large-scale building of strategic roads in the Capital and toward the promotion of public transport[64] it would be premature to assert that motorway building in Greater London is a permanently closed option. There is reason to believe, for example, that one possible alternative being considered is that some strategic roads could be constructed underground.[65]

It has also been suggested that a very much scaled-down set of urban motorways could be built on the surface. According to two authorities,

> ...if urban motorways are considered to be part of a comprehensive planning concept rather than as isolated artefacts, the way is open to remedy most of the environmental problems, and to insert such motorways as can be proved to be essential, into the urban fabric in a civilized way.[66]

Such hard planning projects by their very nature are likely to take some time to put into effect, however. It is therefore important to think in terms of avoiding premature commitment, to consider local feedback and to think, as was suggested earlier, of planning as a comprehensive *process* as well as merely being concerned with *physical* comprehensiveness.

Although soft planning measures are currently in fashion some

---

[63] See on this topic Karl R. Popper, "Of clouds and clocks", in *Objective Knowledge*, Oxford: Oxford University Press, 1972, p. 239.
[64] See GLC, *London: The Future and You* (1973), paras. 24–28.
[65] On this see GLC, *Roads In Tunnel*, London: GLC, 1974. Tunelling is an extremely expensive business, however, and little actual progress has yet been made in this regard.
[66] Walter Bor and John Roberts, "Urban motorways impact", *Town Planning Review*, Vol. 43, No. 4, October 1972, p. 320.

amount of hard planning is inevitable. The point is therefore to view planning as a comprehensive process which makes use of plastic control measures to properly integrate individual physical construction projects with wider soft planning measures in the attempt to achieve strategic urban goals including economy, efficiency, environmental protection and social equity.

In spite of occasional bursts of what F. J. Osborn called "artery driving zeal" the nature of planning in London has fundamentally altered during the period 1943 to 1973.[67] The physical form of the city in its entirety is no longer a matter of supreme concern. It is generally accepted that the type of classical city put forward by Abercrombie and later buttressed by Buchanan is probably practically unattainable.[68] Strategic hard planning measures have, in general, been relegated to a position of secondary importance apart from the continuing recognition that Greater London is now polycentric rather than monocentric in shape, and it is possible that a new cohesive approach will be formulated which consciously relates road and rail considerations to London's polycentric form. For the present of much more concern than London's ultimate form are matters such as balancing the distribution of service and industrial employment, positively directing resources to deal with social problems and limiting new office and hotel developments through the planning control measures available.[69] The heroic Master Planning approach, which the Primary Road Network formed such an important component of, is for the Capital as a whole, and for the near future at least, finished.

In addition to emphasizing the need for contingency planning, more energetic monitoring and the need to relate soft and hard planning measures to one another it is also important to more closely link strategic and tactical concerns. The early GLC, working in close conjunction with the MOT, emerges in some ways as the villain of

[67] Quoted by William A. Robson, *The Government and Misgovernment of London*, London: George Allen & Unwin, 2nd ed., 1948, pp. 425–426.

[68] On the changing utility of form see Melvin M. Webber, "Order in diversity: community without propinquity", in Wingo (Ed.) (1963), p. 52; and see also Britton Harris, "The city of the future", in Larry S. Bourne (Ed.), *Internal Structure of the City*, London: Oxford University Press, 1971, pp. 516–522.

[69] On this see GLC, *London: The Future and You* (1973), paras. 14 and 35.

this study. Matters, however, are more complicated than this. A major part of the GLC's purpose when it was created, as Chapter 2 indicated, was to play a principal role in the planning and building of strategic roads. Opposition arose not because of the GLC did not perform its function with sufficient forcefulness but precisely because it did. Factors other than the GLC–MOT's vigorous approach were involved, however: public opinion, party political and economic considerations all played a part in curbing urban motorway building all over country.

In spite of these qualifications it is nevertheless true that the strategic, top-down approach adopted by the GLC took relatively little cognizance—particularly initially—of local community concerns. Buchanan has written that

> Planning... in my experience cries out for an approach from both ends, working downwards from the big things and upwards from the small. It cries out for broad policies to be settled so that lesser matters can find their place; and it cries out for small fundamentals to be recognized... so that wider policies can be soundly based. Between the two approaches there are constant interactions requiring adjustments or "feed-back" as planners would say.[70]

Participation by public organizations and the public is not merely desirable in planning—it is inevitable; the real question is what form it assumes and at what point in the planning process it enters.

Relations between the GLC, some London Boroughs, and many community groups are not good—partly as a result of the controversy generated by the ring and radial road proposals. Now that this particular confrontation has ended it is possible that better interauthority, relations will begin to become established.[71] It is possible that something along the organizational lines of a "metropolitan forum" could be established which would allow local and borough views to be put forward and defended at a relatively early stage in the planning process and continuing communication links maintained over time.[72] In this way an on-going dialogue could be created which would allow controversy to be canalized and mutual learning

---

[70] Buchanan (1972), p. 47.
[71] See on this topic GLC, *London: The Future and You* (1973), para. 36.
[72] See also on this F. Wedgwood-Oppenheim, D. A. Hart and B. W. Cobley (1974), pp. 58–59.

to take place, so that even party political differences could be fully aired and explored before commitment was entered into.

It could be argued that the business of planning is currently concerned, as the Diffused Mode suggests, with the collection, analysis and presentation of information as well as with the manipulation of physical objects. Monitoring, performance evaluation, resource analysis and policy review are thus all matters of growing interest. A much looser-woven planning strategy supplemented by a regularly and systematically up-dated set of documents would seem to be useful in the near future and would also take cognizance of planning's iterative character. Disjointed incrementation might then be replaced by a kind of "joined incrementalism".

It is now possible to at least tentatively answer the question which has run throughout this study: in what sense is planning a process? As the past 30 years have demonstrated planning in London is an iterative process in at least three different senses: (a) it must pursue continuing alternatives as circumstances alter; (b) it must fuse soft and hard planning measures to create a plastic control system; and (c) it must combine strategic and local concerns by facilitating inter-authority communication and co-ordination.

It should finally be noted that plans—particularly strategic plans—are primarily of interest to planners. As implementation proceeds and plan components change as they are translated into actual effect they become a matter of concern to a much broader spectrum of interest. One of planning's crucial and continuing tasks is therefore to bridge this gap and make planning not only more comprehensive but more comprehensible and therefore more credible as well. The one thing we know with any degree of certainty about the planning process is that plans change.

Bibliography

"A Council for Greater London?" (1960) *Labour Research*, Vol. XLIX, No. 12, December, pp. 204-5.
ABERCROMBIE, SIR PATRICK (1933) *Town and Country Planning*, London: Oxford University Press, Second edition 1943, Third edition revised by D. Rigby Childs 1959.
ABERCROMBIE, SIR PATRICK (1937) *Planning in Town and County*, An Inaugural Lecture in the Department of Town Planning, School of Architecture, University College, London: Hodder & Stoughton.
ABERCROMBIE, SIR PATRICK (1945) *Greater London Plan 1944*, London: HMSO.
ABERCROMBIE, SIR PATRICK (1956) "Remarks at the British Road Federation Conference on Urban Motorways", *Urban Motorways*, London: BRF, p. 31.
ABERCROMBIE, SIR PATRICK and FORSHAW, J. H. (1943) *County of London Plan*, London, Macmillan & Co. Ltd.
ADVISORY COMMITTEE FOR LONDON REGIONAL PLANNING AND TECHNICAL SUB-COMMITTEE, *Report to the Minister of Town and Country Planning*, 1946, London: HMSO.
ALDINGTON, H. E. (1962) "Evidence submitted by the Institution of Highway Engineers", *Miscellaneous Bodies and Private Individuals*, Royal Commission for Local Government in Greater London, Vol. 5, London: HMSO, pp. 164-166.
ALEXANDER, CHRISTOPHER (1972) "A city is not a tree", BELL, GWEN and TYRWHITT, JACQUELINE (Eds.), *Human Identity in the Urban Environment*, Harmondsworth, Middlesex, Penguin Books, pp. 401-428.
ALCOTT, JOAN V. (1960) "Planning and the motor vehicle", *Town and Country Planning*, Vol. XXXVIII, No. 12, December, pp. 403-417.
ALLISON, GRAHAM T. (1969) "Conceptual models and the Cuban missile crisis", *The American Political Science Review*, Vol. LXIII, No. 3, September, pp. 689-718.
ALLISON, GRAHAM T. (1971) *Essence of Decision*, Boston: Little Brown & Co.
ALONSO, WILLIAM (1966) "Cities, planners and urban renewal", in WILSON, JAMES Q. (Ed.), *Urban Renewal*, Cambridge, Mass., and London: The M.I.T. Press.
ALTSHULER, ALAN A. (1965a) "The goals of comprehensive planning", *Journal of the American Institute of Planners*, Vol. XXXI, No. 3, August 1965, pp. 186-195.
ALTSHULER, ALAN A. (1965b) *The City Planning Process*, Ithaca, New York: Cornell University Press.
ARCTANDER, PHILIP (1972) "The process is the purpose", *Journal of the Royal Town Planning Institute*, Vol. 58, No. 7, July-August, pp. 313-315.

Bibliography

BAILEY, MICHAEL (1970) "Both parties stand clear of ringway eruptions", *The Times*, 19 March.
BALFOUR, PATRICK (1938) "Times change, why not the roads?", British Road Federation, London, October (unpaginated).
BANFIELD, EDWARD C. (1961) *Political Influence*, Glencoe: The Free Press.
BAPAT, P. (1969) "Orbital road systems", *Official Architecture and Planning*, Vol. 32, No. 2, February, pp. 158–160.
BARKER, FELIX (1956) *Riverside Highway—The Evening News Plan*, Associated Newspapers, St. Albans.
BAUER, RAYMOND, A. (1968) "The study of policy formation: an introduction", in BAUER, RAYMOND A. and GERGEN, KENNETH J. (Eds.), *The Study of Policy Formation*, New York: The Free Press, pp. 1–26.
BAUER, RAYMOND A. and GERGEN, KENNETH J. (Eds.) (1968) *The Study of Policy Formation*, New York: The Free Press.
BECKMANN, NORMAN (1963) "Our federal system and urban development: the adaptation of form to function", *Journal of the American Institute of Planners*, Vol. XXIX, No. 3, August, pp. 152–167.
BECKMAN, NORMAN (1964) "The planner as a bureaucrat", *Journal of the American Institute of Planners*, Vol. XXX, No. 4, November pp. 323–327.
BEER, STANFORD (1970) "Planning as a process of adaptation" (Ed. JOHN LAURENCE), *OR 69*, London: Tavistock Publications, pp. 31–53.
BEESLEY, M. E. and KAIN, J. F. (1964) "Urban form, car ownership and public transport: an appraisal of traffic in towns", *Urban Studies*, Vol. 1, No. 2, November,
BENDIXSON, TERRENCE (1969) "Box mania", The *Guardian*, Friday, 24 January.
BENDIXSON, TERRENCE (1970) "This mania for motorways", *The Architect and Building News*, 1 January, pp. 41–43.
BERGER, PETER L. and LUCKMANN, THOMAS (1966) *The Social Construction of Reality*, Middlesex: Penguin Books Ltd.
BEVIS, HOWARD W. (1959) "A method for predicting urban travel patterns", *Journal of the American Association of Planners*, Vol. XXV, No. 2, May, pp. 87–89.
BLAKE, JOHN (1968) "The growth of traffic in Greater London", *Surveyor*, week ending 19 October, pp. 34–35.
BLAKE, JOHN (1970) "London's proposed motorways: some unanswered questions", *Building*, 11 September, pp. 92–98.
BLAKE, JOHN (1971) "Shopping and suburban development" in HILLMAN, JUDY (Ed.), *Planning for London*, Harmondsworth, Middlesex: Penguin Books, pp. 77–85.
BOR, WALTER and ROBERTS, JOHN (1972) "Urban motorways impact", *Town Planning Review*, Vol. 43, No. 4, October, pp. 299–321.
BOULDING, KENNETH E. (1956) *The Image*, Ann Arbor: The University of Michigan Press.
BOWEN, MURIEL (1967) "Motorways are GLC priority", *The Sunday Times*, 29 October, p. 3.
BOWER, JOSEPH L. (1968) "Descriptive decision theory from the administrative viewpoint", in BAUER, RAYMOND A. and GERGEN, KENNETH J. (Eds.), *The Study of Policy Formation*, New York: The Free Press, pp. 103–148.
BOYCE, DAVID E., DAY, NORMAN D., and MCDONALD, CHRIS (1970) *Metropolitan Plan Making*, Philadelphia, Penn.: Regional Science Research Institute.

BRANCH, MELVIN (1970) "Goals and objectives of comprehensive planning: in LAWRENCE, JOHN (Ed.), *OR 69*, London: Tavistock Publications, pp. 55–65.
BRAYBROOKE, DAVID (1974) *Traffic Congestion Goes Through the Issue Machine*, London: Routledge & Kegan Paul.
BRAYBROOKE, DAVID and LINDBLOM, CHARLES E. (1963) *A Strategy of Decision*, New York: The Free Press.
BRESSEY, SIR CHARLES and LUTYENS, SIR EDWIN (1937) *Highway Development Survey (Greater London)*, prepared for the Ministry of Transport, London: HMSO,
BRIGGS, ASA (1963) *Victorian Cities*, Middlesex: Penguin Books.
THE BRITISH GROUP OF THE INTERNATIONAL CENTRES FOR REGIONAL PLANNING AND DEVELOPMENT, "Written Evidence", *Miscellaneous Bodies and Private Individuals*, Vol. 3, Royal Commission on Local Government in Greater London, London: HMSO, pp. 170–174.
BRITISH ROAD FEDERATION (1955) *Annual Reports 1954*, London: BRF Ltd.
BRITISH ROAD FEDERATION (1960) *London Needs*, London: BRF Ltd.
BRITISH ROAD FEDERATION (1964) Press Release, "Roads in London: BRF Press Conference", 2 December, p. 6.
BRITISH ROAD FEDERATION PRESS RELEASE (1970) "London ringways: 80 per cent support GLC plan", dated 16 March, 3 pp.
BROWN, LEE and LA MOURY, ANDREA (1971) "Peter Walker outlines new department's major priorities", *Municipal Review*, Vol. 42, No. 493, January, pp. 20–21.
BUCHANAN, C. D. (1958) *Mixed Blessing*, London: Leonard Hill Ltd.
BUCHANAN, C. D. (1962) "Comprehensive redevelopment—the opportunity for traffic", in WILLIAMS, T. E. H. (Ed.), *Urban Survival and Traffic*, London: E. & F. N. Spon Ltd., pp. 1–8.
BUCHANAN, C. D. (1962) Book review "Town and Traffic in the Motor Age, by Professor P. H. Bendtsen, translated by C. Prockewell. Danish Technical Press, 1961", *Town and Country Planning*, Vol. XXX, No. 1, July.
BUCHANAN, C. D. *et al.* (1963) *Traffic in Towns*, London: HMSO.
BUCHANAN, C. D., "Presidential Address—1963", *Journal of the Town Planning Institute*, Vol. 49, No. 10, pp. 334–343.
BUCHANAN, C. D. (1964) *Transport and the Community*, an Inaugural Lecture delivered at the Imperial College of the University of London, 18 February.
BUCHANAN, C. D. (1972) *The State of Britain*, London: Faber & Faber.
BUCHANAN, C. D. and PARTNERS (1969) *The Conurbations*, commissioned by the British Road Federation, London.
BUCHANAN, C. D. and PARTNERS (1970) *North-East London*, a report for the Greater London Council, London: GLC.
BUCHANAN, C. D. and PARTNERS (1971) *Greenwich and Blackheath Study*, a report to the Greater London Council, London: GLC, April.
BUCHANAN, C. D. and PARTNERS (1972) *Greenwich and Deptford Management Study*, a report to the Greater London Council, July.
BUCHANAN, C. M. (1970) *London Road Plans 1900–1970*, Research Report No. 11, December, London: GLC.
CARROLL, J. DOUGLAS (1962) "Adapting urban environments to technology on the reverse", in WILLIAMS, T. E. H. (Ed.), *Urban Survival and Traffic*, London: E. & F. Spon Ltd., pp. 38–45.

CARTER, EDWARD (1962) *The Future of London*, Harmondsworth, Middlesex: Penguin.
"CHANGE AND CHALLENGE" (1962) *Conservative Political Centre*, No. 247, February, London.
CHAPIN, F. STUART, JR. (1950) "How big should a city be?", *Planning Outlook*, Vol. II, No. 1, Autumn, pp. 37–47.
CHAPIN, F. STUART, JR. (1963) "Taking stock of the techniques for shaping urban growth", *Journal of the American Institute of Planners*, Vol. XXIX, No. 2, May, pp. 76–87.
CHAPIN, F. STUART, JR. (1965) *Urban Land Use Planning*, 2nd ed., Urbana, Ill.: University of Illinois Press.
THE CHELSEA SOCIETY (1970) letter "Filter-West Cross Route Chelsea Basin Interchange", dated 25 January, p. 1.
CHERRY, COLIN (1970) "Human communication: technology and urban planning", in JONES, DOUGLAS (Ed.), *Communication and Energy in Changing Urban Environments* (Colston Research Society), London: Butterworths, 1970, pp. 117–130.
CLAYTON, R. (Ed.) (1964) *The Geography of Greater London*, London: George Philip & Son Ltd.
COLLINS, MICHAEL F. and PHAROAH, TIMOTHY M. (1974) *Transport Organisation in a Great City: The Case of London*, London: George Allen & Unwin.
COMMITTEE FOR STAGGERING OF WORKING HOURS FOR CENTRAL LONDON, MINISTRY OF TRANSPORT (1958) *'Crush-Hour' Travel in Central London*, London: HMSO.
COOPER, G. C. (1963) "Towns and traffic", *Journal of the Town Planning Institute*, Vol. 49, No. 5, May 1963, pp. 138–141.
COUNTY COUNCIL OF MIDDLESEX (1962) *Written Evidence from Local Authorities Miscellaneous Bodies and Private Individuals*, Vol. 2, pp. 1–257, Royal Commission on Local Government in Greater London, London: HMSO.
CRAIG, JOHN (1970) "The 1943 London Plan: a perspective", *Official Architecture and Planning*, Vol. 33, No. 12, December, pp. 1075–1078.
CRANE, DAVID A. (1960) "The city symbolic", *Journal of the American Institute of Planners*, Vol. XXVI, No. 4, November, pp. 280–292.
CRAWFORD, DR. K. A. J. (1971) "The 1971 Greater London Transportation Survey", *Quarterly Bulletin of the Intelligence Unit*, September, No. 16, London: GLC, pp. 15–24.
CREESE, NATHAN (1964) "The planning theories of Sir Raymond Unwin 1863–1940", *Journal of the American Institute of Planners*, Vol. XXX, No. 4, November, pp. 295–303.
DAHL, ROBERT A. (1965) *Modern Political Analysis*, Englewood Cliffs, New Jersey: Prentice-Hall Inc.
DAHL, ROBERT A. (1967) "City in the future of democracy", *American Political Science Review* (December), Vol. 61, pp. 953–70.
Daily Mirror (1965) "Super M-way for London", 2 April.
DAILY TELEGRAPH REPORTER (1966) "GLC to be sued over motorway", *Daily Telegraph*, 1 November.
DALAND, ROBERT (1957) "Organization for urban planning: some barriers to integration", *Journal of the American Institute of Planners*, Vol. XXIII, No. 4, pp. 200–206.

Bibliography

DAMER, IAIN and HAGUE, CLIFF (1971) "Public participation in planning: a review", *Town Planning Review*, Vol. 42, No. 3, July, pp. 217–232.

DEEDES, W. F. (1961) "The face of Britain", *Town and Country Planning*, Vol. XXX, No. 12, December, pp. 483–485.

DENINGTON, EVELYN (1970) "London under pressure", *Town and Country Planning*, Vol. 38, No. 2, February, pp. 101–104.

DEPARTMENT OF THE ENVIRONMENT (1973) *Greater London Development Plan — Report of the Panel of Inquiry* (The Layfield Report), Vols. I and II (Appendices), London: HMSO.

DEWEY, JOHN (1927) *The Public and its Problems*, Denver: Henry Holt & Co.

DIMITRIOU, B. (1972) "The interpretation of politics and planning", "The Systems View of Planning", Oxford Polytechnic, Department of Town Planning, Oxford, February, typescript, pp. 5–17.

DOMENICH, THOMAS A. and KRAFT, GERALD (1970) *Free Transit*, a Charles River Association Research Study, Lexington, Firmington, Mass.: D. C. Heath & Co.

DONNISON, DAVID with JUNE BRUEGEL, MICHAEL HARLOW and DOREEN MASSEY (1970) Observations on the Greater London Development Plan", GLBP Inquiry, Background Paper B/603, November, unpublished, pp. 1–11.

DUNN, J. B. (1970) *Traffic Census Results for 1969*, Road Research Laboratory, RRL Report LR 371.

DYCKMAN, JOHN (1971) "New normative styles in urban studies", *Public Administration Review*, Vol. XXXI, No. 3, May–June, pp. 327–334.

The Economist (1968) "Too square?", 27 July, pp. 43–44.

EDDISON, TONY (1970) "How to plan", *Town Country Planning*, Vol. 381, No. 11, December, pp. 519–520.

EDITOR (1964) "Juggernaut and Babel, Inc.", *Town and Country Planning*, Vol. XXXII, No. 1, January, pp. 3–4.

EDITORIAL (1969) *Planning Outlook*, New Series, Vol. VII, Autumn, pp. 5–6.

ELKIN, STEPHEN J. (1974) *Politics and Land Use Planning*, London: Cambridge University Press.

ETZIONI, A. (1964) *Modern Organization*, Englewood Cliffs, New Jersey: Prentice-Hall Inc.

ETZIONI, A. (1968) *The Active Society: a Theory of Social and Political Processes*, London: Collin-Macmillan Ltd., New York: The Free Press.

Evening Standard (1966) "Group fights 'Premature London Motorway Plan'", Friday, 3 June, p. 12.

Evening Standard (1969) "Councillor accuses Tories in M-way row", 27 June.

EVENING STANDARD REPORTERS (1965) "First map of the new urban motorway", *Evening Standard*, 25 March.

EVENING STANDARD REPORTER (1967) "Houseboat owners in bit bid to divert motorway", *Evening Standard*, 27 December.

EVERSLEY, DAVID (1972) "What is London's future", *New Society*, Vol. 22, No. 522, 5 October, pp. 18–20.

"The Face of Britain" (1961) *Socialist Commentary*, September, Special Planning Supplement, pp. i–xxvi.

FAGIN, HENRY (1959) "Organizing and carrying out planning activity within urban government", *Journal of the American Institute of Planners*, Vol. XXV, No. 3, August, pp. 109–114.

FAINSTEIN, SUSAN and NORMAN (1971) "City planning and political values", *Urban Affairs Quarterly*, Vol. 6, No. 3, March, pp. 341–362.
FALUDI, ANDREAS (Ed.) (1973) *A Reader in Planning Theory*, Oxford: Pergamon Press.
FALUDI, ANDREAS (1973) *Planning Theory*, Oxford: Pergamon Press.
FELTON, MONICA (1949) "Democracy in town and country planning", *Political Quarterly*, Vol. XX, No. 1, January–March, pp. 74–82.
FISHER, HOWARD T. (1962) "Radials and circumferentials—an outmoded urban concept?", WILLIAMS, T. E. H. (Ed.), *Urban Survival and Traffic*, E. & F. H. Spon Institute, London, pp. 46–59.
FITCH, LYCE C. (1962) "A transit paradox", *National Civic Review*, Vol. 41, No. 4, April, pp. 181–187.
FOLEY, DONALD L. (1963) *Controlling London's Growth: Planning the Great Wen 1940–1960*, Berkeley: University of California Press.
FOLEY, DONALD L. (1969) "London's motorways: an unwise investment", *Official Architecture and Planning*, Vol. 32, No. 12, December, pp. 1480–1481.
FOLEY, DONALD L. (1972) *Governing the London Region: Reorganization and Planning in the 1960's*, Berkeley: University of California Press.
FORSHAW, J. H. (1943) *Town Planning and Health*, a Chadwick Public Lecture, delivered on 11 November 1943, P. S. King and Staples Ltd., Westminster.
FRIEDMANN, JOHN (1965) "A response to Altshuler: comprehensive planning as a process", *Journal of American Institute of Planners*, Vol. XXI, No. 3, August, pp. 195–199.
FRIEDMANN, JOHN (1967) "A conceptual model for the analysis of planning behaviour, *Administrative Science Quarterly*, Vol. 12, No. 2, September, pp. 225–252.
FRIEDMANN, JOHN and MILLER, JOHN (1965) "The urban field", *Journal of the American Institute of Planners*, Vol. XXXI, No. 4, November, pp. 312–320.
FREIDRICH, CARL J. (1971) "Political decision-making, public policy and planning", *Canadian Public Administration*, Vol. 14, No. 1, Spring, pp. 1–15.
FRIEND, J. K. and JESSOP, W. N. (1969) *Local Government and Strategic Choice*, London: Tavistock Publications.
FRIEND, J. K., POWER, J. M. and YEWLETT, C. J. L. (1974) *Public Planning: The Inter-Corporate Dimension*, London: Tavistock Publications.
GANS, HERBERT J. (1968) "Regional and urban planning", in SHILLS, DAVID J. (Ed.), *International Encyclopaedia of the Social Sciences*, Vol. 12, U.S.A.: The Macmillan Co. and the Free Press, pp. 129–137.
GEDDES, SIR PATRICK (1968) *Cities in Evolution*, New Ed. with an Introduction by Percy Johnson-Marshall, London: Ernest Benn Ltd. (first ed. published 1915).
GLANVILLE, W. A. and BAKER, J. F. A. (1956) "Urban motorways in Great Britain?", British Road Federation (Ed.), *Urban Motorways*, London: BRF, pp. 19–30.
GOLDRICK, MICHAEL (1967) "The administration of transportation in Greater London", London School of Economics, Ph.D. (unpublished).
GORVINE, ALBERT and MARGULIES, S. I. (1971) "The urban crisis: an alternative perspective", *Urban Affairs Quarterly*, Vol. 6, No. 3, March, pp. 263–276.
THE GREATER LONDON COUNCIL (1967) "New roads in West and North Central London", GLC, dated June, unpaginated.

Bibliography 213

THE GREATER LONDON COUNCIL (1967) "London's roads—a programme for action", November, p. 15.
THE GREATER COUNCIL (1969) "Blackwall tunnel", dated January, unpaginated.
GREATER LONDON COUNCIL (1969) *Greater London Development Plan—Statement*, London: GLC.
GREATER LONDON COUNCIL (1969) *Greater London Development Plans—Report of Studies*, London: GLC.
GREATER LONDON COUNCIL (1969) *Greater London Development Plan—Tomorrow's London*, London: GLC.
GREATER LONDON COUNCIL (1969) *Movement in London*, London: GLC.
GREATER LONDON COUNCIL (1969) "A secondary roads policy", Consultative Text, London, GLC, November.
GREATER LONDON COUNCIL (1970) *Transport Evidence—Stage 1*, GLDP Enquiry, London: GLC, November.
GREATER LONDON COUNCIL (1971) *Westway: An Environmental and Traffic Appraisal*, GLDP Background Paper, B. 494, London: GLC, July.
GREATER LONDON COUNCIL (1972) *Greater London Development Plan Statement Revisions*, London: GLC, February.
GREATER LONDON COUNCIL (1973) *London: The Future and You*, London: GLC.
GREATER LONDON COUNCIL (1973) *London: The Future and You—Population and Employment*, London: GLC.
THE GREATER LONDON GROUP OF THE LONDON SCHOOL OF ECONOMICS (1968) *The Lessons of the London Government Reforms*, London: HMSO.
GREATER LONDON COUNCIL (1973) *Minutes for the Years 1964–1973*, London: GLC.
GREATER LONDON COUNCIL PRESS RELEASE (1969) GLC leader calls for new form of public inquiry", 5 June 1 p.
GREATER LONDON COUNCIL PRESS RELEASE 327, (1969) "Dover radial route", 18 June, pp. 1–2.
GREATER LONDON COUNCIL (1969) "Secondary roads—new GLC plan", December, 2 pp.
GREATER LONDON COUNCIL PRESS RELEASE 29, (1970) "GLC to revise spending programme", 21 January, 3 pp.
GREATER LONDON COUNCIL PRESS RELEASE 363, (1970) "Primary roads review—order of priority", 15 July, 3 pp.
GREATER LONDON COUNCIL PRESS RELEASE 397 (1970) "Acklam Road—GLC to start rehousing", 5 August.
GREATER LONDON COUNCIL PRESS RELEASE 584 (1970) "Secondary road scheme submitted", 9 December, GLC, 3 pp.
GREATER LONDON COUNCIL PRESS RELEASE 371 (1971) "New London road a step nearer", 20 August, pp. 1–2.
GREER, SCOTT and MIRROR, DAVID W. (1964) "The political side of urban development and redevelopment", *Annuals of the American Academy of Political and Social Science*, Vol. 352, March, pp. 62–73.
GRIFFITH, J. A. (1966) *Central Departments and Local Authorities*, London: George Allen & Unwin.
GROSS, BERTRAM M. (1971) "Planning in an era of social revolution", *Public Administration Review*, Vol. XXXI, No. 3, May–June, pp. 259–295.

Bibliography

GROSS, EDWARD (1969) "The definitions of organizational goals", *British Journal of Sociology*, Vol. XX, No. 3, September, pp. 277–294.

GRUEN, VICTOR (1965) *The Heart of our Cities*, London: Thames & Hudson.

GUTHEIM, FREDERICK (1969) "The future city and its transportation", *Planning Outlook*, New Series, Vol. VII, Autumn, pp. 7–18.

GUTTENBERG, ALBERT (1960) "Urban structure and urban growth", *Journal of the American Institute of Planners*, Vol. XXVI, No. 2, May, pp. 104–110.

HAAR, CHARLES, M. (1955) "The content of the general plan: a glance at history", *Journal of the American Institute of Planners*, Vol. XXI, No. 2–3, Spring–Summer, pp. 66–70.

HAGMAN, DONALD G. (1971) "The Greater London Development Plan Inquiry", *Journal of the American Institute of Planners*, Vol. 37, No. 5, September, pp. 290–296.

HALL, PETER (1961) "The importance of Finchley Road", *Socialist Commentary*, June, pp. 7–10.

HALL, PETER (1961) "London's missing traffic plan", *Socialist Commentary*, November, pp. 16–19.

HALL, PETER (1969) "Transportation", *Urban Studies*, Vol. 6, No. 3, November, pp. 408–435.

HALL, PETER (1969) *London 2000*, 2nd ed., London: Faber & Faber Ltd.

HALL, PETER (1970) "Transportation", in SELF, PETER J. (Ed.), *London Under Stress* (or the Town and Country Planning Association), Welwyn Garden City: The Broadwater Press, pp. 47–59.

HALL, PETER (1971) "The future London", in HILLMAN, JUDY (Ed.), *Planning for London*, Aylesbury, Bucks.: Hayell Watson & Viney Ltd., pp. 136–150.

HALL, SIR ROBERT (1963) "The transport needs for Great Britain in the next twenty years", Report to the Ministry of Transport, London: HMSO.

HALL, R. K. (1972) "The movement of offices from Central London", *Regional Studies*, Vol. 6, No. 4, December, pp. 385–392.

HALPIN, W. R. C., Chairman, Hampstead Motorway Action Group (1966) "Letter to the Editor", *Daily Telegraph*, 18 July.

HARRIS, BRITTON (1960) "Plan or projection", *Journal of the American Institute of Planners*, Vol. XXXVI, No. 4, November, pp. 265–272.

HARRIS, B. (1970) "Generating projects for urban research", *Environment and Planning*, Vol. 2, No. 1, pp. 1–21.

HART, D. A. (1973) "Ordering change and changing orders: a study of urban policy development", *Policy and Politics*, Vol. 2, No. 1, September, pp. 27–41.

HART, D. A. (1974) "Planning as a process of comprehension", *Town and Country Planning*, Vol. 42, No. 2, February, pp. 116–118.

HAWORTH, LAWRENCE, J. (1958) "An institutional theory of the city and planning", *Journal of the American Institute of Planners*, Vol. XXIII, No. 3, pp. 135–143.

HEAP, DESMOND (1950) "Reflections on the Town and Country Planning Act 1947", *Planning Outlook*, Vol. 1, No. 4, Spring, pp. 4–8.

HENDERSON, ARTHUR (1966) "London's transport and traffic planning problems", *Official Architecture and Planning*, Vol. 29, No. 4, April, pp. 538–539.

HERBERT, GILBERT (1963) "The organic analogy in town planning", *Journal of the American Institute of Planning*, Vol. XXIX, No. 3, August, pp. 198–209.

HERE AND THERE (1961) "Greater London?", *Socialist Commentary*, January, p. 12.

HIGHWAY DEVELOPMENT SURVEY (1937) (Greater London) "The Bressey Report", *Journal of the Town Planning Institute*, Vol. XXIV, No. 8, June, pp. 280–282.
HIGHWAYS AND TRAFFIC COMMITTEE (1966) "The work of the Highway and Traffic Committee 1965–66", London: GLC, Memo, April, pp. 1–30.
HIGHWAYS AND TRAFFIC COMMITTEE (1967) "The work of the Highways and Traffic Committee 1966–69, London: GLC, Memo, April, pp. 1–24.
HILLIER, BILL and LEAMAN, ADRIAN (1973) "The environment paradigm and its paradoxes", *Architectural Design*, August, pp. 507–511.
HILLMAN, JUDY (1970) "Noise could double M-Way rehousing", the *Guardian*, 8 August.
HILLMAN, JUDY (Ed.) (1971) *Planning for London*, Harmondsworth, Middlesex: Penguin Books.
HILLMAN, MAYER and HENDERSON, IRWIN (1973) "Towards a better kind of environment area", *New Society*, Vol. 25, No. 563, 12 July, pp. 75–77.
HIRTEN, JOHN E. (1973) "Needed—a new perception of transportation", *Journal of the American Institute of Planners*, Vol. 39, No. 3, July, pp. 277–282.
HOLFORD, PROF. W. G. (1946) "Transport in relation to Town and Country Planning: with particular reference to Greater London", in, BRITISH ASSOCIATION FOR THE ADVANCEMENT OF SCIENCE, *London Traffic and the London Plans*, a conference held in London on the 12th and 13th September, pp. 102–106.
HOLFORD, PROF. W. G. (1950) "The plans for London", text of a BBC radio broadcast which took place on the Third Programme, 5 April, typescript, pp. 1–8.
HOLMES, DENIS (1965) "Guide for the super-commuter", *Daily Mail*, Friday, 26 March.
HOMES BEFORE ROADS—LONDON COALITION (1970) "London Motorways Inquiry prejudiced", 23 April, p. 2.
HOOVER, ROBERT C. (1960) "On master plans and constitutions", *Journal of the American Institute of Planners*, Vol. XXVI, No. 1, February, pp. 5–24.
HOUGHTON-EVANS (1971) "Town planning and public transport", *Journal of the Royal Town Planning Institute*, Vol. 59, No. 6, June, pp. 264–267.
HOUSE OF COMMONS, SECOND REPORT FROM THE EXPENDITURE COMMITTEE (1972) *Urban Transport Planning*, December, London: HMSO.
HOWARD, EBENEZER (1946) *Garden Cities of Tomorrow*, London: Faber & Faber, first published in a revised edition in 1902.
HUTCHINGS, KEN (1967) "Urban transport: public or private?", *Fabian Research Issue 261*, London: Fabian Society, June.
INSIGHTS (1973) "The motor car wins its biggest victory", *The Sunday Times*, 11 February.
JAMES, JOHN R. (1964) "The next fifty years", *Journal of the Town Planning Institute*, Vol. 50, No. 1, January, pp. 6–11.
JAY, DOUGLAS, M. P. (1969) "Letter to Kenneth Robinson, M.P., Minister of Planning and Land", 29 June, unpublished, unpaginated.
JAY, DOUGLAS (1970) "The cost of urban motorways", *Town and Country Planning*, Vol. 38, No. 2, February, pp. 98–100.
JENKINS, SIMON (1973) "The politics of London motorways", *The Political Quarterly*, Vol. 44, No. 3, July–September, pp. 257–270.

JOHNSON-MARSHALL, PERCY (1966) *Rebuilding Cities*, Edinburgh: Edinburgh University Press.

JONES, COLIN (1969) "Getting London's Motorway Box in perspective", *The Financial Times*, 19 February.

JUSTER, ROBERT J. (1963) "The London traffic survey", *Journal of the Town Planning Institute*, Vol. 49, No. 1, November, pp. 302–306.

KENT COUNTY COUNCIL (1962) "Written Evidence" from Local Authorities, Miscellaneous Bodies and Private Individuals, Vol. IV, *Royal Commission on Local Government in Greater London*, London: HMSO, pp. 1–34.

KING, MICHAEL F. (1965) "50 motorway miles in London", *Evening Standard*, Thursday, 1 April, p. 14.

KING, MICHAEL (1969) "Major GLC breakthrough to cut motorway blight", *Evening Standard*, 13 March.

KING, MICHAEL (1973) "M-ways", *Evening Standard*, 2 July.

KIRWAN, R. M. (1969) "Economics and methodology in urban transport planning", in CULLINGWORTH, J. B. and ORR, J. C. (Eds.), *Regional and Urban Studies*, London: George Allen & Unwin Ltd., pp. 188–212.

KNIGHT, TIMOTHY et al. (1960) "Let our cities live", *Conservative Political Centre*, No. 221, London, December.

KUHN, T. S. (1970) *The Structure of Scientific Revolution*, 2nd ed., Chicago: The University of Chicago Press.

LANGLEY, JOHN (1965) "53 mile motorway plan for London", the *Daily Telegraph*, 2 April.

LEACH, EDMUND (1969) "Planning and evolution", *Journal of the Town Planning Institute*, Vol. 55, No. 1, January, pp. 3–8.

LEIBBRAND, KURT (1970) *Transportation and Town Planning*, translated by Nigel Seymer, London: Leonard Hill.

LEVIN, P. A. (1972) "On decisions and decision making", *Public Administration*, Vol. 50, Spring, pp. 19–44.

LINDBLOM, CHARLES E. (1968) *The Policy Making Process*, Englewood Cliffs, New Jersey: Prentice-Hall Inc.

LINDBLOM, CHARLES E. (1969) "The science of muddling through", in EDWARD V. SCHEIER (Ed.), *Policy Making in American Government*, New York, pp. 24–37.

LOCAL GOVERNMENT CORRESPONDENT (1971) "GLC accused of fatalism over roads", *The Times*, 4 March.

LODER, N. (1971) "City planning by traffic management", *Royal Australian Planning Institute Journal*, Vol. 9, No. 1, January, pp. 34–36.

LONDON BOROUGH OF EALING PRESS RELEASE, 1969, "D-Ring Road—Ealing Council protest to Ministry of Transport", 6 November.

LONDON CHAMBER OF COMMERCE PRESS RELEASE, 1969, "London Chamber gives a 2nd welcome to government's road plans for London and South East", 11 July, pp. 1–3.

LONDON COUNTY COUNCIL (1964) *Minutes of Proceedings, 1946–1964*.

LONDON COUNTY COUNCIL (1951) *Administrative County of London Plan Development Plan 1951—Statement*, London: LCC.

LONDON COUNTY COUNCIL (1951) *Administrative County of London Development Plan 1951 Analysis*, London: LCC.

LONDON COUNTY COUNCIL (1961) *London Statistics 1950–59*, Vol. IV, New Series, London County Council, London.

LONDON BOROUGH OF KENNINGTON AND CHELSEA (1971) *Planning Committee Report*, undated, approx. 22nd April 1971, 12 pages.
LONDON BOROUGH OF WANDSWORTH PRESS RELEASE (1970) "GLC motorway proposals", 8 October, pp. 1–4.
LONDON AND HOME COUNTIES TRAFFIC ADVISORY COMMITTEE, MINISTRY OF TRANSPORT AND CIVIL AVIATION, *London Traffic 1958*, London: HMSO.
LONDON AND HOME COUNTIES TRAFFIC ADVISORY COMMITTEE (1962) "Written evidence", *Miscellaneous Bodies and Private Individuals*, Vol. 5, Royal Commission on Local Government in Greater London, HMSO, London, pp. 245–249.
LONDON MOTORWAY ACTION GROUP, "Newsletter No. 1, March 1969", unpublished pp. 1–8.
LONDON MOTORWAY ACTION GROUP (1969) "Ringway 2", 5 November, unpublished, pp. 1–5.
LONDON MOTORWAY ACTION GROUP (1969) "Objection to the Greater London Development Plan", 5 December, unpublished, pp. 1–3.
LONDON MOTORWAY ACTION GROUP (1970) "Local Appeal Letter launching the Motorway Fighting Fund", 8 May, 1 p. with Special Bulletin.
LONDON MOTORWAY ACTION GROUP, "Statement of objectives", undated, unpublished, pp. 1–6.
LONDON TRANSPORT BOARD (1970) *Annual Report and Accounts 1969*, London: HMSO.
LONG, NORTON E. (1959) "Planning and politics in urban development", *Journal of the American Institute of Planners*, Vol. XXV, No. 4, November, pp. 167–169.
LYDDON, A. J. (1946) "Roads", in British Association for the Advancement of Science, *London Traffic and the London Plans*, a Conference held in London, 12–13 September, pp. 110–114.
LYNAM, D. A. and EVERALL, P. F. (1971) "Public transport journey times in London—1970", *Road Research Laboratory*, RRL Report LR 413, Crowthorne.
LYNCH, KEVIN (1960) "The pattern of the metropolis", in LLOYD RODWIN (Ed.), *The Future Metropolis*, London: Constable & Co., pp. 103–128.
LYNCH, KEVIN and RODWIN, LLOYD (1958) "A theory of urban form", *Journal of the American Institute of Planners*, Vol. XXIV, No. 4, pp. 201–214.
LYON, T. FINDLAY (1948) "After Geddes", *Planning Outlook*, July, Vol. 1, No. 1, pp. 7–19.
LYONS, D. J. (1967) "Technical problems of urban traffic control", *Traffic Engineering and Control*, Vol. 9, No. 1, May, pp. 31–34.
MACMURRAY, TREVOR (1971) "How not to have participation", *Town and Country Planning*, Vol. 39, No. 5, May, pp. 263–266.
MCCONNELL, SHEAN (1967) "The future of city centres", *Official Architecture and Planning*, Vol. 30, No. 9, September, pp. 1266–1275.
MCCONNELL, SHEAN (1967) "Traffic in urban centres", *Official Architecture and Planning*, Vol. 30, No. 11, November, pp. 1631–1640.
MCGOVERN, P. O. (1966) "The city of all our futures", *Town and Country Planning*, Vol. 34, No. 12, December, pp. 543–551.
MCLOUGHLIN, J. BRIAN (1966) "The changing state of British practice", *Journal of the American Institute of Planners*, Vol. XXXII, No. 6, November, pp. 350–355.
MCLOUGHLIN, J. BRIAN (1969) *Urban and Regional Planning*, London: Faber & Faber.

Bibliography

MARPLES, RT. HON. ERNEST (1963) "Opening of the Conference Proceedings", in British Road Federation (Ed.), *People and Cities*, BRF, London, pp. 11–14.

MARLOW, M. (1971) *Repeat Traffic Studies in 1967 in Eight Towns Previously Surveyed in 1963–4*, Road Research Laboratory, RRL Report, LR 390, Crowthorne.

MARTIN, PAUL (1967) "The rape of Old Cheyne Walk", *Sunday Times*, 7 May.

MASSEY, DOREEN B. and CORDEY-HAYES, MARTIN (1971) "The use of models in structure planning", *Town Planning Review*, Vol. 42, No. 1, January, pp. 28–44.

MEDHURST, FRANKLIN (1970) "The planning context", in JAMES, DOUGLAS (Ed.), *Communication and Energy in Changing Urban Environments* (Colston Research Society), London: Butterworths, pp. 21–33.

MEYER, JOHN R. (1968) "Urban transportation", in WILSON, JAMES Q. (Ed.), *The Metropolitan Enigma*, Cambridge, Mass.: Harvard University Press, revised edition, pp. 41–69.

MEYERSON, MARTIN (1956) "Building the middle-range bridge for comprehensive planning", *Journal of the American Institute of Planners*, Spring, pp. 58–64.

MEYERSON, MARTIN and BANFIELD, EDWARD C. (1955) *Politics, Planning and the Public Interest: The Case of Public Housing for Chicago*, Glencoe: The Free Press.

MINISTRY OF HOUSING AND LOCAL GOVERNMENT (1959) *Memorandum of Evidence*, Vol. 4, in Royal Commission on Local Government in Greater London, Memoranda of Evidence of Government Departments, London: HMSO, pp. 105–140.

MINISTRY OF HOUSING AND LOCAL GOVERNMENT, MINISTRY OF TRANSPORT (*et al.*) (1964) *Parking in Town Centres*, Planning Bulletin No. 7, London: HMSO.

MINISTRY OF HOUSING AND LOCAL GOVERNMENT (1966) "PO/RO Conference: Greater London in South East England", Ministry of Housing and Local Government, London, 16 and 17 November, typescript.

MINISTRY OF HOUSING AND LOCAL GOVERNMENT (1970) "Inquiry panel visits Acklam Road", Press Release No. 169, 1 October.

MINISTRY OF HOUSING AND LOCAL GOVERNMENT PRESS RELEASE, 1970, "Mr Walker's satisfaction at outcome of discussions", 5 August.

MINISTRY OF LOCAL GOVERNMENT AND PLANNING (1951) *Town and Country Planning 1943–51*, Cmd. 8204, London: HMSO.

MINISTER OF TOWN AND COUNTRY PLANNING (1946) "Greater London Plan: proposed satellite towns", *The Journal of the Town Planning Institute*, January, Vol. XXXII, No. 2, pp. 68–69.

MINISTRY OF TOWN AND COUNTRY PLANNING (1947) *Memorandum on the Report of the Advisory Committee for London Regional Planning*, London: HMSO.

MINISTRY OF TRANSPORT (1959) *London–Yorkshire Motorway*, London: HMSO.

MINISTRY OF TRANSPORT (1964) *Road Pricing: The Economic and Technical Possibilities*, London: HMSO.

MINISTRY OF TRANSPORT PRESS RELEASE 226 (1963) "Transport Minister opens Blackwall Tunnel approach road", 25 April, pp. 1–4.

MINISTRY OF TRANSPORT AND CIVIL AVIATION (1959) *Memorandum of Evidence*, in Royal Commission on Local Government in Greater London, Memoranda of Evidence from Government Department, London: HMSO, pp. 162–187.

MITCHELL, B. and RAPKIN, CHESTER (1954) *Urban Traffic: A Function of Land Use*, New York: Columbia University Press.

MONSEN, R. JOSEPH JR. and CANNON, MARK W. (1965) *The Makers of Public Policy*, New York: McGraw-Hill.
MONTGOMERY, ROGER (1965) "Improving the design process in urban renewal", *Journal of the American Institute of Planners*, Vol. XXXI, No. 1, February, pp. 7–20.
MUMFORD, LEWIS (1946) "Address to the Town Planning Institute", *Journal of the Town Planning Institute*, Vol. XXXII, No. 5, July–August, pp. 175–179.
MUMFORD, LEWIS (1961) "Letter to R. I. Wolf dated 28th November, 1959", *Journal of the American Institute of Planners*, Vol. XXVII, No. 1, February, pp. 75–77.
MUMFORD, LEWIS (1970) "The highway and the city", in ANDERSON, WALT (Ed.), *Politics and Environment*, Pacific Palisado, Cal.: Goodyear Publishing Co., pp. 169–181.
MUNT, P. W. (1971) "Road traffic in Greater London—results of speed and flow studies 1968–70", *Quarterly Bulletin of the Intelligence Unit*, September No. 16, pp. 3–14.
MUNT, P. W. and WEBSTER, F. V. (1968) "A study of road traffic crossing at cordons round the central area of eight towns with populations ranging from 18,000 to 8 million", Road Research Laboratory Report LR 209, Crowthorne, Berkshire.
MURPHY, CORNELIUS (1972) "New deal for motorway victims", *Official Architecture and Planning*, Vol. 35, No. 2, February, pp. 81–84.
NEW SOCIETY PRESS RELEASE (1970) "Urban motorways not popular with Londoners", 9 December, 2 pp.
NORTH KENSINGTON AMENITY TRUST (1971) "Inauguration at Town Hall, Kensington", 5 February, unpaginated.
OAP (1966) "The future of London in peril", *Official Architecture and Planning*, Vol. 29, No. 4, April, pp. 559–561.
OAP (1971) "The GLDP inquiry: Stage 1 transport", *Official Architecture and Planning*, Vol. 34, No. 6, June, pp. 471.
OAP, Leader (1966) "London's traffic: the price of confusion", *Official Architecture and Planning*, Vol. 29, No. 4, April, p. 527.
OSBORN, F. J. (1945) "The Garden City Movement; a revaluation", *Journal of the Town Planning Institute*, September, October, Vol. XXXI, No. 6, pp. 193–207.
OSBORN, F. J. (1963) "Letter to the Editor", *Journal of the Town Planning Institute*, Vol. 48, No. 9, November, p. 325.
OSBORN, F. J. (1971) "The history of Howard's 'Social Cities'", *Town and Country Planning*, Vol. 39, No. 12, December, pp. 539–545.
OWEN, WILFRED (1961) "Managing the transportation system", in BANFIELD, EDWARD C. (Ed.), *Urban Government*, The Free Press, New York, pp. 510–514.
OWEN, WILFRED (1972) *The Accessible City*, The Brooking Institutions, Washington D.C.
PARLIAMENTARY DEBATES (*Hansard*) (1965) *House of Commons Official Report for the Session 1964–5, comprising the period from 26th October to 9th November 1965*, Fifth Series, Vol. 718, London: HMSO.
PARLIAMENTARY DEBATES (*Hansard*), *House of Commons Official Report, 1965, Session 1965–6, comprising period from 22nd November to 3rd December*, Fifth Series, Vol. 721, London: HMSO, no date.
PARLIAMENTARY DEBATES (*Hansard*), *House of Commons Official Report, 1966,*

Session 1966–67, comprising period from 28th November to 9th December 1966, Fifth Series, Vol. 737, London: HMSO, no date.

DIRECTOR OF THE PEABODY TRUST (1970) "Comments on the Greater London Development Plan", GLDP Inquiry, Background Paper B605, December, unpublished, pp. 1–3.

PEARSON, NORMAN (1956) "Land use and transport systems", *Planning Outlook*, Vol. IV, No. 1, pp. 41–52.

PERRY, C. A. (1939) *Housing for the Machine Age*, New York: Russell Sage Foundation.

PLANNING CORRESPONDENT (1966) "Motorway for London 'premature'", the *Guardian*, 12 January.

PLANNING CORRESPONDENT (1970) "Sound of Silence...", the *Guardian*, 12 August.

POLITICAL CORRESPONDENT (1967) "GLC Box Road plan criticized", the *Guardian*, 30 November.

PLOWDEN, S. (1972) *Towns Against Traffic*, London: Andre Deutsch.

PLOWDEN, W. (1971) *The Motor Car and Politics 1896–1970*, London: Bodley Head Ltd.

PLUMMER, DESMOND (Con.) (1966) "Letter to the Editor", *Daily Telegraph*, 18 July.

POPPER, KARL R. (1972) "Of clouds and clocks", in KARL R. POPPER, *Objective Knowledge*, Oxford: Oxford University Press.

PROUDLOVE, J. A. (1964) "Traffic in towns: a review", *The Town Planning Review*, Vol. XXXIV, No. 4, January, pp. 253–268.

PURDOM, C. B. (1945) *How Should we Rebuild London?*, London: J. M. Dent & Sons.

RABINOVITZ, F. F. (1969) *City Politics and Planning*, New York: Atherton Press.

THE STANDING JOINT COMMITTEE OF THE R.A.C., A.A. AND R.S.A.C. (1962) "Memorandum on London Traffic Administration, *Written Evidence from Local Authorities, Miscellaneous Bodies and Private Individuals*, Vol. 1, London: HMSO, pp. 410–12.

RASMUSSEN, STEEN (1937) *London: The Unique City*, London: Cape.

RAYFIELD, F. A. (1956) "Reports at the British Road Federation Conference on Urban Motorways", BRF (Ed.), *Urban Motorways*, London: BRF, pp. 31–32.

READE, ERIC (1969) "Contradictions in planning", *Official Architecture and Planning*, Vol. 32, No. 10, October, pp. 1179–1185.

REGAN, DAVID (1966) "The expert and the administrator: recent changes at the Ministry of Transport", *Public Administration*, Vol. 44, December, pp. 149–169.

REINER, THOMAS, A. (1963) *The Place of the Ideal Community in Urban Planning*, Philadelphia: University of Pennsylvania Press.

Report of the London Planning Administrative Committee, London: HMSO, 1959.

RESEARCH COMMITTEE OF THE TOWN PLANNING INSTITUTE (1960) "Urban traffic problems", *Journal of the Town Planning Institute*, Vol. XLVI, No. 2, January, pp. 39–43.

REYNOLDS, D. J. (1966) *Economics, Town Planning and Traffic*, Institute of Economic Affairs, London.

RHODES, GERALD (1970) *The Government of London: The Struggle for Reform*, London: Weidenfeld & Nicolson.

RHODES, GERALD (1972) "Highways, Traffic and Transport", in RHODES, GERALD (Ed.), *The New Government of London: The First Five Years*, London: Weidenfeld & Nicolson.
RHODES, GERALD and RUCK, S. K. (1970) *The Government of Greater London*, London: George, Allen & Unwin.
RICHARDS, J. M. (1943) "London plans", *Geographical Magazine*, Vol. XVI, No. 1, May, pp. 1–13.
RIEMER, SVEND (1971) "The nucleated city", *British Journal of Sociology*, Vol. 22, No. 3, September, pp. 231–239.
"Ringway rift", *Evening Standard*, 21 March 1973.
ROBINSON, I. (1965) "Beyond the middle-range bridges", *Journal of the American Institute of Planners*, Vol. XXXI, No. 4, November, pp. 304–312.
ROBINSON, KENNETH, MINISTER OF PLANNING AND LAND (1969) "Letter to Douglas Jay", unpublished, pp. 1–2.
ROBSON, WILLIAM A. (1948) *The Government and Misgovernment of London*, London: George Allen & Unwin Ltd. 2nd ed.
RODWIN, LLOYD (1970) *Nations and Cities*, Boston: Houghton Mifflin Co.
RONDINELLI, DENNIS A. (1973) "Urban planning as policy analysis: management of urban change", *Journal of the American Institute of Planners*, Vol. 39, No. 1, January, pp. 13–22.
ROTH, S. J. (1964) "Town planners and road pricing", *Town and Country Planning*, Vol. XXXII, No. 8 and 9, August–September, pp. 366–368.
The Royal Academy Planning Committee's Interim Report (1942) "London replanned", Country Life Ltd., London, October, pp. 1–27.
ROYAL COMMISSION ON LOCAL GOVERNMENT IN GREATER LONDON 1957–1960, *Report*, London: HMSO, October 1960, Cmnd. 1164.
ROYAL COMMISSION ON LOCAL GOVERNMENT IN GREATER LONDON, Written Evidence from Local Authorities, Miscellaneous Bodies and Private Individuals, 1962, *Local Authorities—Administrative County of London*, Vol. 1, London: HMSO.
ROYAL COMMISSION ON LOCAL GOVERNMENT IN GREATER LONDON (1959) *Memoranda of Evidence from Government Departments*, Vol. 4, London: HMSO.
RUBENSTEIN, JAMES (1969) "The Motorway Box", unpublished thesis presented to the University of Chicago, Chicago.
SAGASTI, F. and ACKOFF, R. (1971) "Possible and likely futures for urban transport", *Socio-Economic Planning Sciences*, Vol. 5, No. 5, October, pp. 413–428.
THE HONOURABLE MR. JUSTICE SCARMAN (1962) "Town and country planning and the public", *Journal of the Town Planning Institute*, Vol. XLVIII, No. 7, July–August, pp. 188–191.
SCHNEIDER, L. M. (1968) "Urban mass transportation: a survey of the decision making process", in BAUER RAYMOND, A. and GERGEN, KENNETH, J. (Eds.), *The Study of Policy Formation*, New York: The Free Press, pp. 239–280.
SCHNORE, L. T. (1971) "The city as a social organism", in BOURNE, L. S. (Ed.), *Internal Structures of the City*, New York: Oxford University Press, pp. 32–39.
SELF, PETER (1961) "Highway folly", *Town and Country Planning*, Vol. XXIX, No. 8, pp. 305–306.

SELF, PETER (1961) *Cities in Flood; The Problems of Urban Growth*, (2nd ed.), London: Faber & Faber Ltd.
SELF, PETER (1965) *Bureaucracy or Management?*, an Inaugural Lecture, London: G. Bell & Sons.
SELF, PETER (1970), "Opinion: a planning charade", *Town and Country Planning*, Vol. 38, No. 8, September, pp. 366–369.
SELF, PETER (1971) *Metropolitan Planning*, The London School of Economics: London: Weidenfeld & Nicolson.
SELF, PETER (1972) *Administrative Theories and Politics*, London: George Allen & Unwin.
SELF, PETER (1974) "Is comprehensive planning possible and rational?", *Policy and Politics*, Vol. 2, No. 3, March.
SENIOR, DEREK (1971) "London in the region", in HILLMAN, JUDY (Ed.), *Planning for London*, Harmondsworth, Middlesex: Penguin Books, pp. 39–48.
SHEPEARD, PETER, STEPHENSON, GORDON and LING, ARTHUR (1950) "The New London, text of a BBC radio broadcast which took place on the Third Programme, 28 March, typescript, pp. 1–11.
SMALLWOOD, FRANK (1965) *Greater London*, Indianapolis: The Bobbs-Merrill Co. Ltd., Inc.
A Socialist Strategy for London—Labour Party Manifesto (1973) London: The Castle Press.
SOUTH-EAST ENGLAND YOUNG LIBERAL FEDERATION, "The Motorway Box briefing", undated, unpublished, 4 p.
SOUTH EAST JOINT PLANNING TEAM (1971) "Strategic plan for the South East, Strategies and Evolution, Vol. 4, London: HMSO.
STARKIE, D. N. M. (1973) "Transportation planning and public policy", *Progress in Planning*, Vol. I, No. 4, Oxford: Pergamon Press.
STEERING GROUP, COLIN, BUCHANAN *et al.* (1963) *Traffic in Towns*, London: HMSO.
STEIN, C. S. (1966) "Radburn planning; an American experiment", *Official Architecture and Planning*, Vol. 29, No. 3, March, pp. 301–314.
STEPHENSON, PROFESSOR GORDON (1951) "Hopes and fears for the London plans", from an address given to the Town and Country Planning Association National Conference, 4 and 5 October, typescript, pp. 1–7.
STEWART, J. D. (1971) *Management in Local Government: A Viewpoint*, London: Charles Knight.
STEWART, J. D. (1974) *The Responsive Local Authority*, London: Charles Knight.
STOLLMAN, J. (1971) "Getting from here to there", *Planning*, Vol. 37, No. 10, November, pp. 161–162.
STOTT, P. J. (1967) "Structure and management", *Traffic Engineering and Control*, Vol. 9, No. 1, May, pp. 35–39.
SUMMERSON, SIR JOHN (1967) "Letter to the Editor", *The Times*, 21 November, *The Sun* (1965) "12,500 families must move", 26 May.
SUTHERLAND, ALASDAIR C. (1958) "Land use and local traffic in the Central Area", *Planning Outlook*, Vol. IV, No. 4, pp. 48–53.
SWINTON, CAPTAIN G. (1906) "London Traffic", *Journal of the Society of Arts*, 2 March, pp. 437–449.
SWINTON, CAPTAIN G. (1924) *London: Her Traffic—an Improvement and Charing Cross Bridge*, London: John Murray, pp. 90.

"Talking about London Government" (1960) *Labour Research*, Vol. XLIX, No. 1, January pp. 13–15.
TAYLOR, NICHOLAS (1969) "The motorway juggernaut", *The Sunday Times*, 26 January.
TETLOW, JOHN and GOSS, ANTHONY (1968) *Homes, Towns and Traffic*, 2nd ed., London: Faber & Faber.
THOMAS, WYNDHAM (1961) "The growth of the London Region", *Town and Country Planning*, Vol. XXIX, No. 5, May, pp. 185–193.
THOMAS, WYNDHAM (1964) "Buchanan Report", *Town and Country Planning*, Vol. XXXII, No. 1, January, pp. 10–12.
THOMSON, J. M. (1971) "Transport: the motorway proposals", in HILLMAN, JUDY (Ed.), *Planning for London*, Harmondsworth, Middlesex: Penguin Books, pp. 86–98.
THOMSON, MICHAEL (1969) *Motorways in London*, London: Gerald Duckworth & Co. Ltd.
THOMSON, MICHAEL (1971) *Transportation Strategy in London*, GLDP Inquiry Proof E12/20 prepared for the London Motorway Action Group and the London Amenity and Transport Association, London: typescript, January.
THE TOWN PLANNING INSTITUTE (1962) "Evidence", *Written Evidence from Local Authorities, Miscellaneous Bodies and Private Individuals*, Vol. V, London: HMSO, pp. 425–436.
TRIPP, ALKER (1938) *Road Traffic and its Control*, London: Edward Arnold & Co.
TRIPP, ALKER (1942) *Town Planning and Road Traffic*, London: Edward Arnold & Co.
TRIPP, SIR ALKER (1946) "Traffic", in British Association for the Advancement of Science, *London Traffic and the London Plans*, a conference held in London on 12 and 13 September, pp. 100–102.
TUSLER, CARL (1970) "A motorway in London: learning from Western Avenue Extension", the *Surveyor*, 24 July, pp. 30–34.
UNWIN, RAYMOND (1911) *Town Planning in Practice*, 2nd ed., London: T. Fisher Unwin.
UNWIN, RAYMOND (1929) "Memorandum No. 1", *First Report of the Greater London Regional Planning Committee*, December, London: Knapp, Drewitt & Sons Ltd., pp. 8–26.
UNWIN, RAYMOND (1933) "Memorandum", *Second Report of the Greater London Regional Planning Committee*, March, London: Knapp, Drewitt & Sons Ltd., pp. 12–92.
UNWIN, SIR RAYMOND, (1938) Some notes from his presidential address in the Section of Architecture, Town Planning and Engineering, at the Annual Congress of the Royal Institute, July 1938, p. 439, *Journal of the Town Planning Institute*, Vol. XXIV, No. 12, October.
VICKERS, SIR GEOFFREY (1968) *The Art of Judgement: A Study of Policy Making*, London: University Paperbacks, Methuen.
VICKERS, SIR GEOFFREY (1968) *Value Systems and Social Processes*, Harmondsworth, Middlesex: Penguin Books.
VICKERS, SIR GEOFFREY (1972) "Commonly ignored elements in policymaking", *Policy Sciences*, Vol. 3, No. 2, July, pp. 265–266.
VIGARS, LEONARD (1967) "A reprieve from motorway threat", *Evening News*, 1 November.

WALLING, ROBERT (1965) "And London may lead the way", *Evening Standard*, 31 March.
WEBB, SIDNEY and BEATRICE (1913) *The Story of the King's Highway*, London: Ingrave Dunn & Co. (reprinted by Frank Cass & Co., 1963).
WEBBER, MELVIN M. (1963) "Order in diversity: community without propinquity", in LOWDON WINGO, JR. (Ed.), *Cities in Space*, Baltimore: The John Hopkins Press, pp. 23–54.
WEBBER, MELVIN M. (1965) "The roles of intelligence systems in urban systems planning", *Journal of the American Institute of Planners*, Vol. XXXI, No. 4, November, pp. 287–296.
WEDGWOOD-OPPENHEIM, F., HART, D. A. and COBLEY, B. (1974) "An exploratory study of strategic monitoring", a report to the Department of the Environment, Birmingham, October, typescript. (Forthcoming, *Progress in Planning*, Vol. 5, Part 1, Oxford: Pergamon Press.)
WEISMANTEL, WILLIAM L. (1959) "Dante's Inferno: the first land use model", *Journal of the American Institution of Planners*, Vol. XXV, No. 4, November, pp. 175–179.
WEST LONDON ARCHITECTURAL SOCIETY (1970) "West Cross Route statement", 23 April, pp. 1–2.
WILCOX, DAVID (1969) "The Motorway Box—2 GLC pledges", *Evening Standard*, 19 April.
WILCOX, DAVID (1970) "LMAG appeal", *Evening Standard*, 9 May.
WILCOX, DAVID (1971a) "The Greater London Development Plan", in HILLMAN, JUDY (Ed.), *Planning for London*, Harmondsworth: Penguin Books, pp. 17–36.
WILCOX, DAVID (1971b) "Keeping the car out of Central London", *Evening News*, 27 October.
WILCOX, DAVID (1972) "GLC Tories shelve half of those highly controversial road plans", *Evening Standard*, 5 September.
WILLIAMS, DAVID D. (1971) "The modal split", *Town Planning Review*, Vol. 42, No. 2, April, pp. 181–194.
WINGO, LOWDON (1963) "Urban space in a policy perspective: an introduction", in LOWDON WINGO, JR. (Ed.), *Cities and Space: The Future Use of Urban Land*, Baltimore: The John Hopkins Press, pp. 3–21.
WISE, M. J. (1961) "The crisis for British planning", *Town and Country Planning*, Vol. XXIX, No. 5, May, pp. 179–184.
WOLF, R. J. (1961) "Letter to Lewis Mumford dated 18 November 1959", *Journal of the American Institute of Planners*, Vol. XXVII, No. 1, February, pp. 74–75.
WOOD, PETER (1963) "Studying traffic in towns", *Journal of the Town Planning Institute*, Vol. 49, No. 8, Sept./Oct., pp. 265–271.
WOODS, S. (1972) "The role of the architect in community building", in GWEN BELL and J. TYRWHITT (Eds.), *Human Identity in the Urban Environment*, Harmondsworth: Penguin Books, pp. 376–393.
WRIGHT, MYLES (1963) "Planning ideas", *Journal of the Town Planning Institute*, Vol. 49, No. 10, December, pp. 349–356.

Index

"A" ring (see also Ring roads) 74, 77, 107, 135
Abercrombie, Professor Patrick 7, 43 ff., 53 ff., 56 n., 56–57 ff., 75 n., 81, 93 ff., 96, 98 ff., 104 ff., 113 ff., 135 ff., 142 ff., 147, 150 n., 153, 159 n., 180, 184, 185, 188, 189, 194, 200, 204
  concept of urban order 3
  county of London plan 175
  "geometry" 71 ff.
  Greater London plan 1944 40 n., 54, 176, 186
  influence on London planning 54
  London's major defects 59–60
  on "drawing-board planning" 65
  organic concept of city 56
  planning in town and country 63
  road plan, role in town planning 71, cf. note re: Tripp p. 71
  sources of his thought 57
  static vision of future 56
  town and county planning 39 n., 56 n.
Abercrombie, Professor Patrick and Forshaw, H. H., county of London Plan (1943) 57 n.
Abercrombie Plans 10, 36, 61, 87
  recapitulation 83 ff.
  replanning from top and bottom simultaneously 83
  population growth halt 84
Abercrombie–Buchanan
  "geometry" 143, 147; "hierarchy" 143, 147
  plans contrasted 101 (table)
  road hierarchy 147
  "movement systems" 153
Abercrombie and Forshaw 153 n.
Accidents 66, 68

Advisory Committee for London Regional Planning 45 n.
Aldous, Tony 113 n.
Alexander, Christopher 81 n.
Allison, Graham T. 183 n., 187 n., 192 n.
Alonso, William, "Cities and city planners" 59 n., 200
Altshuler, Alan 117, 126, 199 n.
  The City Planning Processes 14, 15 n.
American traffic experience 31
Andrews, C. D. 52 n.
Arterial roads 71, 75, 76
Ash, Maurice, A Guide to the Structure of London 39 n., 144 n., 145 n.
Aucott, Joan V., "Planning and the motor vehicle" 35 n., 92 n.
Autobahn 70
Autostrada 70

"B" ring 74, 77, 108, 135, 136 n.
Bailey, Michael 157 n.
Baker, J. F. A. 108, 109, 179
Balfour, Patrick 103 n.
Banfield, Edward C. 13 n., 157, 162 n., 185 n.
Banfield, Edward C. and Meyerson, Martin, Politics, Planning and the Public Interest 26 n.
Barker, Felix, Riverside Highway—The Evening News Plan 28 n.
Barlow Commission Report 60
Bauer, Raymond and Gergen, Kenneth J., The Study of Policy Formulation 27 n.
Beckman, Norman 201 n.
Beer, Stafford 10 n.

226   Index

Beesley, M. E.   146
Beesley, M. E. and Kain, J. F., "Urban form, car ownership and public transport; an appraisal of traffic in towns"   147 n.
Bell, Daniel   7
Bellamy, Alec, "The 1943 London Plan: a perspective"   55 n.
Bendixson, Terence, "Transport: the two cities"   166 n.
"Biological triad"   63 n.
Blackman   16
Blake, John   144
 "London's proposed motorways: some unanswered questions"   145 n., 163 n.
 "Shopping"   147 n.
 "shopping and suburban development"   144 n.
Blanfield, Edward C.   6 n.
Blau, P. M.   190 n.
Bloomsbury   81, 82 (diag.)
Board of Trade, *Reports of the London Traffic Branch*   42 n.
Bor, Walter   203 n.
Bor, Walter and Roberts, John   79 n.
Bossom, Sir Clive, M.P. for Leominster   30
Bow Group   112
Boyce, David E.   183 n.
Branch, Melvin, "Goals and objectives of comprehensive planning"   19 n.;
 Planning: Aspects and Applications   18 n.
Braybrooke, David   21 n.
Braybrooke, David and Chas. E. Lindblom, *A Strategy of Decision*   17
Bressey, Sir Charles   122 n.
Bressey, Sir Charles and Lutyens, Sir Edwin
 Royal Academy Plan   57 n.
 Highway Development Survey 1937 (Greater London)   70 n.
 Bressey Report   73, 74, 79 n.
 Bressey proposals   143
British Rail   120, 154
British Rail and GLC financial policy   155

British Road Federation   29, 108, 109 n., 124 n., 125, 125 n., 150, 160, 167, 178, 179
 People and Cities   27 n.
Britton, Harris   11 n.
Brown, George   48 n.
Brown, Muriel   132 n.
Buchanan, Colin   3, 6 n., 86, 88, 92, 93, 94, 97 n., 98 ff., 104, 114, 124, 131, 136 ff., 142 ff., 147, 180, 184, 185, 188, 189, 194, 200, 204, 205
Buchanan, Colin and Abercrombie, Patrick
 geometry, "movement systems"   147, 153
 plans contrasted   101 (table)
Buchanan, C. M.
 London Road Plans   57 n.
 London Road Plans 1900–1970   153 n.
 Mixed Blessing   99 n., 100 n., 164
 N.-E. London   149 n., 150 n.
 Traffic in Towns   88 ff., 146, 148 n., 150, 175
 Transport and the Community   95 n., 108 n.
Buchanan Report   88, 94
Buchanan, Colin and Partners   123 n.
 Consultants to GLC   88, 145
 The Conurbations   149
 North-East London   165 n.
Burgess, Ernest W., spatial analysis in "The growth of the City"   63 n.
Burnham, Daniel   53
Butler, R. A. B.   112

"C" ring   74, 77, 135
Camden, London Borough of   159
Canalization of Traffic   101, 125, 126, 137, 139, 145, 151, 164, 200
Car ownership, effect on London's growth   39
Carroll, J. Douglas   25
Cars, penetrating power of   92
Carter, Edward   44 n., 102, 107 n.
 The Future of London   26 n.

Index

Cellular completeness 85
Cellular groupings, cellular structure 78 ff., 85, 148
Central London 69
Central London Plan (1943) 55 ff.
Chadwick, G. 199 n.
Change, dealing with inducing 2, 5 ff.
Change, incorporating in planning 13
Chapin, F. Stuart, *Urban Land Use Planning* 96 n.
Chelsea Boat Owners' Association 159
Cherry, Gordon E. 10 n.
Chief Planner, Ministry of Housing and Local Government 105 n.
Cities in Evolution by Patrick Geddes 58
City Cybernetic 193
City Mechanistic 188, 193
City of London 63 n.
City Organic 184, 188, 193
City Planning Processes by Alan Altschuler 14
City Politics and Planning by Francine Rabinovitz 14
Cobley, B. W. 202 n., 205 n.
Cohesive policy made 182 ff., 191, 195 ff.
Collins, M. F. 191 n.
Collins, Michael F. and Pharoah, Timothy M., *Transport Organization in a Great City* 155 n.
Commons, House of 48–49
Communal London, Community London 62–63, 78
Communities 78, 79, 80
Community area amenities 68
Community opposition 172 ff.
Community, sense of 80–81
Compensation 163
Comprehensive planning 199, 203, 204
Conduits 98
Conservative Party 113, 129, 173 ff.
Containment (*see also* Green Belt) 61
Contingency planning 201, 202, 204
Cooper, G. H. C. 122 n.
"Corridors of opportunity" 123
County of London Plan 10, 73, 74, 93, 95, 147, 151
Craig, John 53, 111 n., 136 n.

"The 1943 London Plan: a perspective" 55 n.
Crane, David A. 91 n.
Crawford, K. A. J., "The 1971 Greater London Transportation Survey" 161 n., 176
Creese, Walter 5
Crosland, Anthony, Secretary of State for Local Government and Regional Planning 160 n., 169
Crowther, Sir Geoffrey 94 n., 100 n.
Cullingworth, J. B. 13 n.
Cumbernauld New Town 91

"D" ring 74, 77, 129, 131, 135, 136
Dahir, James 80 n.
Dahl, Robert A. 34; *Modern Political Analysis* 34 n.
Davidoff, Paul 194 n.
Decanting of population 61, 64, 66, 67, 84
Decentralization (*see also* London polycentric form developing) 147
Decentralization of outer London 64
Deckman, Norman 196 n.
Denington, Mrs Evelyn, Deputy Leader of Labour Opposition on GLC 123, 172
Density controls 86
Department of Scientific and Industrial Research 108
Derwent, Lord 125 n.
Deutsch, Karl 193
"Development and Compensation—Putting People First" 163 n.
Development Control 50
Development Plan *Review* 1960 108, 109
Development Plans: a Manual on Form and Content 12 n.
Dewey, John 193 n.
Diffused Policy Mode 192 ff., 195 ff., 206
Director of Traffic 51
Disjointed incrementalism 197, 206
an iterative planning 21 ff.; contrasted 22

Index

Donnison, David et al., *Observations on the Greater London Development Plan* 158 n.
Downs, Anthony 13 n.
Doxiadis, Constantine 6 n.
Dror, Gehezkial 22 n.
Dykman, John 16 n.

Edmonds, Richard 105, 123
Elkin, Stephen J. 194 n.
Elliott, Sir John, Chairman of London Transport Executive 28
Environment, Department of the (*see also* Ministry of Transport) 163, 199
formed 169
Environmental areas (Buchanan) 147, 148
crude traffic capacity 89 ff.
"E" Ring 136
"E" Ring Road 74, 77
Etzioni, Amatai 21; *The Active Society* 21 n.
Evening News 28
Evening Standard 30
Eversley, David 174 n., 180 n.
Expenditure on roads 110
Explanatory Memorandum 12
(Town & County Planning Act, 1947) and 12 n.
Express arterial roads 76

Fabian Society 112, 113
Factored Policy Made 186 ff., 192, 195 ff.
Fagin, Henry and Schnore, Leo F., eds., *Urban Research and Policy Planning* 15 n.
Faludi, Andrea 182 n.
Farhi, Andre 183 n.
Finchley Road 106
Fitch, Lyce C., *Urban Transportation and Public* 40 n.
Foley, Donald L. 10 and n., 11, 43 n., 114 n., 121 n.
Forshaw, J. H. 65 n., 79, 81 n., 105, 136; *Town Planning and Health* 147

Forshaw J. H. and Abercrombie, Prof. Patrick 54; *County of London Plan (1943)* also 54 n.
Forshaw and Abercrombie 153 n.
Freeman, Fox (jorden) 111, 112 n.
Friedman, John 24 n., 186, 197 n., 199 n.
Friedman, John and Miker, John, "The urban field" 144 n.
Friend, J. K. 6 n., 114 n., 183 n., 191 n.; *inter alia, Public Planning: the Inter-Corporate Dimension* 14 n.
Functional components of London 61 ff., 78, 80, (diag.)
and road system hierarchy 81
Future, planning for 5 ff.
Future of Development Plans, 1964 12

Gaitskill, Hugh 448
Gans, Herbert, "City planning in America" 56 n., 118, 181
Garden Cities of Tomorrow by Ebenezer Howard 58
Garden City principles applied to London 58
Geddes, Patrick 7 n., 57–58, 63
Cities in Evolution 58
influence on Abercrombie 57
Glanville, W. H. 108, 109, 179
Glazer, Nathan 80 n.
Goldrick, Michael 47 n., 119 n., 120, 121 n., 127 n.
the administration of transportation in Greater London 154 n.
Goodman, Paul and Percy 91 n.
Goodwin, Sir Reg
Leader of Labour Opposition on GLC 172
Leader of GLC 175
Gorvine, Albert 12 n.
Goss, Anthony and Tetlow, John, *Homes, Towns and Traffic* 40 n.
Grade-separation 110
Greater London Council 1, 3, 4, 31, 48 ff., 148, 150 ff.
British Rail financial policy 155
broadens transport powers 155
cost-benefit study 163
department of planning and transportation formed 169

Greater London Council (*cont.*)
elections, April 1970   157
elections, Feb. 1973   174
Environmental Effects of the Construction of Primary Roads—illustrative examples   149 *n*.
London's roads—a programme for action   154 *n*.
MOT plans, opposition to   159 ff.
MOT proposals   129ff., 139, 142ff, 151, 163, 189, 190, 194, 205
Movement   38, 165 *n*.
New Roads via West and North Central London   164 *n*.
Planning policy   2
a secondary roads policy   165 *n*.
Services   49 *n*.
strategic road planning and urban order   24
to control all principal roads   155
to tackle planning and traffic problems   53
Tomorrow's London   31 *n*.
Urban Design Bulletin   165 *n*.
Westway: An Environmental and Traffic Appraisal   166 *n*.
Greater London Development Plan (1969)   7
comparison with 1929 plan   8
introduces increased concept of control   8, 50, 128, 131, 133, 144, 149, 156, 157, 176, 189 *n*., 190
Greater London Development Plan Inquiry   167 ff., 173, 192, 195
first regional plan (1929)   7
Inquiry-conclusions   170 ff.
opposition to   160 ff.
Report of Studies   35 *n*.
Statement Revisions   168 *n*.
Greater London Group   52 *n*., 140 *n*.
Greater London Plan   10, 75 *nn*., 76 (map)
Greater London Plan (1944)   43, 55 ff., 76 (map), 103, 106 *n*., 136 *n*., 137, 145, 184
Greater London roads, authority for   41
responsibility for   41
Greater London Transportation Survey   161 *n*.
Green Belt   49 *n*., 61, 63–64, 74, 84, 85, 118, 185

Greenwich   159
Gresham Cooke, R., M.P. for Twickenham   29
Griffith, J. A. G.   110 *n*.
Gross, Bertram   158 *n*.
Guardian Planning Correspondent   158 *n*.
Guen, Victor, *The Heart of Our Cities*   68, 68 *n*.
Gutheim, Frederick, "The future city and its transportation"   36 *n*.
Guttenberg, Albert, "Urban structure and urban growth"   36 *n*.

Hagman, Donald G.   134 *n*.
Hall, Peter   37, 65 *n*., 103 *n*., 112, 139 *n*., 182 *n*.
London 2000   26
Hall, Sir Robert (*et al*.), *The Transport Needs of Great Britain in the next Twenty years*   34 *n*.
Halpin, W. R. C.   163 *n*.
Hampstead Motorway Action Group   159
Harris, Britton   10, 23 *n*., 204 *n*.
Harrison, M. L., "Development control"   61 *n*.
Hart, D. A.   181 *n*., 202 *n*., 205 *n*.
Hawley, Amos   58 *n*.
Heap, Desmond   11 *n*.
Henderson, Irwin and Hillman, Mayer, "Towards a better kind of environmental area"   149 *n*.
Herbert Commission   43 ff., 117 *n*.;
Report   54 *n*.
Herbert, Sir Edwin   43
Herbert, Gilbert   184 *n*.; "The organic analogy in town planning"   59 *nn*.
Hierarchical road system   104, 137 ff., 184, 188, 200
Higgins, Christopher   103
Highway construction   46
Highway Development Survey, 1937   74 (Greater London)   127 *n*.
Highway planning   46
Hillman, Mayer   118 *n*.

Index

Hillman, Mayer and Henderson, Irwin, "Towards a better kind of environmental area" 149 *n.*
Holden, C. H. and Holford, W. G., *Reconstruction in the City of London* 63 *n.*
Holford, Sir William 58–59 and 59 *n.*
Holford, W. G. and Holden, C. H., *Reconstruction in the City of London* 63 *n.*
Holleb, Doris B. 11 *n.*
Holmes, Denis 126 *n.*
Homes Before Roads 159
Housing 106, 168
Housing and Local Government, Ministry of 36–37, 37 *n.*, 55, 104 *n.*, 105 *n.*, 169
Housing substandard 165
Howe, Geoffrey, M.P. for Bebington 30
Howard, Ebenezer 57, 58 and 58 *n.*
  Garden Cities of Tomorrow 58
  influence on Abercrombie 57–58, 64 *n.*
Hunt, R. N. and Webster, F. V., *Road Research Laboratory Report* 32 *n.*
Husband & Co. 123 *n.*
Hutchings, Ken, "Urban transport: public or private" 128 *n.*, 165 *n.*
Hyde Park Corner underpass 31

Industrial Population, Report of the Royal Commission on the Distribution of 60 *n.*
Inner London Motorway 171, 174
Inner ring road 72, 74
Inner Urban Ring 63–64
  City of London "punched out" of 63 *n.*
Inns of Court 81
Inter-authority problems 51
Iterative planning 2, 3, 11 ff., 13, 14, 23, 24
  and disjointed incrementalism 21 ff.;
  contrasted 22
  and error-elimination 18

Jackson, Eric W. 106 *n.*
Jacobs, Jane, *The Death and Life of Great American Cities* 60 *n.*
James, J. R. 105 *n.*
Jay, Douglas, M.P. 159, 161 *n.*, 162 *n.*
Jeffreys, Rees 153
Jenkins, Simon 109 *n.*, 180 *n.*
  The Politics of London Motorways 162 *n.*
Jessop, W. N. 6 *n.*, 114 *n.*, 183 *n.*
Johnson-Marshall, Percy, *Rebuilding Cities* 42 *n.*
Joseph, Sir Keith 50 *n.*
Juster, Robert J. 112 *n.*

Kahn, Louis 91
Kain, J. F. 146
Kain, J. F. and Beesley, M. E., "Urban form, car ownership and public transport an appraisal of traffic in towns" 147 *n.*
Kensington and Chelsea, L. B. of 168
Kent, County of, and the Greater London Plan 55
Kent, T. J., *The Urban General Plan* 15
King, Michael F. 103 *n.*, 125 *n.*
Kirwan, R. M. 36, 118 *n.*
Knight, Timothy 112 *n.*
Korn, A. and Samuely, F. J. A., "A master plan for London" 57 *n.*
Kress, Paul F., *Social Science and the Idea of Process* 14 *n.*

Labour Party 113, 129, 157, 172 ff.
Lambeth, London Borough of 158
Land requirements for road system 134
Land use and transportation 12
Land use planning 2, 36
  integration with road planning 113 ff.
  transportation surveys 116
Layfield, Frank 160, 201
Layfield Inquiry (*see also* GLDP Inquiry) 160 ff.
Leach, Edmund 6 *n.*
Le Play 63 *n.*
Levin, P. H. 190 *n.*

Index

Lewisham, London Borough of 159
Lindblom, Charles 21, 22 n., 192, 197
  The Policy Making Process 174 n.
Lindblom, Chas E. and Braybrooke, David, *A Strategy of Decision* 17 n.
Llewelyn-Davies, Lord 193 n.
Local area 148
Local authority boundaries 47
  co-operation 86
Local Government in Greater London, Royal Commission of 36, 37 n., 104 n., 110 n., 117, 119 n.
Local Road System 131, 138
London (*see also* Greater London; Greater London Council; County of London)
London, Administrative County of, Development Plan (1951), First Review 5, 104, 107 n.
London Amenity & Transport Association (LATA) 159, 168, 171, 193, 194
London & Home Counties Traffic Advisory Committee 28, 29 n.
London as a "nuclear city" 38
London Borough 49 ff.
London Boroughs 140, 179, 188, 205
London Boroughs Association 50 n.
London, car usage decreasing 161
London, Central Area of 64, 72, 78, 84, 90, 91
London, City of 48 n., 49
London County Council (LCC) 37, 38, 41, 49
London County Council, Abercrombie and Forshaw,
  County of London Plan (1943) 54
  Administrative County of London Development Plan 1951—
  Analysis 38 n.
  Administrative Development Plan Statement 1951 41 n.
  "Written evidence" 41 n.
London employment figures falling 161
London Government Act of 1888 37
London Government Act, 1963 48 ff., 49 n., 103, 150, 156 n.
London Government: Proposals for Reorganisation 48
London—Great Fire of 1666 41

London Highway Division 154
London's major defects 59–60
London Motorway Action Group (LMAG) 159, 167, 168, 171, 194
  "Appeal Letter" 165 n.
  "Ringway 2" 165 n.
London Passenger Transport Area 38
London Passenger Transport Board (later London Transport Executive) 37–38, 37 n., 40, 49 n.
London pattern of growth 38
London Plan (1943), County of 43, 54–55, 67, 105, 135, 136, 145, 184
London Policy Division 154
London, polyceretric form developing (*see also* Decentralization) 144
London population figures falling 161
London Road System 75
London roads, Report of the Committee on 111 n.
London's physical defects 96, 99
London's road pattern, history of 41–42
London's roads, expenditure on 42
London Traffic Management Unit 47 n., 51
London Traffic, Report of the Royal Commission on (1905) 96 n.
London Traffic Survey (LTS) (*see also* London Transportation Study) 111 ff., 127, 145, 146, 156, 189, 201
London Transport 45, 120, 154, 155
  debt 155
  executive 155
  executive report, 1958 28
  in 1958 28 n.
London Transportation Study 127, 128, 131, 161, 189
Long, Arthur 108 n.
Long, Norton E., "Planning and politics in urban development" 158 n.
Lords, House of 48–49
Lutyens, Sir Edward 122
Lutyens, Sir Edwin and Bressey, Sir Charles
  Bressey Report 74
  Highway Development Survey 1937 (Greater London) 70 n.
  Royal Academy Plan 57 n.

232 Index

McDonald, Chris   183
McLoughlin, J. Brian   9 n, 10 n., 199 n.
Macmurray, Trevor   193
Maitland   79
Marguilies, Samuel L.   12 n.
Marples, Rt. Hon. Ernest, Minister of Transport   27, 30, 111, 126
Marsh, Richard, Minister of Transport   152 n.
Marshall, T. H., *The Population Problem*   61 n.
Massey, Doreen B. and Martyn Cordey-Hayes, "The use of models in structure planning"   147 n.
Master Planning   181, 189, 197, 201, 204
Master Plans/Planning   2
Mechanistic London   62–63, 78
Medhurst, Franklin   195
Meier, Richard L.   193 n.
Metropolitan Police   51
Metropolitan Roads   50, 51
Meyerson, Martin   183 n.
Meyerson, Martin and Banfield, Edward C., *Politics, Planning and the Public Interest*   26 n., 174 n.
Middlesex, County of   55
Miller, John and Friedmann, John, "The urban field"   144 n.
Mitchell, Robert B.   116 n.
Modal Split   107 n.
Monitorius   9
Montgomery, Roger   199 n.
Monumental London   62–63, 78
Morrison, Lord   49 n.
Motorway Box (*see also* Ringway One)   13, 102, 103, 104, 121 ff., 157, 202
   opposition to   158 ff.
Motorway Ring   173
Motorway Rings abandoned   175
Mumford, Lewis   80 n., 142
Murphy, Cornelius   179; "New deal for motorway victims"   166 n.

National road network   75
Neighbourhood precincts (*see also* Cellular groupings, cellular structure)   79, 80, 81

New Towns   61, 83, 84
Nicholas, R.   109 n.
Nisbet, Robert, *Social Change and History*   20 n.
Niven and Pepler's ring road proposals   75 n.
North Circular   74, 129, 131, 173
North-East London   145
Nugent Committee   111 n.

Optional traffic increasing   164
Orbital roads   170, 171
Order, in relation to change   5
Organic analogy in town planning   58 ff.
Osborn, Sir Frederick   58; "The Garden City Movement: a revaluation"   58 n.
Osborn, F. J.   204
Outer Country Ring   63–64
Outer Orbital Route   135
Outer Ring   129
Owen, Wilfred   67 n., 112 n.; *The Accessible City*   35 n., 156 n.

Parking controls   109
Parking, off street   51
Parliamentary Debates   29 n., 30, 31
Participation in planning   205
Pearson, Norman, "Land use and transport systems"   39 n.
Pedestrian segregation   91
Pepler and Niven's ring road proposals   75 n.
Perloff, Harvey S.   9 n.
Perrin, Constance   13 n.
Perry, Clarence, *Housing for the Machine Age*   67 n.
Pharoah, Timothy   191 n.
Pharoah, Timothy M. and Collins, Michael F., *Transport Organization in a Great City*   155 n.
Planning Advisory Group PAG Report   9
Planning, as a continuous process   13, 182
   as a learning process   177
   as a *process*   11, 197, 203, 204, 206

Index 233

Planning (*cont.*)
concept of 16 ff.
hard 137, 138, 142, 177 ff., 192, 194, 200, 203 ff.
increases as rate of change increases 6
makes future more acceptable 6–7
operation fluid 13
physical-prescriptions 87 (table)
process 2, 15, 16
public 14
soft 178 ff., 203 ff.
spiral, composition of 19 ff.
traditional 93 ff.
Plastic control system 203 ff.
Plowden, Stephen 78 n., 128 n.
Plummer, Sir Desmond 129 n., 180
Policy planning 13
Political parties, need for co-operation 86
Politicization of planning process 176, 179
Polycentric City 194, 204
Popper, Karl 203 n.
"Of clouds and clocks" 18 n.
The Poverty of Historicism 20 n.
Population to be reduced 61
Poverty, Planning and Politics by Stephan Thernstrom 14, 15
Power, J. M., *inter alia, Public Planning: The Inter-Corporate Dimension* 14 n.
Precincts 98, 147, 148
Principle of planning 137
Precincts neighbourhoods (*see also* Cellular groupings, cellular structure 79, 80, 81
Primary Road Network 1, 127 ff., 143, 144, 145, 147, 148, 151 ff., 155, 156, 168, 172, 174, 175, 177 ff., 189, 199, 201, 204
cost of 134, 163
fall of 142 ff.
Primary System 2
Private passenger-carrying vehicles in London 26 ff., 32 ff.
Process, concept of, in planning 14
Proudlove, J. Alan 88
Public Planning 14

Public Planning: the Inter-corporate Dimension by J. K. Friend, J. M. Power and C. J. L. Yewlett 14 n.
Public transport 155–156, 171
network in London 35
Purdom, C. B. 184 n.; *How shall we Rebuild London?* 69 n.

Rabinowitz, Francine 20 n., 176, 197 n.;
City Politics and Planning 14
Radburn, New Jersey 85 n.
Radial Motorways 110, 122 ff., 133, 180, 200
Radial Roads 74
Railway Termini 74
Rapkin, Chester 116 n.
Rasmussen, Steen 80 n
Rayfield, F. A. 108
Reconcentration of inner London 72
Regional Development Authority (*see* Regional Planning Authority)
Regional Planning Authority 86
Regional Planning Board 61 n.
Reith, Lord 54
Report of the Royal Commission on the Distribution of the Industrial Population 60 n.
Report of the Royal Commission on London Traffic 27 n.
Reynolds, D. J., *Economics, Town Planning and Traffic* 164 n.
Rhodes, Gerald 46 n., 47, 51 n., 52 n., 127 n., 190 n.
Rhodes, Gerald and Ruck, S. K., *The Government of Greater London* 38 n., 155 n.
Richards, J. M. 192 n.; "London plans" 66 n.
Riermer, Svend 81
Riley, D. M. 9 n.
Ring-radial-cross system 65, 73
Ring-radial road system 84, 146
Ring Road 73, 74, 75, 76, 77, 84
System 104, 107, 121, 122, 133, 188, 194, 200
Ring Roads, concentric (*see also* Spatial components of London) 63 ff., 64

234 Index

Ring Roads (cont.)
  (diag.), 77, 85
  in fortified continental towns 75
Ringway One 131, 133, 135, 168, 171, 172, 173
  cost of 162, 163
  west cross route 159
  and party politics 172
Ringway Three 135, 168
  Two 129 n., 133, 135, 168, 172, 173
Ringways 173
Riverside Highway—the *Evening News* Plan, Felix Barker 28 n.
Road building plans reduced 173
Road constructions, large scale 152
Road "hierarchy" 69, 92
  network 148
  network physical form 73
Road Plan 73
  (Abercrombie's) purpose-dependent 73
Road Planning 65 ff.
  Strategic 14
Road Research Laboratory 28; *Report*, Hunt, R. N. and Webster, F. V. 32 n.
Roads, approach 85
Roads, approach or local 70
Roads, arterial 69, 85
Roads, at expense of local environment 148 ff.
Roads congestion 26 ff.
  of people? 39
Roads for access to buildings 68
Roads for movement from place to place 68
Roads, local 50
Roads, sub-arterial 69, 85
  three basic types 85
Roberts, John 203 n.
Roberts, John and Bor, Walter 79 n.
Robinson, Kenneth, Minister of Planning and Land 161 n.
Robson, Professor William 42, 45 n., 49 n.; *The Government and Misgovernment of London* 42 n., 74 n.
Robson, William A. 96 n., 204 n.
Rodwin, Lloyd 7 n.
Royal Academy Planning Committee, "London replanned" 57

Royal Commission on Local Government in England 52 n.
Royal Commission on London Traffic, Report of the 27 n.
Royal Institute of British Architects 160
Royal Institute of Chartered Surveyors 51 n.
Ruck, S. K. 47 n., 51 n., 52 n., 127 n.
Ruck, S. K. and Rhodes, Gerald, *The Government of Greater London* 38 n., 155 n.

Samuely, F. J. A. and Korn, A., "A master plan for London" 57 n.
Sandys, Duncan, Minister of Housing and Local Government 39
Schnore, Leo T., "The city as a social organism" 58 n., 59 n.
Schnore, Leo F., and Fagin, Henry, *Urban Research and Policy Planning* 15 n.
Schon, Donald 7 n., 184 n.
Schools—neighbourhood focus 80
Scott, Sir Harold, Metropolitan Commissioner of Police 27
Scott, P. F., "Structure and Management" 28 n.
Scott, W. Richard 190 n.
Secondary Road network 145, 166, 171
  system 131 ff., 138; cost of 163; demand would exceed capacity 165
Self, Peter J. 8 n., 50 n., 113, 114 n., 115 n., 140 n., 149, 169, 200
  Metropolitan Planning 150 n.
  "Town planning in Greater London" 54 n.
Sharpe, L. J. 46 n.
Shepeard, Peter 108 n.
Silkin, Lewis 87 n.
Silverman, David 196 n.
Simon, Herbert, *The Sciences of the Artificial* 59
Simon, Herbert A. 188 n.
Skeffington Report 187 n.
Smallwood, Frank 45 n., 48
Smith, Dudley, M.P. for Brentford and Chiswick 30

Index

Social Science and the Idea of Process, by Paul F. Kress 14 *n*.
South Circular 74, 77, 129, 131, 173
Spatial components of London (*see also* Rings, concentric) 61, 63 ff., 95
  differentiated by road networks
  geometric symmetry 83
Starkie, D. N. M. 116 *n*.
Stein, Clarence 85 *n*.
Stepney 106 *n*.
Stollman, Israel, "Getting from here to there" 37 *n*.
Stott, Peter 128, 179
Strategic Centres 144
  Highways 148
  Planning (road) 14
Strategic road planning and urban order 24
Strategy of Decision, A, David Braybrooke and Chas. E. Lindblom 17
Stephenson, Professor Gordon, "Hopes and fears for the London plans" 56 *n*.
Sub-arterial roads 71
Suburban Ring 63–64
Suburban Shopping Centre Growth 144
Sutherland, Alasdair C. 178 *n*.
Swingler, Stephen, Secretary for Parliamentary affairs 30–31
Swinton, G. S. C. 103 *n*.

Tetlow, John and Goss, Anthony, *Homes, Towns and Traffic* 40 *n*.
Therstrom, Stephan, *Poverty, Planning and Politics* 14–15
Thomas, Wyndham 54; "The growth of the London Region" 55 *n*.
Thomson, J. Michael, *A Transportation Strategy for London* 65 *n*.
Thomson, Michael 121 *n*., 128 *n*., 160 *n*., 161, 162 *n*., 163 *n*., 164 *n*., 179 *n*., 194 *n*.
(*et al*.) *Motorways in London* 153 *n*.
Through Traffic 66
von Thunen's rings 38 *n*.
The Times 157
Toffler, Alvin 7 *n*.

Tory Party 48
Tower Hamlets, London Borough of 159
Town & Country Planning Act (1932) 12; (1947) 12, 45 *n*., 185
  Explanatory Memorandum 12
Town & Country Planning Act 55
Town & County Planning Act (1962) 12; (1968) 11, 12–13
  land use and transportation 12
Town & Country Planning Association 160
Town & Country Planning, Minister of 55 *n*., 104
Town and Country Planning Regulations, 1965 50 *n*.
Town planning and control of change 7
  as a set of harmonious relationships 7–8
  and concept of control increases 8
  attempt to achieve flexibility not new 10
  should both control and reflect change 8 ff.
Town planning, classical approach to 2
Town Planning Institute 51 *n*.
Town Planning unitary and adaptive approaches 10
Town Plans to become strategic decision documents 9–10
Traffic and urban structure, relationship between 87 ff.
Traffic architecture (Buchanan) 91
Traffic, physically canalization 65 ff., 67, 96
Traffic circulation 66
Traffic congestion 26, 42, 65 ff., 68
Traffic control, policy for 148 ff.
Traffic—crude capacity of environmental area 90
Traffic, different purposes of 68 and *n*.
Traffic direction 72
Traffic in given area not unalterable, fixed (Buchanan) 91
  absolute limits to (Buchanan) 90
Traffic in towns 92, 93, 94, 95 *n*., 96, 100 *n*.
  (Colin Buchanan) 87, 88
Traffic, inessential, optional 90
  essential 90

236 Index

Traffic, integrated with architectural considerations (Buchanan) 91
Traffic management 46, 47, 78 ff., 85, 109
   powers 51
Traffic problem, London 25 ff., 83, 89 ff.
Traffic restraint measures 171
Traffic safety 97
Traffic, segregation of long-distance from local 66
"Traffic thrombosis" 27
Traffic through 47, 85
Traffic, two kinds 68
Transport, balance between private and public 153
Transport in London (white paper) 154
Transport (London) Act, 1969 51, 155
Transport, Minister of 104, 106, 111, 114
Transport, Ministry of 30, 41 n., 50, 51, 105 n., 108, 109, 110, 115, 118 ff., 129 ff., 140, 148, 150, 154, 163, 178 n., 188, 189, 204
   "Memorandum of Evidence" 41 n.
   supports Primary Road Network 168
Transport planning 155
Transport, private and public 4
   volumes contrasted 43, 44 (table)
Transport problem, London 25 ff.
Transportation and Land Use 12
Transportation Planning 36, 40
Transportation Policy and Programme (TPP) 203
Tripp, Alker 70 nn., 71 nn., 78 n., 81, 97 ff.; also 97 n., 98 n., 101 n., 125 n., 137, 139, 141
Tripp, H. Alker, Assistant Commissioner of Metropolitan Police 69, 69 n.
Trunk roads 50
Tunnel, roads in 203

Unwin, Sir Raymond 57–58, 67 n., 137
   influence on Abercrombie 57
   quotation 5, 7
   ring analysis of London 63 n.
   Town Planning in Practice 39 n., 68, 68 n.

Urban motorways 151
Urban order 142
   concept of 177, 181, 187, 194, 200; abandoned 175
   concept of Abercrombie and 2, 3
Urban rooms 92
Urban rooms (Buchanan) 148

Vehicles, of different types in London traffic 32, 33 (table)
Vickers, Sir Geoffrey 6 n., 100 n., 183
Vigars, Robert 132

Webb, Beatrice and Sydney 25
Webber, Melvin 197, 204
Webber, Melvin M., "The roles of intelligence systems in urban systems planning" 174 n.
Webster, F. V. and Hunt, R. N., *Road Research Laboratory Report* 32 n.
Wedgwood-Oppenheim, F. 202 n., 205 n.
Welfare, Jonathan, "Programme, budgeting: the experience at Milton Keynes" 18 n.
Westway 166
Westway: an Environmental and Traffic Appraisal 148 n.
Wilcox, David 160, 173 n.
Williams, David G. 107 n.; "The modal split" 150 n.
Wilmott and Young 167
Wilson, James Q., "Urban transportation" 66 n.
Wingo, Lowdon, Jr. "Urban space in a policy perspective: an introduction" 154 n.
Wolf, R. I. 102
Wood, Peter 111 n.; "Studying traffic in towns" 148
Wood, S., "The role of the architect in community building" 92 n.
Works and Planning, Ministry of
   Abercrombie, Professor P., *Greater London Plan 1944* 54

"X" and "Y" roads 74, 75

Yewlett, C. J. L., *inter alia*, *Public Planning: the Inter-corporate Dimension* 14 n.

Yewlett, C. J. L. 191 n.
Young and Wilmott 167
Young Liberal Federation (South-East England), "The motorway box briefing" 153 n.

LIBRARY AND TECHNICAL INFORMATION
Urban and Regional Planning Series

The terms of our inspection copy service apply to all the above books. A complete catalogue of all books in the Pergamon International Library is available on request. The Publisher will be pleased to receive suggestions for revised editions and new titles.

OTHER TITLES IN THE SERIES

CHADWICK, G. F.
A Systems View of Planning (Volume 1)

BLUNDEN, W. R.
The Land Use/Transport System: Analysis and Synthesis (Volume 2)

GOODALL, BRIAN
The Economics of Urban Areas (Volume 3)

LEE, COLIN
Models in Planning: An Introduction to the Use of Quantitative Models in Planning (Volume 4)

FALUDI, ANDREAS
A Reader in Planning Theory (Volume 5)

COWLING, T. M. and STEELEY, G. G.
Sub-regional Planning Studies: an Evaluation (Volume 6)

FALUDI, ANDREAS
Planning Theory (Volume 7)

SOLESBURY, W.
Policy in Urban Planning: Structure Plans, Programmes and Local Plans (Volume 8)

MOSLEY, M. J.
Growth Centres in Spatial Planning (Volume 9)

LICHFIELD, N., KETTLE, P. and WHITBREAD, M.
Evaluation in the Planning Process (Volume 10)

SANT, MORGAN E. C.
Industrial Movement and Regional Development: the British Case (Volume 11)